SOMETHING FUNNY HAPPENED

ON THE WAY TO MY 80TH BIRTHDAY

by

Elmer Mulhausen

authorHOUSE®

AuthorHouse™
1663 Liberty Drive, Suite 200
Bloomington, IN 47403
www.authorhouse.com
Phone: 1-800-839-8640

First published by AuthorHouse   1/8/2009

ISBN: 978-1-4389-2288-1 (sc)
ISBN: 978-1-4389-2289-8 (hc)

Library of Congress Control Number: 2008910190

Printed in the United States of America
Bloomington, Indiana

This book is printed on acid-free paper.

CONTENTS

POEMS

DEDICATION

I dedicate this book to three of the most wonderful women in the world.

Ruth Mixer Mulhausen Lassiter, my mother was/is a true Saint. My father left when I was ten years old. He never offered any financial or parental help to our family. Mother sacrificed and raised us on her own. She was very devout. Although I rebelled at various points in life, her teachings about right and wrong and about God never left me. Any strength of character I might have came through her.

Carrie Evelyn Crow Mulhausen was my child bride. We raised each other as we raised our children. We were married for fifty years through thick and thin. Her untimely death in 1998 broke my heart. I don't know how she put up with me all those years, but I will always love her.

Jo Ann Albright Mulhausen is now my wife and best friend. In my wildest dreams, I couldn't imagine ever marrying again, but God had a very special one for me. She is a most remarkable woman and has a heart as big as all outdoors. She is unselfish to a fault. She has had an unbelievable life, and my goal is to make her happy in the time I have left.

ACKNOWLEDGEMENTS

Jeanne, Sarah and Mary Mulhausen for illustrations.

Elizabeth Dierksen for transcription.

Sandy Bogovich for proofing.

Jo Ann Mulhausen for patience.

FORWARD

I retired from the State Farm Insurance Companies in 1993 after thirty-four years of service. Evelyn and I traveled and really enjoyed life for the next five years. We celebrated our 50th Anniversary and life was good. Then Evelyn suddenly passed away in 1998 leaving me grief stricken.

A dear friend, Beverly Sharp, told me that a grief seminar at her church had been very helpful after her husband died. The Custer Road United Methodist Church in Plano, Texas offered this seminar semi-annually. The seminar had six sessions over six weeks. I signed up for the next one available.

In the first session, our leader suggested that we buy a large spiral notebook and keep a daily journal of our thoughts, memories and pain. The journal was helpful for me. In the second session she suggested that we try writing something creative along with our journaling. I began to write some crude poetry. First I wrote some greeting cards, then began to put some old stories into verses. I tried some political satire but then Bill Clinton left office. I lost my inspiration. Later, I began writing some spiritual and patriotic things.

One of our seminar participants lost his sixteen year old daughter to a drug overdose. He wrote a beautiful song about her as his creative effort. Thinking about his pain helped relieve some of mine. At least Evelyn lived nearly sixty-eight years.

I continued writing for my own amusement and shared with friends and family when I could corner them. A few actually suggested that I write a book. When I did decide to write this book, I hated to bore people with one poem after another. I decided to separate the poems with vignettes of life. I relate my spiritual journey over seventy-nine years from a very strict up bringing to rebellion. I returned to a spiritual life as a young married man and began to refine my beliefs. I again spent many years un-churched and outside the will of God. When Evelyn died, I returned to church, worship and spirituality. I tell this to provide my family and friends an example and message that you can come back to your faith.

Most of my poems try to be humorous. I always thought God had a sense of humor but that may be somewhat presumptuous. I have noted that some of the finest people I know have a sense of humor and I can say with certainty that God loves people with a sense of humor. Some of my poems may border on the risqué. To all my Christian friends, I say if you might be offended, please fast forward past pages with an asterisk by the title. I really don't want to offend anyone.

Many old stories, clichés and ideas came from someone else. I never set out to be a plagiarizer, but I just can't remember who to give credit or discredit. Over eighty years you hear a lot from a lot of people. I can't remember whether I made up some stories or heard them from someone else.

From being widowed at age seventy, I have come a long way. A lot of funny things have happened on the way to my eightieth birthday.

I have remarried. Jo Ann and I moved to Bosque County, Texas, and we are happy operating our Lakehaven Bed and Breakfast on Lake Whitney.

I feel a little humility when someone refers to me as a poet, but down here in this part of Texas we have cowboy poets. Now that's a title I can aspire to. I've never ridden the range. I don't know anything about working cattle, but I did write a couple of verses using the word cowboy. I'll start this book with them and maybe become a semi-cowboy poet.

HIGHER EDUCATION

The cowboy took his seat next to a Harvard
man on a cross country flight.
And they had a lively conversation while
traveling through the night.

By his own admission, the Harvard man was
an expert in every category,
So the cowboy listened patiently
to story after story.

After a while, the cowboy said he had never
flown with a Harvard grad.
Since they had not mentioned their schools,
the chap was both intrigued and glad.

"Cowboy, how in the world did you know where
I received my education?
Was it my great knowledge of news, history,
or was it my legal occupation?"

"Was it my exquisite manner or
my perfect grammar and expression?
Knowing how you know where I was educated
is my burning obsession."

"Please tell me, could it be the traditional cut
of my ivy league clothes?"
"No, truthfully sir, I saw your class ring
while you were picking your nose."

BUCK JONES FROM MULESHOE, TEXAS

The skinny cowboy strolled
into a crowded Manhattan bar.
"Hey, there's Buck Jones from Muleshoe, Texas,"
came a voice from afar.
A Yankee questioned the odds of one being
recognized in such a place.
"Not odd at all." Buck replied,
"People all over the world know my face."

"Governors and Kings know me
just like the elites in this city."
"Fat chance," said the annoyed Yankee,
"Just name one celebrity."
"I'll bet you a hundred dollars I know Mayor Giuliani, sir."
"You're on cowboy."
So they got Rudy on the line,
their acquaintance to concur.

After winning, Buck said, "How about five hundred
I know Governor Pataki?"
The Yankee took the bet, confident that his governor
wouldn't know this lackey.
The Yankee lost again when the governor greeted
Buck on the phone.
The Yankee grew irate as the crowd joined in.
Now they weren't alone.

Someone yelled, "How about the President,
do you know him, too?"
The desperate Yankee said,
"I'll bet a thousand that Bush won't know you."
The bartender connected the speaker to the phone
to benefit every spectator.
The excitement grew as they all hear
the White House operator.

3

"Tell the President that Buck Jones is on the line,
if it won't trouble ya."
After a pause a familiar voice came over the speaker,
"This is George-double-ya."
"Junior, how are you? How's Laura and the girls?
This is Buck Jones."
"We are great, how's Mabel and the kids,
and you, you old bag of bones?"

"Gee, its great to hear from you.
How is everybody down in Muleshoe?"
As the conversation continued,
the enchanted crowd watched the Yankee stew.
And then again, someone shouted,
"Bet Buck doesn't know the Pope."
The Yankee lightened up, I'll get even he thought-
the Pope is my only hope.

The excited crowd started exchanging bets
and the Yankee was relentless.
"Ten Thousand Dollars that you don't know the Pope
and I'll pay the expenses,
for our trip to the Vatican where I'll
gladly prove your deception."
The next day, the huge crowds prevented
their getting a Papal reception.

So Buck and the Yankee joined the St. Peters crowd
and through field glasses
looked up to the window where the Pope
was to address the masses.
Buck said, "You stay here by this column
while I work my way inside.
When the Pope comes out to speak,
I will waive to you from his side."

The Yankee's heart sank as he saw Buck appear
and waive from the door.
Could this be true? Is that the Pope?
Or is it a scam I'm falling for?
"Who's that on the balcony?" He asked, grabbing a tourist-
while getting reckless.
"Don't know that guy in the robes
but the cowboy is Buck Jones from Muleshoe, Texas."

Arriving With the Great Depression

I was born at Asherton, Dimmet County, in South Texas in 1928. Dad was there working on the rural electrification project. We moved when I was an infant. I have no memory of life before Oklahoma City during the "Great Depression". No one had any money and I guess we had even less.

We never owned a home. We moved from one rent house to another. I can remember ten houses or apartments. When we couldn't pay the rent, we moved in with Grandma Haswell, who owned her homestead. We were poor, but Mother exhibited such faith and positive attitude that I don't really ever remember worrying about it.

Sometimes Dad was home. Sometimes he was away while working or looking for work. He was an electrician and law enforcement officer.

I was in the third grade at Putnam City Elementary School the last time I remember Dad being home. He left to work re-construction of the Great Mississippi floods and to marry his lady friend, Hazel Poore. That was about 1936.

Most of my father's family retained the old German spelling of our name, Muhlhausen. Some of the family Americanized the name by dropping the first "h". Our dropping of the h occurred before my memory. My father, Elmer Muhlhausen, was angry in later years that my brother and I dropped the "h" and blamed my Mother. However, we have discovered old documents where he signed without the "h" in his younger years.

We visited Muhlhausen Germany while on a trip to Munich. We discovered there is a Muhlhausen in about every province. It is a common name meaning mill house. The largest city is now in France and spelled Mulhouse. Through history, this border city has passed back and forth between France and Germany. It was spelled Muhlhausen when in Germany.

When we visited the Bavarian Muhlhausen between Munich and Nuremberg, we didn't find any old unclaimed inheritance. We also escaped all old tax liens.

My Grandma Haswell had a homestead about the 2700 block of South Eastern Avenue, in Oklahoma City. The area was oil fields and semi-rural in those days. Grandma had lost most of her acreage and royalties to outlaw oil operators. The oil boom of the late 20's and early 30's was rough and wild.

Oil drilling raped the land. The creeks turned to salt water and overflow oil. Much vegetation was killed leaving scars on the sandy landscape. In my first memories of Grandma's house, we illuminated with kerosene lamps and had outdoor plumbing.

An oil company had dug a pit adjacent to the creek that ran by Grandma's house. They built some apparatus on the creek to skim escaped oil off the surface and divert it into the pit. A pumper-truck came from time to time to reclaim the oil. There was a plank foot-bridge about thirty-six inches wide across the creek and by this pit.

When I was about three years old, a better-off relative had given me a cast off tri-cycle. I had a good time riding that tri-cycle in the back yard while all the adults were inside. That foot-bridge looked exciting and challenging to me, so I rode down the hill and crossed it. When I got to the other end, I had a problem - - there were some steps down, so I had to turn around. Yes, while turning around, I fell into the oil pit.

I did manage to grab a plank at the top of the pit and hang on. I managed to keep my face above the oil. My feet couldn't reach the bottom of the pit.

Our bulldog, "Old Buddy" was the only other creature around. He started barking. Then he started running from the pit to the house and back again. He finally managed to get someone's attention, and they pulled me out of the pit.

Mother, Grandma, and some other lady put me into a number three wash-tub and started scrubbing me with a brush and home-made lye soap. The other lady was an aunt or one of my older sisters. Mother said my face was the only part of my body not covered by oil. They did laundry then by hand with a scrub board and tubs outside, so I'm sure they burned my clothes.

I don't remember whether they recovered my tri-cycle or not.

Author, Elmer Mulhausen, looking for something funny
(December 1928)

EVEN A GOOD BIRD CAN
MAKE A BAD TERN

Up North in Alaska one beautiful fall eve,
a majestic flock of terns prepared to leave
on their unbelievable migration of thousands of miles
from Alaska to the tropics, over land, sea and isles.

Meanwhile in California, the Sheriff doing his duty
made a huge pot bust and hauled off his booty
to an incinerator with a chimney so high
that the smoke wouldn't harm folks passing by.

The burning contraband turned the sky black and blue,
while on the horizon, our terns came into view.
They were magically drawn to the smoke it seems,
an amazing event defying our wildest dreams.

In a formation so tight it appears they are cloned
flew straight into the smoke, leaving not a tern un-stoned.

MOTHER'S FAMILY

My Mother's maiden name was Dolly Ruth Mixer. I regret that I know very little about her life before knowing her as my mother. Mother didn't talk much about herself. Mother was all about others. I am positive that Mother was the most perfect, righteous, loving, hard working person I have ever known. Outside the patriarch, Abraham, in the Bible, Mother is the best example of faith ever revealed to me.

My birth and childhood coincided with the great depression. I'm sure a lot of people have considered me bad news. My parent's failed marriage added to the economic misery, but Mother never let us feel fear or be depressed over our circumstances.

In the thirties, there were very few jobs even for the men of the home. Women stayed home and cared for the children. When Dad left for good, Mother had to find work. At first, the only thing available was domestic. Most jobs were temporary. I can remember her working in homes where there was a new baby or the housewife was sick. Sometimes she took in ironing.

I learned about one desperate time, long after it occurred. Mother hadn't worked for several weeks and we were completely out of groceries. She learned about a house cleaning job, but it was on the other side of Oklahoma City. Mother never owned a car while we were growing up. There was good bus and street car service in Oklahoma City. The fare was only a dime, but she didn't have a dime.

The afternoon before the potential job, our life insurance man dropped by to collect on the nickel and dime policies; Mother told him about the situation. The life insurance salesman loaned her a dime, so she could go to the job. I can't remember his name, but he will always have a place in my heart. That was life in 1938.

Later, Mother got a steady job during the school year at a school cafeteria. Then, she was employed by the Work Progress Administration (W.P.A.) as a pre-school attendant. That program sent her for some college courses, and she became a teacher. I am a political conservative now, but I am thankful for that liberal program that came along when needed. World War II ended the depression and the W.P.A. Mother's career path changed again.

My brother, Harold, was called to active duty in the Marine Corps in July, 1950. Mother had completed her long hard job of raising and supporting her children. Now she could think of herself. Mom's whole world and social life was wrapped up in her church. She was totally dedicated. She met a widower in her church whose family was also grown. Cecil Lassiter was a fine decent man that we learned to love. Mom and Cecil married in 1952. We were all very happy for them.

Cecil worked for a steel fabricating company. Mother later opened her own day care center and Cecil helped her in the business. Mom was doing what she did best: loving and caring for children. They did well.

My Mother, Ruth Mulhausen Lassiter and Cecil Lassiter (1952)

In 1956, Harold built a new home. Cecil and Mother bought Harold's little G.I. home. She was nearly sixty years old and living in her very first owned home. I also think it was Cecil's first owned home. God is good.

The pre-school made Mom happy, but the physical work became too much: she and Cecil semi-retired to being the custodians of the church.

Cecil was diagnosed with prostate cancer in the late 1960's. Surgery seemed to be successful, but cancer re-appeared in his bladder in 1972. After Cecil passed away, Mom went to visit my sister, Orissa, in Washington.

When Mom came home, she was suffering a lot of pain. She had been complaining about arthritis for two or three years. Her doctor put her in the hospital for tests. Her arthritis turned out to be bone cancer.

Mom went to the hospital for the first time when she was 74 years old. She had all four of her children at home. On our last visit, Mom was unable to raise her knees. She said she didn't want to live disabled or with constant pain. She said she was going to ask the Lord to take her. I knew God always answered Mom's prayers, so Evelyn and I insisted on staying with her on that night. Mom told us she was very peaceful, and insisted that we go home to our children. She died in her sleep that night, July 31, 1973.

I served as executor for Mom's and Cecil's estate. Cecil had five adult children and Mother had four. I survived. All the children, spouses and their children got mementos. There was about two hundred thirty dollars left for each child after everything was sold and the bills paid.

The legacy of love and life's lessons was priceless.

My Grandmother Haswell's maiden name was Clara Burden. Her family lived in Missouri. She married my birth Grandfather, Daniel Mixer.

He was a chief or captain in the Sedalia, Missouri fire department. He passed away before I was born.

It is rumored that Grandma had an interim marriage, but she didn't talk about that. She did talk a lot about pioneer days. One story was about Jesse James "borrowing" their horses. It seems he traded for, rather than stole the horses, but they didn't have a choice.

I can't remember the details about her coming to Oklahoma and getting a homestead. From my first memory, her husband was Calvin Haswell. My most vivid memories are of him in bib overalls and starched shirt in his rocking chair. He rocked me while telling stories and singing funny songs.

One day he harvested some peanuts and was cleaning them for storage. I kept eating the fresh peanuts. They were real small and a little green and probably fit only for livestock feed. He called them goobers. He told me, "Elmer, you are eating too many goobers. If you keep eating them, you are going to get the fantods"
I asked, "What is the fantods?"
"It's about the same as the pahseeah".
"What's the pahseeah?"
"It's about the same as the fantods."
"Well, Grandpa, what's the fantods?"
"You keep eating those goobers and you are going to find out."

Grandpa died while I was very young, before I started to school. I missed him very much. When Grandmother reached her nineties, she went to live with Mother. She remained sharp and precious until her death.

Grandma and Grandpa Haswell about 1933

Bad News – Good News *

Popa and Mama Brodsky agreed on a
resolution for the new year.
They would move away from the city's mean
streets and all the mischief there.

Give the kids a chance with farm animals.
Get close to the land.
So without a clue about country life,
they moved the whole Brodsky clan.

They wanted to start with pigs so they
bought a sow to breed.
Their neighbors had a big Berkshire boar
to fill the need.

The Brodskys' named their sow Marge,
and were ready for some action,
but they had no clue on loading a
sow for transport to the transaction.

They lifted and wrestled, tugged and pulled
before getting Marge into the trailer.
Then off to the neighbor's with little
Ted riding in back as Marge's jailer.

All went well in the breeding shed,
until loading for the return trip.
The Brodsky clan got muddy and exhausted
just trying to get a grip.

The Brodskys' arose bright and early the
next morning with great anticipation.
They ran out to see the little pigs, but
missed their expectation.

Alas – no pigs! – but they were determined,
so went through the task again.
They intended to own a litter of pigs –
they just didn't know when.

After three tough but unproductive trips
to the breeding shed,
the next morning, only little Ted
felt like checking Marge's bed.

Ted came running back into the house with
news and all aglow.
There's still no pigs, but Marge is already
in the trailer rarin to go.

Uncle Roy Mixer was my Mother's youngest brother. He and Aunt Helen built a small frame home next door to Grandma's house. They had five sons. George was born between Harold and me. Harry was just younger than Harold; then came Richard, Warren and Harvey.

Since my Dad was seldom home, Uncle Roy filled a special role in my life. He included Harold and me in all their family fishing and camping excursions. We boys spent many afternoons across the road hunting with our dogs. I owe Uncle Roy a deep debt of gratitude.

In 1951, after I had started my family, Uncle Roy bought a farm near McCloud, Oklahoma. Then it was a sad day in my life when Uncle Roy passed away in 1955. Aunt Helen died two years later. George, a navy veteran, was living with his family in Pennsylvania. He returned to the farm to raise Warren and Harvey with his own children. Harry and Richard had already graduated.

George lives at Blue Lake, California now. Richard had a very successful career as a pipe fitter and construction superintendent. He helped build the Alaska pipeline. He and his wife, Karlene, live in Palm Springs, California. Warren, a Marine veteran, lives in Portland, Oregon. Even with the odds against him, Harvey did finish high school and college. He now lives in Seminole, Oklahoma and works as an industrial traffic manager in Shawnee.

For some reason or other I have always been closer to Harry than the other boys. Harry retired from the Marine Corps as the proto-type first Sergeant. He and his wife, Pat, live at Vista, California.

I talked to Harry on the telephone last week. He asked if I still remember taking him snipe hunting when he was about eleven years old. I did, and we had a good laugh.

I'll explain for those who may not know the fine tradition of snipe hunting. The hunt is done at night, preferably a very dark night. The perpetrators tell the uninitiated that snipes are small, delicious birds that run up and down crop rows. The victims are taken to the far end of crop rows and instructed to kneel down holding open sacks so the snipe run into the sacks. The perpetrators are supposed to go to the other end of the field and drive the snipe down the rows into the waiting sacks, but instead, they go to the house laughing and betting on how long it will take the victims to come home!

Harry was a high tempered red head. People, who know Harry today as a fine mature Christian gentleman, wouldn't believe what a mouth he had then. When he finally came home that night, he gave me the most complete cursing I have ever had.

My Aunt Clara was my Mother's younger sister. She was married to Bert Tubbs. They lived in a rural oil field area southeast of Oklahoma City. James was the oldest, then Jack, Bill and Tommy. Elizabeth was the oldest daughter, then Betty Jean. Jo Ann was the baby sister of the family.

James and Jack served in World War II. Bill was just a little older than me. We both served right at the end of the war. Since Bill and I were about the same age, most of my memories of the Tubbs family center on adventures Bill and I had. Bill and I would be total buddies for a while, then have a big fight and not see each other for a long period of time.

When we were pre-school age, Bill and I ran off from his house. We went swimming in a polluted, salt water creek. We couldn't swim, but we held on to a pipe and kicked our feet. Finally big brother James found us. He took us to Aunt Clara's house kicking and screaming in our oil stained clothes. We crawled under their house trying to escape Uncle Bert' switch; I don't remember how that adventure ended.

Some relatives said I was a bad influence on Bill, while others said Bill was a bad influence on me.

When we moved to the north side of Oklahoma City, our brindle bulldog "Old Buddy" couldn't stay out of fights. Finally, he killed a dog, so we shipped Buddy to Aunt Clara's house out in the country.

Then, in addition to seeing the Tubbs family, we liked going to see old Buddy till he died.

Bill and I roamed the rural area swimming in stock ponds and oil field circulation tanks. We survived the tanks, but a lot of children in those days did not. The insides of those wooded tanks were very slick with moss and hard to climb out of.

Kitchens Lake was our favorite fishing hole. It was really a large stock pond, but seemed like a big lake to us. One day, four of us found an abandoned wooden boat at Kitchens. We got aboard and pushed off. Luckily, there was a bucket on board. The boat had a huge leak. Three could fish while one bailed furiously. When the bailer got tired, there would be a near fight to name the next bailer. However, we knew that if we stopped bailing for just a short while, we would sink. We took turns. The fish were biting that day. We didn't sink and caught a nice stringer of fish.

Bill got out of the Sea Bees before I was discharged from the Marine Corps. When I got home, I went looking for Bill. I found him roofing a house. He told me that so many people had postponed home improvements during the war, the business was booming. Bill's brother in law, Floyd Hall, was in the home improvement business. Bill suggested that we go into the business together.

We both knew that I was not handy with tools. However, I did have a little money from my separation. I would sell. Bill would do the work. I started knocking on doors and sold our first job the next morning.

We didn't even have a car. I walked to Bills job site. At noon we drove the construction company's pick-up to the office. We borrowed contract forms and FHA home improvement loan applications. We drove to the lumber yard, purchased materials, and then delivered them to our first job site. Bill quit his job and we were in business. We bought a 1933 Ford together. We were also proud of the first business cards of the "T. and M. Construction Company".

After three jobs in Oklahoma City, the finance company where we took the contracts and FHA loan applications, questioned my age. They said I was too young to sign a contract and receive the loan proceeds. So, Bill and I hit the road to find another market. We went to Anadarko, Oklahoma where the Bureau of Indian Affairs or some tribal government, helped fund Indian's home improvements.

We were doing well, but I was selling and contracting more jobs than we could do. We were in over our heads and about ready for our inevitable fight.

We met a couple of girls and had double dates. One of the girls was Evelyn, my future wife. One day, I told Bill that I was getting too serious about Evelyn and I planned to not see her for a while. Then I discovered Bill was calling her. He told her I was planning to break up and he asked her for a date. Well, we had our fight.

We sold our incomplete contracts to Bill's brother-in-law. We had been in business nine weeks. After everything was divided, we had a pretty nice profit by 1947 standards.

I didn't see Bill Tubbs for the next fifty years. I believe it was in 1999 that my cousin, Harry Mixer, visited Oklahoma City from his home in Vista, California. I went to Oklahoma City at the same time to see Harry and other relatives.

We learned that our cousin Jo Ann Tubbs Hast was back in the Oklahoma City area. Harry, my sister Betty Ruth and I went to see Jo Ann and her husband Billy Hast at their home in Edmond. We were also fortunate to see Elizabeth, Jo Ann's older sister, who was visiting from Arkansas.

Jo Ann, the baby of the Tubbs family, grew up to marry the pastor of their neighborhood church. Billy Hast also owned a plumbing business. After he and Jo Ann married, he sold his business and became a full time missionary. Jo Ann and Billy spent most of their lives in Puerto Rico. Billy has retired and they returned to the Oklahoma City area. We had a great time visiting and discovering Billy and Jo Ann's wonderful family.

Jo Ann told us that Bill Tubbs was in an assisted living facility. Harry and I went to see him. Bill and I had not seen each other since we were nineteen or twenty years old. It seemed like I was talking to his dad, Uncle Bert.

Bill was suffering from complications of diabetes and in a wheel chair. We had a very good visit and filled in fifty years. I'm thankful we had that chance. He passed away a short time later.

Mother had sisters in Missouri but I never really got to know them. Her oldest brother, Clay Mixer, managed a cement plant in Dewey, Oklahoma. He and Aunt Eva lived on a farm north of Dewey. I went to visit for a week one summer and enjoyed it.

Uncle Orren owned a furniture business and lived in Palestine, Texas. I never really got to know him, but did connect with his son, Orren, Jr. after we were adults.

Orren doesn't like to be called an artist. He is a cowboy that paints horses. Orren and his wife Evelyn, live on a ranch at Arcadia, Oklahoma. He raises prize longhorn cattle, collects antique farm and ranch equipment and paints in his studio.

My last visit with him was about five years ago. He was a spry eighty-year-old. He lamented that he didn't have any of his original paintings to call his own. He paints on commission from prominent horse owners and never catches up. He said he planned to stop and paint something for himself. I sure hope he has done that.

He has painted for a lot of famous people including Ronald Reagan and Paul Harvey. I'm very proud to display a couple of his signed prints in my home.

MISSING

The flyer on the door had a rather direct text,
with the sender's identification and this plea next.
Missing; three-legged terrier with a broken tail.
He's friendly, black and white, a recently neutered male.

We really need your help, we want him here,
even though you might say, he's had a rough year.
He lost that right eye and left ear to a pit bull named Buckey.
You'll know my pet when he answers to the name of "Lucky".

Paternal Grandparents Family

My memories of my paternal grandparents, Richard H. and Annie Sheets Muhlhausen, are very dim. They both died when I was very young.

One of Dad's older brothers, Alvin, died in World War I. Uncle Harry was an aviator in World War I. He lived in Tulsa, but did move to Oklahoma City before he died.

My Uncle Clarence, maintained a job and owned his home throughout the depression. His wife, Aunt Perle, was a jewel and I loved her. Their son, Clifford, died in World War II. Most of their children were too old for interaction with me except Kenneth. He managed one of the best seafood restaurants in Oklahoma City for a number of years – Evelyn and I enjoyed seeing him and having a night out at Hermann's on several occasions.

Uncle Zed Willet married my Dad's sister Fannie. Uncle Zed managed a lumber yard throughout the depression and seemed quite prosperous to us. My cousin, Lloyd Willet, was a year or so older than me. I sure enjoyed his hand me down clothes and discarded toys. His younger sister, Lois Jean, earned her doctorate and enjoyed a long career teaching at the University of Oklahoma. Uncle Zed and Aunt Fannie were always good to us and we enjoyed visiting their family. Lloyd lived his adult life in Wichita, Kansas. Both he and Lois Jean are now deceased.

Uncle Roy Mulhausen was the entrepreneur of the family. He created businesses in Galveston, Texas, Oklahoma City and in Portland, Oregon. My best memory of him was when Harold and I visited him and Aunt Grace in Portland. We had spent the summer at Dad's in Bremerton, Washington. We spent a week in Portland on our way to Los Angeles. This was the summer between my 9th and 10th year in high school.

Their two daughters were older than Harold and I. They both reside at White Salmon, Washington now. Carol and her husband Doug

Holliston have visited Oklahoma City through the years and we enjoyed seeing them.

Our cousin, Zane was about the same age as Harold and I. We got to know Zane and he has been back to this part of the country to visit from time to time.

Zane was an engineer, but his dream was wine. He became a very good vintner. In the 1980's, Zane and his wife had vineyards and a winery near Beaverton, Oregon. It was called the Chehalem Mountain Winery. They made some very good wines and we took great pride in serving "Mulhausen" wine. Sadly, marital problems caused the demise of that enterprise.

Dad's older sister, Minnie, married Will Skorkowsky. I never really knew them, but I was fond of their son, William. He was more like an uncle than cousin because of our age differences. He and his wife, Eleanor, lived on acreage near Harrah, Oklahoma. He was a long time employee of Oklahoma Gas and Electric Company. He even did contract work for their power plant construction jobs after he was eighty years old.

When I was five or six years old, I spent a week visiting William and Eleanor. Harrah was a hot bed for amateur baseball. Their town team had produced several major league players including the famous Waner brothers. William played on the town team and I enjoyed watching him play. Preparation for dinner each evening was equally exciting. William rang the neck of a chicken every evening for our fried chicken dinner. After about three days, I asked if I could ring the chicken's neck. William decided to let me try. But rather than the necessary tight twisting, wrist action, I extended my arm and swung the chicken around windmill style. That chicken's neck must have stretched twelve inches long. William quickly and mercifully took the chicken and quickly finished the job.

I didn't know Dad's younger brother, Uncle Stewart, until I was an adult. He had moved to Pueblo, Colorado and owned a rental equipment business.   When I moved to Shawnee, Oklahoma, I was pleased to discover that his daughter and my cousin, Ana Jean, lived there. She was married to Fred Lancaster and operated a dance studio where my daughter, Teresa, took dance lessons. That was in the sixties. She later moved to Colorado to join her father in the rental business. I just learned that she has returned to Tulsa after her second husband passed away. She is now Ana Jean Bishop. I am looking forward to seeing her sometime soon.

THANKSGIVING PRAYER

Dear Heavenly Father, we gather around this table
with thankful hearts.
Thank you for space to move, air to breathe and
all of creation's parts.

Thank you, that from all the eons of time,
we were born in our generation.
And with all the places in the world, we were born
in this nation.

Thank you for all the medical miracles and
creature comforts of this age,
for the standard of living we enjoy and the
freedom on America's stage.

Thank you for sound minds, eyes that see and
ears that hear,
for flowers, blue skies, a baby's smile, an embrace
from those held dear.

Thank you for the beautiful memories and hopes;
for the joys that lie ahead,
for pain overcome, for goals achieved, for all
the paths we have tread.

Thank you for family and for all the
wonderful times we share.
Let us never take your blessings for granted,
may we be thankful and care.

Thank you for our Savior and for your forgiveness,
though undeserved,
for all those protecting our freedoms,
for all who have served.

Thank you for this wonderful food and the
loving hands of preparation.
Please join us as we eat, laugh, give thanks
and enjoy loving conversation.
Amen

Psalms 136:1-4

My Sisters and Brothers

My sister Orissa was my parent's first child. My sister, Betty Ruth, was born about five years later. I was next, about four years behind Betty. I am two and a half years older than my younger brother, Harold.

Orissa left home to marry when I was in about the second grade. She always lived in another state so I have very few memories of her while growing up. Orissa's first marriage failed and she later married Alvin Shultz. During World War II they lived in Glendale, California and both worked in the defense industries.

Al was a creative mechanic. Al and Orissa made a trip to Oklahoma one summer before car air conditioning. Al had modified his car's air vents to include a box for ice or water and little burlap curtains. That device air cooled their car especially out in the arid desert.

I saw Al and Orissa again when I was a high school sophomore in Los Angeles. When I was a Marine stationed in Southern California, Orissa and Al hosted my buddy Lloyd Ervin and I many weekends. We really appreciated those good times.

After World War II, Al inherited a farm in Quincy, Washington. His parents had dry-land-farmed a large acreage. Now that water was coming from the Grand Coulee Dam project on the Columbia River, all their kids could get wealthy on smaller tracts with the help of irrigation. It was an empty promise. Al and Orissa struggled for thirty-five years. They worked side jobs and farmed just to make ends meet. I visited them in 1954 and helped Al with some of the irrigation. It was back-breaking work.

Orissa became public relations director for the Washington branch of the National Farm organization. She wrote articles and testified before Congress and State Legislatures on the plight of the American Family Farmer. We loved Orissa, but learned to keep the conversation away from the economy or politics. She was a zealot!

They adopted a son, Ryan, and a daughter, Ruth Ann. We see or hear about Ruth Ann from time to time but haven't heard from Ryan since the 1970's.

Orissa died in 1985 and Al followed her a few years later.

My sister, Betty Ruth, is my next older sibling. She helped Mother care for her two younger brothers while we were growing up, so I guess she earned the right to keep giving us direction even into our seventies.

Betty married C. W. Millus at a very young age. We called my brother-in-law, Walter, back then but he became "Chuck" in later years. Betty and Chuck struggled to make ends meet in those years before the great depression ended. At the outset of World War II, they moved to Los Angeles where Chuck worked in the ship yards. I lived with them briefly at the start of my sophomore year in high school.

Chuck went into the Navy and Betty moved back to Oklahoma City. Betty and Chuck had four children, Charles W. Jr., Betty Sue, Martha and Terry. Betty and Chuck divorced many years ago. Chuck remarried, but Betty never did. Chuck passed away a few years ago.

Betty had a career at the Federal Aviation Administration and has now retired from government service. She is a loyal and devout member of Southern Hills Baptist Church in Oklahoma City. Betty is a wonderful sister and I love her dearly. We talk on the phone often and visit when we can. She and her children celebrated her 80th birthday at our place shortly before we opened as a bed and breakfast.

C.W. Millus Jr., Betty's oldest son, lives with his wife, Bobby in Moore, Oklahoma. He also goes by Chuck, although we called him "Butch" when he was a child. Chuck has a career as a systems consultant in the banking business. He also builds and races drag race cars. Betty Sue is married to Jim Sloan. They live on a ranchette between Edmond and Guthrie, Oklahoma. They are both retired and are big NASCAR fans.

Martha is married to Carl Lumpkin. They are both retired and live near Tuttle, Oklahoma. Betty's son Terry and his wife Barbara live in Arlington, Texas. Terry is a construction inspector and also does some professional bass fishing. Betty's has a large number of grand children and great grandchildren.

Dad's last visit with children
L to R: Orissa Shultz, Elmer Mulhausen, Elmer Muhlhausen,
Betty Ruth Millus, Harold Mulhausen

HAPPY BIRTHDAY BETTY RUTH

On your special day please know
that someone loves you.
Know that you are in our
thoughts and our prayers too.

Have a wonderful birthday
That's full of cheers,
and keep having those birthdays
For many more years.

Love,
Elmer and Jo Ann, 2004

I have always loved my younger brother Harold very much, but we did have our sibling fights while growing up. I am two and a half years older than Harold, but he was a little bigger for his age than I was. He was also more athletic, so the fights were closer than they should have been. He had a fiery temper and I really did try to just defend myself rather than be a bully. However, one time I did throw him into a book case. He hit his head on a corner and suffered a nasty gash about an inch from his eye. I felt terrible but he was tough to defend when he attacked me. Another time, we were boxing and I knocked him out. Yes, I was severely punished both times.

All through elementary school until I left for junior high school, Harold got me into a number of school yard fights. It seemed that he delighted in starting something, then calling on me for help. On my very last day at Robert E. Lee Elementary School in Oklahoma City, I was standing in center field playing work up softball. I looked up and saw Dean Hite walking toward me. Dean had a large entourage following him. He had a "hit" list (although he had another name for the list). It was the last day of school, so Dean was going around the school yard settling grudges.

Dean just walked up to me and swung at my face. I had no idea we were going to fight. His first blow closed my left eye and knocked me to the ground. I got up swinging, but Dean circled to my blind side. I don't think I landed many punches. Dean gave me the worst whipping I ever had. I later learned that I was on the list because Harold had some run in with Dean. Harold told Dean that he would have Elmer kick his tail. I was sure glad to get out of the same school with Harold and move on to Capitol Hill Junior High.

When I came home from the Marine Corps, Harold and our younger cousins complained to me about a neighborhood cowboy near Grandma's house. He had gotten his kicks by roping the youngsters. One of my cousins had a rope burn on his neck. I saw the accused drive up to our neighborhood grocery a few days later. I walked up to the car window to admonish him. The cowboy wasn't in a mood to be admonished and started out of the car to get me. I felt pretty tough then, but this fellow looked like a formidable opponent. I decided to get in the first punch while he was still getting out of his car. I swung as hard as I could, but he saw it coming and started closing the door. My fist hit the edge of the car door full force, rendering my right hand useless. Luckily, some men at the store intervened before I got another "Dean Hite" whipping. I went home to doctor my bleeding knuckles. I decided then and there that I would rather be a lover than a fighter.

All stories aside, Harold and I did have a good time growing up with each other. We hunted, fished, camped out and played a lot of pick up ball games. I always wanted to play on the Capital Hill High School football team, but I was too small for the line and too slow for the back field. I couldn't quite make the varsity. Harold did make the team. He played full back on the state championship team – I was very proud of him.

Harold joined the Marine Corps reserves while he was still in high school. I completed my reserve enlistment two weeks before the Korean War. I felt a little guilty when the unit was called for active duty. Harold went to war, and I stayed home. I didn't re-enlist because I had a young wife and toddler son.

Harold married Betty Jo Baker. They had two sons, Chris and Mike. Chris lives in Hot Springs, Arkansas. Sadly, Mike contracted Multiple Sclerosis. and passed away in 1997 at the age of 43. Harold and Betty have a large number of grandchildren and great grandchildren. Harold and Betty both had careers at Tinker Air Force Base in Oklahoma City and both retired early. Betty was a secretary and Harold was an engineer technician and became an expert in electronic welding.

Harold didn't talk about his war-time experiences for a number of years. It wasn't until he retired that he became very active in veteran's activities. He wrote "Korea – Memories of a U.S. Marine" (Mocedon Publishing Co.) and contributed to "Voices from the Korean War" (The University Press of Kentucky).

The battle around the Chosin Reservoir in the Korean War is one of the most courageous battles in American history. The veterans of that battle have regular re-unions and name their organization "The Chosin Few". I try to honor my brother and the other brave participants of that battle in the following pages.

Harold is president of the Oklahoma Korean War Veterans and held many other offices in groups such as the "Chosin Few". He recently hosted a reunion of his Marine Regiment.

Betty Jo has returned to college and is determined to get her degree, even though she is in her seventies.

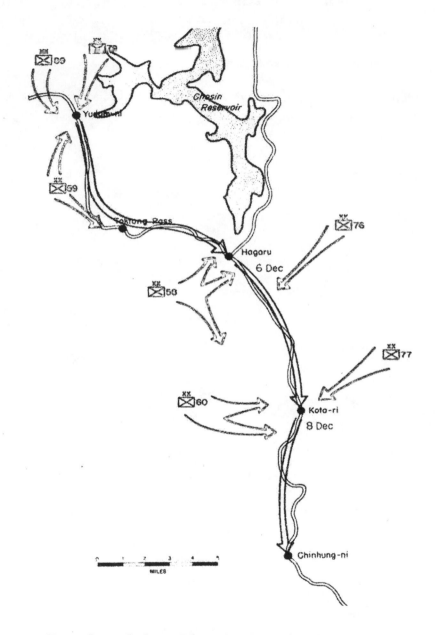

Battle of the Chosin Reservior

CHOSIN FEW

My brother Harold, had left his young wife Betty
just a few weeks before,
as a member of the Marine Reserves who were called
up for the Korean War.

He shipped into Korea as a replacement,
and joined Company A,
First Battalion, Seventh Regiment who were
fighting their way

From the coast to the Chosin Reservoir,
then on to the Chinese border.
Quickly dividing North Korea was General
MacArthur's daring order.

He planned to end the war now – Korea's
army was in disarray.
But suddenly China entered the war and
their huge numbers changed the fray.

Lead forces of the First Marine Division
reached Chosin Reservoir at Yudam-ni.
But this division was strung out for over
twenty-five miles to Koto-ri.

Then all along this extended deployment
one cold, snowy morning,
twelve Chinese army divisions attacked
our forces without warning.

General MacArthur had failed to plan for
the Chinese entering the fray.
Although the marines were surrounded,
They battled courageously, come what may.

They were outnumbered twelve to one,
the weather tormenting and drear.
"Retreat? Hell, no!" the commander declared,
"We will attack to the rear!"

There was one road to the coast through rugged
mountains, ice and snow.
Although it had been breached in many places,
and our forces divided, it was the only way to go.

From Yudam-ni, through the Tokoing Pass,
into Hagaru, fighting raged.
To the front, on the rear and on the flanks
the enemy was engaged.

Those rugged, icy and bloody,
seventy-eight miles to the sea
became the stage for one of the most
courageous battles in all of history.

Harold at nineteen had known little violence
in his young life.
Now all around him, both friend and foe are dying
from freezing and from strife.

It is December Fourth, nineteen fifty,
on a frozen Korean pass.
The Seventh Marines are fighting their way
through a huge Chinese mass.

It's Harold's twentieth birthday,
but rather than fun and candle lighting,
his only awareness is of numbing cold,
hunger, fatigue and bitter fighting.

He has no concept of time.
Days have no end or beginning.
If he is still alive,
then surely they are winning.

MARCHING TO THE SEA

The fight into Hagaru took seventy-nine hours,
to Koto-ri another twenty-two.
Mortal words can't describe the misery
and the courage of these Chosin Few.

At Hagaru's makeshift airstrip,
supplies were flown in and wounded evacuated.
Confidence began to build
and even victory was anticipated.

But at Koto-ri, there was more bad news.
A bridge had been destroyed,
across that only road,
making it impossible for our vehicles to be deployed.

An urgent call was made for a portable bridge
to be air-dropped.
But a thick blinding snow storm closed in;
no flights till it stopped.

The situation was becoming more perilous.
If the marines were to survive,
They needed clear skies, air support,
and that bridge to arrive.

But temperatures plunged to forty below
and it snowed two more days.
On his knees in the snow, a chaplain prayed
and looked up into the haze.

Then through a break in the clouds,
he spotted a beautiful star peeking through.
The Chaplain raised a frozen tent flap
and told the marines inside what God would do.

He told them that at home and here,
They were being lifted up in Prayer.
God knew and loved each one of them personally.
Yes, God did care.

He had made known his promise,
with a beautiful star in the sky.
Tomorrow, the sun would shine.
Our air support would fly.

The marine's spirits lifted with the news
about the star of Koto-ri.
They began to sing "From the Halls of Montezuma,
to the shores of Tripoli".

One can only imagine the thoughts
of those Chinese freezing in the night,
listening to those singing marines
that they would have to fight.

Thirty-three years later,
those survivors made that star peeking through,
that "Star of Koto-ri"
the logo for their organization, "The Chosin Few".

The next morning as the sun shined,
bridge sections were dropped despite all fears.
And the dangerous icy chasm
was spanned by courageous engineers.

Harold's company again took the point
as they fought out of Koto-ri.
They swept the hills beside the road
on that last bitter battle to the sea.

A shot knocked the heel off Harold's boot.
He fell from a ridge, became buried in the snow.
After carrying wounded to the road,
he didn't know where to go.

Many marines lost their units in bitter fighting,
but with the help of God
found the strength and courage to pick up the
fight with another squad.

On December tenth, the first of the marines
broke through to the land of living.
They were evacuated to ships, for showers,
shaves, hot food and thanksgiving.

Rarely in the annuls of military history
has a force been so assailed
with such overwhelming numbers and
natural elements - - yet prevailed.

Seventeen medals of honor were awarded
for this campaign
and well-deserved; though not accounting for
all the courage and the pain.

Because every single member of the "Chosin Few"
are genuine heroes we all agree.
Their sacrifice reminds us once again,
that freedom is not free.

Those Chosin Few, along with all heroes
who defend the red, white and blue,
from the revolution, to the present, and
those in the future, too.

Deserve our deepest gratitude
and respect for their sacrifice.
For us and for our allies –
Freedom purchased at an indescribable price.

Epilogue –

After all these years, I am finally able to write these lines honoring
my brother Harold L. Mulhausen and his comrades in arms reverently
remembered as the Chosin Few. I honor the members of the First
Marine Division and the remnants of all other United Nations forces
that joined them in the fight from the Chosin Reservoir. I also honor
the Navy, Air Force and Marine aviators who flew 3,700 close support
sorties and 830 helicopter missions.

The commandant reported to the Secretary of the Navy that from October 26th to December 15th, the Marines suffered 4,418 battle casualties and 7,350 non-battle casualties (freezing and frostbite). Of the total, 718 died of battle wounds. The division arrived at the Hungnam Port at about 50% of original strength.

I reverently honor these and all the United Nations casualties. I revere every precious drop of blood shed for our cause.

In Christian retrospect, I'm also saddened by the estimated 37 to 50 thousand Chinese casualties. A large percentage of those ill-clothed, ill-equipped Chinese soldiers froze to death in the bitter cold.

When Harold reached his evacuation ship, he showered and shaved for the first time in 50 days. He had lost 47 pounds. During the course of that battle, he had hot food only four times.

Rather than being shipped home, Harold and his surviving buddies were re-deployed into South Korea where they fought for nearly another year. Harold got home to his wife, Betty, on December 3, 1951. That was exactly one year after the epic battle into Hagaru. The next day, he celebrated his 21st birthday.

Harold and Betty still live in Oklahoma City where the Marine Reserve 20th Infantry Battalion was activated in July 1950. Harold still suffers from the frostbite on his feet.

SCHOOL YEARS

My first school was Wheeler Elementary in Oklahoma City. My Mother attended the first parents' open house when I was in the first grade. Each of we students went to the blackboard to demonstrate how we could write our ABC's and numbers.

When I went to the board, my Mother put her head on the desk and cried. My teacher, Mrs. Thompson, patted Mother on the back and said, "That's alright Mrs. Mulhausen. Elmer can read pretty good."

My handwriting hasn't improved over these past 73 years. I sympathize with and commend Elizabeth Dierksen who transcribed this manuscript, much of it handwritten. Elizabeth's business is "Girl Friday Secretarial Services" in Waco, Texas.

Before attending second grade, we moved to the North side of Oklahoma City and I attended Putnam Heights Elementary. We lived for a while on North Pennsylvania Avenue and also on North Florida behind my Aunt Perle and Uncle Clarence. Their home faced N. W. 33rd Street.

In the summer, I went swimming at the Harding Junior High School pool. Bobby Miller and I walked the five or six blocks to Harding. We were taught to be very careful crossing Classen Blvd. We waited patiently for the green light, and then crossed quickly.

One summer day, my Uncle Clarence, a meat salesman, called on the grocery store at 33rd and Classen. While there, he saw a car run over a little boy. A second boy ran off. Uncle Clarence rushed home and asked my Mother,
>"Where is Elmer?"
>She said, "He went swimming with Bobby Miller".
>"What was he wearing?"
>"A little blue seersucker outfit," she answered.
>"Ruth, Elmer has been hit by a car. Let's go to the hospital".

When they got to the hospital, they were told that the unidentified little boy was D.O.A. They rushed to the funeral home and were ushered in to make an identification - - well, it wasn't me.

By that time, several Aunts and Uncles and cousins had been notified of my untimely death. Two older cousins drove to the Harding pool. They rushed into the pool and spotted me. They were actually angry - - "get out of there! Come home!" We were furiously dried and rushed home to a room full of crying relatives. Mother grabbed me and about squeezed me to death. I was passed around the room from one relative to another. I had never been hugged so much and I had no idea why.

Well, we didn't have any money, but we did have love.

I went to a different school each of my first three years. I was in the third grade at Putnam City when Mom realized Dad wasn't coming back home. Putnam City was on the northwest edge of Oklahoma City. Mom moved the family to the south side in an area called Capitol Hill. Mom rented a small house adjacent to Robert E. Lee Elementary School.

With the exception of a partial year in California, I then stayed with my group of friends through Lee, Capitol Hill Junior High and then through graduation at Capitol Hill High School. I became a true dedicated, maroon blooded Capitol Hill Redskin throughout school and now as an as an alumnus.

My first buddies in the fourth grade were E. G. Stewart and Leslie Smith. I can't recall the exact grades when we were joined by Gordon Grider and Edmond Campbell. Jim Hamil was a grade behind us but became a part of our fraternity. As time went along, our gang included Lloyd Ervin, Ralph Hunter, Dick Hildebrand, Euless Stapp and others.

E.G. was one of those kids who always seemed three or four years older than the rest. He probably started shaving when he was twelve. He drove a produce delivery truck when he was fourteen. In high school he became an all state tackle on the football team. Of course, he was the biggest of our gang and I was at the other end of the scale. I was the last to have a voice change so my first nick name was "Peeps".

We were notorious for nicknames to embarrass each other or as a result of a concocted story or practical joke. Some were temporary and some hung on. E. G. was "Zeke", Leslie was "Leers", Gordon was "Candy". Edmond was "Stick". I endured at one time or another "Mooch" and then "Smooch".

Next to spouse and family, school boy bonding is one of life's most important relationships. My buddies in our old gang were very important to me. We had extreme loyalty to each other.

Some might say we were bad. We were mischievous. We really enjoyed a good practical joke, but didn't do anything really bad. We didn't steal, vandalize or use dope. Yes, most of us started smoking at fifteen or sixteen and there were a couple of alcohol incidents. We were involved in a few fist fights, but never any weapons. Our zealous pursuit of sex was more talk than action. Oh yes, we did skip school a few times.

We loved sports. Some were good, and others of us tried. E. G., Leslie, Stick and Dick lettered in football and we had a couple of lettermen in basketball and baseball. Jim became a sports official. He served high school sports in Oklahoma City for a number of years. Capitol Hill High School had award winning bands and choirs, but none of our gang had musical talent.

Lack of talent didn't keep us from singing however. Bus and street car fare was a dime then. That included transfers to other routes and going to the end of the line and back. On numerous occasions we spent a whole evening riding street cars for a dime a piece. We gathered in the back singing old folk songs, telling jokes and just hanging out.

We constantly looked for stunts that would produce a laugh. When we went downtown, we stood on a sidewalk and all looked up to the top of the buildings. This was contagious. When a large crowd had blocked the sidewalk looking up for whatever, we moved on. A few restaurants at that time had plate glass windows. Sometimes we lined up and pressed our faces up against the glass looking in. The reaction of patrons near the window was good for a laugh. We moved on before a confrontation with managers or the police.

Sometimes we hailed a city bus. When it stopped or delayed starting to wait for us, one of us would place a foot on the step and tie a shoe. Then we thanked the route driver for providing a place to tie the shoe. We were the only ones that thought our stunts were funny. I would like to tell about the night we put a goat on the third floor of Capitol Hill High School, but I can't remember the details.

At the last high school reunion I attended, Jim Hamil gave me a picture of our little league baseball team. We were probably about twelve years old, and sponsored by the C.R. Anthony Department Store. Jim, who has retired as the city attorney for Oklahoma City, pointed out that only three or four of us in the picture still survive. Memories and heartaches are all part of life.

Jimmy Johnson and Mary Lou Jones are friends from that fourth grade class and still surviving alumni. Mary Lou married Bill Waller. Jimmy operated the Capitol Hill Funeral Home for a number of years. Jimmy's personal view of our dwindling numbers inspired him to join with others in organizing reunions. I appreciate his efforts.

*C.R. Anthony Department Store Dodgers, Oklahoma City 1941 or
1942. Kneeling: Jack Kerr, Chris Gers, Jim Hamill, Keith Smith, Elmer
Mulhausen, Jack Hoskins, and Horton Smith. Standing: Billy Smith,
Vin Johnson, E.G. Stewart, Coach Leo Smith, Dave DeGraffenreid,
John Hisel and Hoyt Estes.*

THE FOOD CHAIN

A fly, flying lazily over a river clear
said to himself, "self it's hot up here.
If I drop six inches, the water will make it cooler,"
while just below swam a trout already cooler,
thinking, "If the fly drops six inches, not a bunch,
I'll leap out of the water and have some lunch."

Up on the shore behind a tree a bear took it all in.
"If the fly drops and the trout jumps I'll grab him then,
I'll have some lunch." While a hunter across the river
viewed the scene with anticipation that made him quiver.

The hunter's rifle lay on his knees as a quick snack he catches,
and plots, "the fly drops, the trout jumps, when the bear snatches,
I'll grab my rifle and shoot the bear in the chest.
A trophy I've always dreamed of, my very best."

Now down in the brush near the hunter's feet,
hid a mouse also savoring something to eat.
The mouse raised his head to see and plan his act,
thinking, "The fly drops, the trout jumps with fly intact.

The bear will grab the trout while coming out of the wood.
The hunter will reach for his rifle and drop his food.
And I'll have a delicious lunch, oh lucky me."
Not knowing that overhead a hungry cat was in the tree.

The cat observing the plot which I won't repeat,
thought, "when the mouse leaves the bush I'll get to eat."
And then it happened with amazing precision,
just like watching a show on television.

The fly dropped six inches to be cooler, and then crunch.
The happy trout leapt out of the water and had his lunch.
The trout was so fully satisfied when he sailed,
into the claws of the bear where he was impaled.

47

The bear smacked his lips while across the stream,
the giddy hunter was about to realize his dream.
The hunter grabbed his rifle and dropped his snack,
as he shot the bear, the mouse got lunch and darted back.

Simultaneously, the cat leapt from the tree,
not calculating how quick the mouse to be.
She landed on the steep bank and fell into the stream.
Does all this drivel have a moral or a scheme?
Not really, but on one thing you can bet,
when the fly drops six inches something gets wet.

ADOLESCENCE

I landed my first real job when I was thirteen years old. I had done odd jobs such as yard work and setting pins at the bowling alley, but this was real employment. We had a real job interview setting the hours, duties and compensation. I was going to school, so it was a part-time job. I can't recall the hours per week, but I vividly remember the compensation.

Mr. and Mrs. Stumpf owned and operated a little grocery store right across the street from us. My older friend, George Douglas and good buddy, Gordon Grider already worked at the store so I applied too. We agreed to a salary of $6.00 per week. I would draw three dollars in cash and get $3.00 worth of experience.

I can say that the $3.00 of experience was more valuable than the $3.00 cash. That German couple believed in, practiced and taught the work ethic. My first assignment was to restock some shelves. But first, Mrs. Stumpf showed me how to wash those old painted, wooden shelves with soap and water. I finished that first assignment while Mrs. Stumpf was checking out customers at the cash register. I stood by waiting for the next assignment. I noticed a dirty look or two but didn't really compute it. As soon as Mrs. Stumpf finished with the customers, she turned on me like a hungry lioness. She told me there are two kinds of people who will never amount to a hill of beans. The first kind never did what they were told to do. The second kind did only what they were told to do. She said there is always work to do in a grocery store. You never stand around idle. She told me that I had enough sense to find something useful to do.

I have never forgotten. She didn't ever have to correct me twice. That was just the first of many lessons. We three boys received a foundation for the work ethic. George grew up to be a successful home builder in Oklahoma City. Gordon owned a chain of super markets and became a millionaire. I had a very satisfying career in the insurance industry and supported my family.

Although Gordon was more successful financially, I wouldn't change places with him. He had two failed marriages. He bought a farm to get away from business stress and lost a leg in a hay bailing accident.

I was working and living in Columbia, Missouri in 1975 when my school boy buddy E. G. Stewart called me. He had sad news that Gordon had terminal brain cancer. E. G. organized a reunion dinner for our old school gang. We were all about forty-five years old at the time. I really enjoyed seeing every body. That was the last time I saw Gordon.

Elmer Mulhausen, E.G. Stewart and Gordon Grider

On Sunday, December 7th, 1941, I was walking on South Lee Street in Oklahoma City looking for a pick-up softball game. A neighbor came out and yelled to me, "We are at war! The Japanese have bombed Pearl Harbor!"

I didn't know where Pearl Harbor was, but I quickly found out. Our family huddled around the living room radio and heard about the horrors of war. Of course there was no T.V. then. The radio demanded our intense attention as President Roosevelt talked to us and mobilized the nation. Everything changed.

Able bodied men went into the armed forces. Other men and women went into the war industries. Unlike later conflicts, this whole nation went to war. Groceries, gasoline, tires and all scarce commodities were rationed. War is terrible. No one likes it. But, I do admire total effort and dedication to a cause. We were united. We were all involved. We won.

I hate it when we have our young, our best, fighting and bleeding for our country, while civilian life continues as usual. We can't have guns and butter at the same time. While some families are grieving lost sons, the rest of us shouldn't go on as if nothing is happening. We should suffer together. When one American goes to war, we should all go to war. We should go to win. We should not stop short of victory.

World War II was a terrible thing, but it should serve as a history lesson on what we can do when we are all united. Korea, Viet Nam, Somalia and the current conflict are some examples of the opposite. I despise political posturing that divides our efforts in time of war.

Everyone old enough remembers when they heard about Pearl Harbor. That's also true about the victory over Japan in World War II. On VJ Day, when World War II ended, the streets were filled with spontaneous celebrations. Most remember too, where they were and what they were doing when they heard about the Kennedy assassinations and the terrorist attacks on 9-11, 2001.

Boxing was a very popular sport in the thirties and forties. Our local parks had summer boxing for boys from around ten or eleven through fourteen or fifteen years old. Our nearest park was Oliver Park. We had a coach, training area and a real ring. We put on boxing matches for the neighborhood every Thursday night. Merchants like the C.R. Anthony Department Store donated prizes for the winners. So, I was a prize fighter at an early age.

Various parks in Oklahoma City developed teams, so some Thursdays were matches between the park teams. This was a "farm" program for the Golden Gloves. At about age fifteen, the better boxers joined the Oklahoma City Golden Gloves and tried to make the Oklahoma City Boxing Team.

My memory fails me to the point that I can only remember the wins. Butch Gose was one of the better boxers in the program. He was my age and he had a younger brother Harold's age. Butch graduated to the Oklahoma City Boxing Team and compiled an impressive record in amateur boxing.

My most vivid and proud memory of boxing was the night I boxed Butch and Harold boxed Butch's younger brother. It was our lucky night. Harold and I both won. We were awarded brand new dress shirts that were badly needed.

When I was old enough to consider trying out for the city team, Harold and I traveled to Bremerton, Washington to spend the summer with Dad. When I returned to Oklahoma City, I visited the Golden Gloves Gym one time. I didn't like the effect boxing seemed to have on some of the older boxers. Mom was against my continuing to box and I just didn't have the motivation to endure the rigors of training and sacrifices to make weight. I boxed some again when I was in the Marine Corps, but concluded that boxing was not my calling.

I started noticing girls when I attended Capitol Hill Junior High School in Oklahoma City. I thought the prettiest girl in the whole school was Ruth Ann Myers. She was so pretty and I was so shy, I never told her so or asked her to any of our parties.

I did make the mistake of sharing my admiration with some classmates. Jimmy Fortenberry was a very clever guy and decided to help me by writing Ruth Ann a note and signing my name to that note. I can't remember any more details except that I was embarrassed nearly to tears and hopping mad.

In the school hallway, I told some other boys about Jimmy's little trick. I told them that I was so mad that I would punch Jimmy in the nose for two cents. Well, Bobby Jessupp reached in his pocket and pulled out two cents. Now, I was honor bound. I couldn't back down. We followed Jimmy out into the school yard. I walked up to him and punched him in the nose. That was it. It was all over and I felt kind of cheap.

I went to school in Los Angeles the first half of the tenth grad, then returned to Capitol Hill High School midyear. When I saw Jimmy, he told me that he had a terrible time. He said that I had broken his nose and he had to have surgery. I apologized. He said that he didn't get mad. He got even. Jimmy was our high school year book editor our senior year. When our senior yearbook came out, my picture was not to be found anywhere in the year book. Jimmy said, "I got even".

Ruth Ann and I were not in the same social circles in high school. Later at high school reunions Ann and I visited. As an adult, she dropped the "Ruth". The pretty girl became a beautiful woman. She was happily married to Ed Dooley who had been a football star at one of our rival high schools. I was happily married to Evelyn.

A few years later, Ann lost Ed. I was still happily married to Evelyn and had to quell feelings of attractions at subsequent reunions.

On a trip to Oklahoma City after Evelyn had passed away, I remembered that attractive widow. I had a crush on her fifty-seven years previously. Wouldn't that be an item if we got together now that we are seventy years old? I called Ann and took her to dinner, and we had lunch together a couple of other times.

We had a wonderful time talking about our lives, families and careers. Ann had become an accomplished water color artist. However, I didn't detect any fires of romance from her. Maybe it was too soon after Evelyn's death, but I didn't get fired up either. Our becoming an item was not to be.

Between my ninth and tenth grades, my brother, Harold and I spent the summer with Dad and Hazel in Bremerton, Washington. Dad was a master electrician at the Navy yard. Dad also taught electricity at the high school. When school started, we went to Los Angeles to live with my sister, Betty Ruth and her husband, Chuck Millus. I attended John C. Fremont High School. During this time, Mother worked as a live-in domestic with the famous composer, Sammy Fain and his wife in Beverly Hills.

Finally, in the middle of the school year, Mom, Harold and I returned to Oklahoma City. We were a family together again. I returned to my beloved Capitol Hill High School and all my running buddies.

Family in Los Angeles in 1943
Sitting: Charles Millus Jr. on C. W. Millus's lap, Betty Ruth Millus,
Sue Millus on Grandmother's lap, Ruth Mulhausen,
Orissa and Al Schultz
Standing: Harold and Elmer Mulhausen

THE MONUMENT

Peace is illusive on the beautiful isle of Cypress
and even danger lurks.
Because racial hatred is historical there
between the Greeks and the Turks.

Massive peace efforts by the United Nations
have failed time and again.
So they made a buffer zone between the two,
but hate prevails like its always been.

Although not in an actual war, they yell insults
and curses across the Zone.
Day in and day out, louder and more profane,
continuing the hateful tone.

One fateful day a Greek soldier and his Turk counterpart
yelled insults, the air to pollute.
Then the Greek turned his back, dropped his pants,
bent over and gave a vulgar salute.

The young Turk was enraged from the tip of his toes
to the top of his head,
prompting him to pick up his rifle, aim
at the young Greek, and shoot him dead.

Soon after, mournful Greeks built a marker
on this place of iniquity,
so all who pass see the high cost
of hatred, even if born in antiquity.

Hopeful that this marker would serve
this senseless act to impugn,
it will always reverently be referred to
as the Monument to the Moon.

CAPITOL HILL HIGH SCHOOL

At Capitol Hill High School a group of us played shinney on an abandoned tennis court during our lunch hour. Shinney is hockey on concrete rather than on ice. The puck is a tin can beaten into a solid mass. Our shinney sticks were home made from a group of trees on the south edge of our campus. Sometimes the design of our shinney sticks got creative. There were no rules.

One player cut a limb from a tree that had a fork on the end. He trimmed the fork so that the puck would fit into it perfectly. When he could get control of the puck into the fork on the end of his stick, he just pushed it down the court like he was pushing a push broom. It was a sure score.

I decided that our team had to be just as creative. I cut a limb out of a tree shaped like a baseball bat, only bigger and heavier. The next time the opponent cradled the puck into his "push broom" and started down court, I was ready. I approached him and swung my club in a huge arc chopping motion down onto his stick. I swung with all my might. I aimed for mid-stick but landed the blow about six inches below his hand. It must have felt like a huge electrical shock because he instantly dropped his stick. My teammates got the puck and scored.

The opponent went down on one knee from the blow but quickly jumped up ready to fight. We danced toward each other like a couple of game cocks. High school boys of that day were usually egging on a fight, but surprisingly my friends jumped between us and pulled me back.

My antagonist had come to high school from a different junior high school so I didn't know him. His name was Herschel Acton. He was the state Welter Weight Golden Gloves champion. He went on later to win the national championships and international championship. Later, Herschel and I became friends. I'm thankful that my buddies intervened and saved my hide.

The Redskin Theatre and the Capitol Hill Bowling Alley were principle hang outs when I was in school. Even if we couldn't afford to bowl, or to buy a movie ticket, we still enjoyed hanging out. If we had a real special occasion or date to impress, we went to Beverly's Fried Chicken. That was across town but the classiest place in the forties.

One evening while we were hanging out at the bowling alley, a girl told us an alarming story. She had been dating a boy from Northeast High School. Someone had painted their school. That guy accused Capitol Hill students of the vandalism and vowed revenge. We were innocent of those charges. He told her that three car loads of painters were headed for our school.

We quickly recruited a platoon of guys and went to protect our school. We had a lot of fun standing around joking, when sure enough, three car loads of boys pulled up to the curb in front of the school.

We hid in the shrubbery along the front of the school. I peeled off my new coat to be ready for action. As soon as our prey was inside the gate, we came out of the bushes and surrounded them. Some of our girls slipped out and let the air out of their tires.

Well, it was just too funny to get mad enough to fight. A couple of guys did dance around pretending to throw punches, but it was mostly talk. There was enough commotion that neighbors called the police. A couple of police cars showed up, and we scattered.

After escaping, I remembered my new coat. I tried to sneak back when a spot light caught me full in the face. I ran around the corner of the school right into the mid-section of a policeman. I nearly knocked him down and of course he took me into custody.

They took four or five of us downtown. We were questioned, lectured and scared to death. A patrolman confirmed that the cars with flat tires were full of paint. Those cars were towed in.

The detective in charge told the patrolman to take us home. I told the patrolman about my coat and talked him into taking me to the school rather than home. I did retrieve my coat.

I noticed lights at Bob Lane's home across the street. Evidently his folks had gone somewhere, because a party was going on in their home. I decided to join the party.

Students from both schools were having a good time together. Of course, the Northeast boys were worried about their cars and how to get home. Some of our guys took them home. Later on, I served in the Marine Corps with one of their guys, Harry Ratliff.

One Sunday afternoon, a group of us were at the Redskin Theatre. Someone mentioned that Capitol Hill had a home baseball game. My buddy, Stick Campbell was playing on the team, so we decided to go. None of us had a car, so we started walking the eight or nine blocks to the school.

I didn't know Bob, one of the boys who had joined us. As we walked down the street (which was unpaved) Bob spotted his friend Jerry's car stuck in a bar ditch. I didn't know Jerry either. These guys must have gone to a private school. Jerry lived about a half block down the street, so Bob went to his house to inquire about what had happened. Bob returned with the car keys and asked if we could all help get the car out of the ditch. Jerry was sick in bed.

While we were pushing and shoving, trying to get the car out, a police patrol car drove up. The policemen asked what we were doing and we told them. Then, the police informed us that the car was stolen and they had been watching it. We quickly directed the police to Jerry's house. We went with them to confront Jerry.

Jerry's family was not home. He was in bed with a fever and a rash. He told the police that he had stolen the car. He didn't know any of us except Bob. Although Bob had been with Jerry Saturday night and ridden in the car, he said Bob didn't know it was stolen.

The police called into the station. They were told not to bring that sick kid down there, but bring the rest of us in for a formal statement. We were told we would be released after making a statement. We thought this was great fun riding in back of the squad car. We did duck down when we thought someone we knew might see us, but this was just another adventure. We sang "If I had the wings of an Angel, over these prison walls I would fly".

At the police station, it wasn't funny anymore. We were photographed, finger printed and thrown into jail. The place stunk. The food was garbage and the characters scary. We were held overnight so that detectives coming on shift Monday morning could question us. When I was questioned, the detective kept trying to make me change and contradict myself. I went back to the cell and was recalled in about an hour. I was asked to sign a typed statement. There were several errors and I would not sign until those errors were corrected. About that time, the detective learned we were all in the same cell. He threw a fit and said no wonder we all told the same story.

We had been in a large cell with a lot of inmates. It was called a drunk-tank. We were re-assigned to smaller cells and had no other contact with each other. I was in a cell with a man who said he had killed his wife and a one-armed man who said he was a career criminal. That helped me sleep well.

Unknown to us, when Jerry's father returned on Sunday, he went in to take a shower. Jerry got out of bed, got the car keys out of his father's pocket and took off. Police arrested Jerry six days later in Milwaukee. He had joined the Merchant Marines and was driving around until his ship left.

Also, unknown to us, our parents, pastors, relatives and school principal were all clamoring to get us out. The law then allowed police to hold someone seventy-two hours for investigation before filing charges or releasing them. Since the confessed thief had escaped, this detective decided to hold onto what he had. A few hours before the seventy-two hour deadline, I was released by myself. I had no idea what was happening with the others. I left the police station and started walking to find a business where I could call home. Before I could call, I was arrested again for investigation and returned to jail. I was feeling mighty lonesome.

Within three or four hours though, we were all released to the waiting arms of a delegation of parents, pastors and other well-wishers. Evidently this group had gotten our story to some official. No charges were ever filed on us. I do know Jerry was returned to Oklahoma City, but I never heard his punishment.

When I got home, all I wanted was a bath, clean clothes and a decent meal. I itched for a month. Never once in my life have I ever considered committing a crime. This experience may have contributed to my commitment to stay straight.

After completing my junior year of high school a group of boys proposed a daring adventure. They said that the oil fields near Casper, Wyoming was desperate for workers. They were paying $1.25 per hour. I was working as an office boy for 40 cents an hour. Three or four of us agreed to hitchhike up there and get rich.

That trip never happened. I was able to talk Mother into letting me go, but the other parents put a stop to the trip. I had already quit my job. Gordon Grider said that he would like to go, but we changed our destination from Wyoming to the wheat harvest in Northern Oklahoma and Kansas. When I went by to get Gordon, his father had told him he could not go and that he would call the police and report him as a runaway if he did go.

I carried my ditty bag on down the street and came across Richard Kessee mowing his yard. He asked where I was going and I told him the wheat harvest. He went in and told his Mother that we were going fishing. He packed a bag and went with me. We walked to the highway and started hitch hiking.

We got as far as Alva, Oklahoma where he wrote a post card to his Mother telling her the truth. We were late for the harvest, so we slept in a stubble field. We went on into Kansas the next morning. World War II was still going on and the farmers were desperate for help. We were hired right off the highway, but had to work for two different farmers. We got separated. Richard went on North with the harvest. I stayed with the same farmer until he had plowed his fields. I was paid $10.00 a day for harvest and $5.00 a day for plowing. Room and board and laundry were furnished, so I didn't collect until I left. It was pure profit. I was rich, so I went home and opened a bank account.

In the mean time, Gordon had made his parents miserable for not letting him go. They took notice of my bank account and told him good riddance when he asked to go with me to the peach harvest in Colorado. I hit the highway again with Gordon.

We stopped at Gunnison, Colorado and worked on a ranch north of town for a few days. We slept in a bunkhouse with the cowboys while we worked hay. We went on to the peach harvest at Grand Junction, but didn't like what we saw. We decided to go see Yellowstone Park and headed north. We ran out of money at Jackson, Wyoming and worked at the Blue Bird Cafe for several days. We were trying to reach a movie set at Grand Teton, but were recruited before getting there.

We left Jackson for Yellowstone. We caught a ride with a soldier and his wife. He had just received a medical discharge. We agreed to buy the gasoline if we could tour the park with them.

We enjoyed a great tour of the park, but now time was running out. We got to Oklahoma City at 4 a.m. the day school started. I didn't go to bed so I could get to school on time. I learned more that summer than in all my senior year classes.

ECUMENICAL DAWNING

Gordon and I reached Jackson Hole just as we ran out of money.
A man approached me on the courthouse square and said, "Sonny,
     I need some help. Could you boys come to work for me?"
He owned the Blue Bird Cafe, the nicest in town it was plain to see.

     A movie was being made and the rodeo was in town.
     Business was booming, without enough help to go around.
          So, Gordon and I became bus boys for a few days.
     We cleaned up, replenished our funds before going our ways.

The movie company dined at the Blue Bird with the money crowd.
We learned not to mention the little casino in the back out loud.
     The owner seemed curious about me and invited me to lunch.
He was a very nice man and I welcomed a respite from the crunch.

     He told me the history of the settlement in Jackson Hole.
Pioneers from Salt Lake had made a new Mormon town their goal.
          I enjoyed lunch, his lesson and the restful break.
     He told me he was Mormon as he finished his wine before cake.

Then I told my benefactor that my Oklahoma Mormon friends,
     considered even drinking coffee, let alone wine as sins.
He smiled and said, "Oh, we are Jack Mormons in Jackson Hole".
Then it dawned on me, "I'm a Jack Baptist, I have found my role."

As graduation time approached, the question was whether to enlist or wait to be drafted. Some of my friends and I did not want to live with our lives on hold, so decided to enlist as soon as we graduated. We decided to enlist in the smallest unit possible to enhance our chances of staying together. We tried the Coast Guard, but they wouldn't take me. I was too small.

We heard that the Marine Corps had an enlistment option guaranteeing assignment to aviation units. That sounded like the best chance for some of us to stay together. Several of us enlisted. My buddies E. G., Gordon and Leslie waited to be drafted into the army.

E.G. Stewart, Mother and I

That decision to enlist for aviation duty was a good one for two reasons. First, several of us did stay close during our service. Secondly, budget cuts caused the Marine Corps to offer us early discharge. When congress changed the Army Air Corps to the Air Force as a separate branch of service, they questioned the need of the other branches of service needing aviation units. The Marine Corps did win the debate to keep squadrons for close air support to ground troops and some supply purposes. The Marines still had too many people committed to aviation with the reduced role. I jumped at the chance for an early discharge.

My military service was very unremarkable. World War II ended. The Cold War began. It is truly sad that so many Japanese were killed by atomic bombs. On the other hand, it is my opinion that even more lives were saved by the early surrender caused by the bombs. Amphibious landings were very costly in lives on both sides. The last, largest and most costly landing was to be on the Japanese coast. The invasion of Japan would have killed more Japanese and Americans than any battle except the European invasion. I would have been in that operation.

After boot camp, I was assigned to VMF452, a squadron in Marine Air Group 12. Physically, we were stationed at El Toro near Santa Anna, California. Occasionally, we went to sea on an escort air craft carrier for training exercises along the coast. We were on twenty-four hour alert to go to any hot spot in the world, so we drew overseas pay. In a conflict, our squadron of F4U Corsairs would have provided close air support to a battalion making an amphibious landing and/or fighting within a couple of hundred miles inland.

My job was maintaining the oxygen and CO_2 systems on the aircraft. When aboard ship, I doubled as a flight deck crewman. Our aircraft carrier, the Bedoing Straits was not one of these large super ships. It was a small freighter with a flight deck on top of it. It carried only one squadron.

Personnel in a marine squadron were trained for infantry combat. Our role was to be close to a battalion and that might have required our defending an air strip close to the battle lines. I drew extra pay as an expert rifleman. I also served as a bartender at the El Toro Leatherneck Club. That provided opportunities to supplement my fifty dollar a month base pay.

My only action consisted of fighting a forest fire in the mountains and climbing up to a crash on a mountainside. All other adventures took place on leave. When I visit with combat veterans, I refer to myself as a 'Hollywood Marine.'

MARINE COUSINS

James Tubbs, WW II

Elmer Mulhausen

Harold Mulhausen, Korea

Terry Millus, Viet Nam

Harry Mixer, Viet Nam 2 Tours

Warren Mixer, Viet Nam

Harvey Mixer

Phillip Mixer

MY MISSPENT YOUTH *

My misspent youth indicates my mother wasn't a goose.
Nor did I become a fan of the more modern Doctor Seuss.
While some were being educated on nursery rhymes,
I discovered that virtue becomes its own punishment sometimes.

Are we reading our kids some really harmful stuff?
Beanstalks reaching the sky-come on! Enough is enough.
And that giant on the beanstalk is as tasteful as a Clinton cigar.
And really, can you make any sense of wishing on a star?

All those stories hinting that you can depend on a fairy
make me suspicious and like Mary, quite contrary.
Leftist leaning Mother Goose needs some political centering
and Goldilocks should be jailed for breaking and entering.

Teaching kids that a tortoise can outrun a hare is a lie as great
as teaching them that celibacy is an inherited trait.
How about old Disney coming along and making us love a mouse?
The three pigs should have applied to HUD for a better house.

That little nymphet who lived in a shoe — without a clue,
I'll bet Planned Parenthood could have told her what to do.
Little Bo Peep should have been turned in to the humane society.
And Little Miss Muffet's weird diet caused the spider's impropriety.

What about that original party crasher, old Cinderella baby?
Dancing in slippers made of glass. Believe that? Oh, maybe.
But that crazy rhyme about the cow jumping over the moon–no way,
I would rather bet on a piss ant eating a bale of hay.

CIVILIAN AGAIN

When I came home from the Marine Corps, my cousin, Bill Tubbs and I did a little home improvement business. That didn't last long. Then I went to work for the Western Electric Company as an installer of telephone central office equipment. My starting wage was eighty-two cents per hour with a six cent raise in three months.

I considered this a temporary job because I planned to enter college in the fall. I got married and postponed school for a year. The next year, Evelyn was expecting and I put college off another year. Well, my temporary job turned into a twelve-year career.

Western Electric was the manufacturing and installation division of the Bell System. AT&T was the mother company of Western Electric as well as each of the geographic Bell Telephone Companies and AT&T Long Lines, which provided long distance service between them. AT&T also transmitted all the radio and television networks. There were a few independent companies but it was a virtual monopoly. When the justice department broke up the Bell System, Western Electric became AT&T. Later it was spun off as an independent company and became Lucent Technologies. Ironically, now one of the geographic Bell Companies, Southwestern Bell has now acquired other regional companies and AT&T.

I wasn't a really valuable employee in my early years with Western. I had never been good with tools or a good craftsman. I'm still not. I may be the worst handyman in Bosque County. I did recognize that most of our crewmembers seemed content to do basic work and not that interested in learning circuitry. I wanted to learn how the system worked. Because of Mr. and Mrs. Stumpf's early training, I was determined to compensate for my craft clumsiness and find a way to profit my employer.

I took an electronics course on my own at night and requested every school or course the company offered. Gradually, I became adept at wiring miscellaneous circuits, transitioning new equipment into the existing system, testing and trouble shooting. Sometimes management placed more experienced craft level employees in charge of up to six other employees. That duty had a handsome bonus of ten cents per hour extra. I needed every penny.

Eventually, I evolved into the role of taking a helper or small crew out to do small jobs. Sometimes I played a key role on large installations. At that time we were changing towns over from manual switch boards to dial systems. On these jobs I did early planning to help management determine the number of people needed at each stage of the job and to sequence assignments for better efficiency. During the bulk part of the job, I was in charge of a crew. Then as the installation wound down, I did testing and trouble shooting.

I worked in the days before electronic switching. We installed step-by-step or crossbar electromagnetic switching systems. Electronic circuits then used vacuum tubes. That was in the days before transistors and chips.

My cousin, Bill Tubbs and I worked together for a while right after I came home from the service. One Saturday afternoon, we met two girls at the Redskin Theatre. They wouldn't let us take them home, but did give us their telephone numbers. Shortly thereafter, I called Evelyn Crow and asked her for a date. She wouldn't go unless it was a double date, so Bill dated her friend, Christine Robinson.

The four of us went out two or three times a week for a while until Bill tried to date Evelyn. In his defense, I did tell Bill that I planned to back off for awhile as I was getting serious too quickly. He did make me mad, though, so that ended the foursome. I kept dating Evelyn to protect my territory. Yes, we both got serious rather quickly. Before long, we admitted we were in love.

We knew we were too young to get married. I wasn't making enough money, either. Today, young people make other arrangements. But in 1947, when people with our upbringing were in love, they got married. We met in April and married on September 25th. We had a simple family ceremony in J. W. and Helen Booker's home. Helen was Evelyn's older sister.

Evelyn and I moved into what we considered a doll house. In reality, it was probably just a shack on the back of a neighbor's lot. It was good to be neighbors with Helen and J. W. for many reasons. They helped look after us. I was making eighty-eight cents an hour. We didn't own a car. When Bill and I split, we sold our jointly owned car. I got to my various Western Electric job sites by bus or a ride with a co-worker.

In those days, when a man married a woman, he committed to supporting her as very few women worked outside the home. We budgeted very closely. Obviously, we didn't have any extra money, but we didn't miss any meals either. I packed a brown bag for lunch at work. We didn't buy anything until we had the money.

Not many people expected much from our marriage. We overheard Evelyn's neighbors betting whether or not we would last six months. When John was three or four months old, they were enchanted with the beautiful baby. We still didn't have a car. They offered to trade their new car for our baby. They really thought they would be saving the baby. Evelyn and I had many laughs in later years about that incident.

J. C. and Alene Crow were Evelyn's parents. Popa Crow was the true patriarch of the family. His word was final. At the time I met Evelyn, he was an assistant manager at a large service station. He had owned a service station at one time. He and Alene had both worked at an aircraft plant during the war. Earlier in life he drove a truck and did other blue collar work. They managed their money well and were independent. Popa Crow arranged for me to work part time at the service station to supplement my income. I worked several second jobs. I tried selling vacuum cleaners door to door. I also sold milk for my brother-in-law, J.W.

Evelyn's Parents, J.C. and Alene Crow

Evelyn had an older brother, Harlan Crow that worked in the oil field exploration business. He and his family always lived a long way from us. They visited every three or four years, but we had very little interaction with them.

Christine was Evelyn's other older sister. She was married to Harvey Cass. We three son-in-laws looked up to Popa Crow for direction and always did our best to please him. He dearly loved his grandchildren and they idolized him.

Throughout our early married life, we had a lot of good times with the Crows and Evelyn's sister's families. J. W., Harvey and I were fishing companions. J. W. and Helen owned a boat. All the family went to the lake frequently to camp, cook out and water ski.

J. W. and Helen had three daughters that we were always close to. We loved Betty Jo, Linda Kay and Shirley. Betty Jo was around six years old when Evelyn and I married. We were with her quite a bit before we married. I don't know if we were baby sitting her or if she had been assigned to chaperone us. Later in life, we also became close to Betty Jo's children. Betty's first marriage failed and she is now married to Rick Luttrell. Whenever we can get to Oklahoma City, Jo Ann and I love to visit with Betty Jo, Rick and Shirley.

Christine and Harvey Cass had two sons, Ron and Jimmy. Ron and his wife, Glenda, live in Enid, Oklahoma. Jimmy and his wife, Carol, live in Piedmont, Oklahoma. We always enjoyed the Cass family. My oldest, John, was close enough in age to have many adventures with Ron and Jimmy. After Harvey's death, Christine owned a restaurant in Hennesee, Oklahoma. When it burned down, she was unable to replace it. She was long past retirement age any way. She lives in a retirement community now in Kingfisher, Oklahoma.

I just talked to Ron's wife, Glenda, on the telephone. She and Ron are planning a trip down to see us. I'm really looking forward to seeing them. They haven't met Jo Ann, so we are looking forward to that as well.

On one outing with the Booker and Cass families, we camped along the lake shore a good distance from the boat ramp. Later in the afternoon we noticed a severe looking cloud approaching. We decided it was time to break camp and get the boat out of the water. It was my turn to ski, so rather than miss my turn; I decided to ski across the lake as we headed for the boat ramp.

J. W. was driving the boat, and Harvey was also in the boat. About half way across, the thunderstorm hit with strong winds and blinding rain. The waves were immediately six to seven feet tall. I was at the end of the ski rope and couldn't even see the boat. When I hit a wave, the rope nearly jerked from my hands. After going over or through a wave the rope went slack. I finally went down.

J. W. told Harvey they had to turn around and get Elmer. Harvey said "he is already drowned, we have to save ourselves." Luckily, they were

73

able to pull me out of the lake and we reached the ramp area. The ramp was in a protected harbor, so we were able to load. Just as we pulled the boat out of the water, the storm ended and all was quiet.

Harvey denied saying that I was already drowned, but it made a good story for kidding him for many years.

I enjoyed my job at Western Electric. I enjoyed the camaraderie of fellow employees and the challenges of the job. We had good benefits and a union contract.

When I started, I had an attitude against unions and refused to join. Before long, I learned why unions were needed in that era. Not long after I married, several of us were transferred to Lubbock, Texas. One of the transferred men questioned the terms of the transfer. The steward on the job looked at our papers. Sure enough, we were shorted some money and time allowance for reporting. When confronted, management quickly corrected the "error".

Many people who knew me during my executive days would be surprised to learn that I did join the union and worked for fair treatment of employees. I did take my turn several times serving as job steward.

Another time, I did some extensive wiring low enough that I had to work on my knees on a concrete floor. I developed a severely inflamed knee and spent two or three days in the hospital. The doctor told me not to work on my knees for a week or two. That enraged my supervisor who said my injury was not job related. He refused to pay the medical bills and threatened to fire me. Our job steward intervened and the crew threatened to walk off the job. The supervisor relented.

Incidents like that were not uncommon. I only had those two during my twelve years, but our union did play an important part.

During my insurance career, I never observed a situation where a union was needed. I think that over time labor organizations have been like a swinging pendulum. There have been times of labor abuse demanding help from union organizations. Then as unions became more powerful over time, then union leaders many times became the abusers. Power breeds corruption and abuse.

Over the years management has also become more professional and enlightened. If that trend continues, union membership will continue to decline.

Of course, most of my supervisors were good and also friends. I did enjoy the job. I didn't like the travel and short notice transfers. I didn't like night work. Any work that might interrupt service was done between 10:00 P.M. and 7:00 A.M. A night shift was never long enough to become accustomed to sleeping days. I didn't like the fear of lay offs. The size of our work force depended on the Bell System's annual growth budget, which was never steady. I was never laid off but many friends with less seniority were.

I did quit in 1950. I was sent to a job in Borger, Texas. After a couple of weeks, Evelyn wanted to join me. We couldn't find a place to live. I was staying in a boarding house. The proprietor said that Evelyn and John could stay with me if Evelyn worked for her. John was about a year and a half old and Evelyn was newly pregnant. When morning sickness started, she couldn't handle the work. She and John went home. A few weeks later, she miscarried.

I wanted to be with her, and asked my supervisor for a transfer home to Oklahoma City. He said he couldn't transfer me, so I turned in my tools and went home. I spent several days looking for a job to no avail. After a week, I went by the district superintendent's office just to see who might be around and visit. The superintendent asked what I was doing there and I told him my story. The superintendent wasn't aware that I had quit. The supervisor in Borger never turned in my resignation. They said they could use me in Oklahoma City, and I was transferred home. I was greatly relieved.

I appreciated Western Electric giving me a job when I was a boy and allowing me to keep it while I grew up.

My stay in Borger was not without a laugh or two. At that time Borger wasn't the flower garden of the world. Phillips Petroleum was the principle employer. They had their own community of company homes just outside of town. They also had a carbon black plant. When the wind was right, you could smell it. That wind also carried a fine mist of carbon black. Anything or anybody left outside was soon speckled with black.

The town sorely needed something to be proud of. Community leaders wanted a nice hotel downtown, but no hotel company would build one. Finally, visionary leaders formed a local corporation. Citizens bought shares and bonds in their local corporation. The citizens personally financed a beautiful downtown hotel. They were proud of this accomplishment. Now they had a central meeting place, a social center and quality lodging for travelers doing business in Borger.

Dedication of the hotel called for a big civic celebration. Even Texas governor, Allen Shivers came for the event. An eighteen-wheeler flatbed oil field truck was driven into the vacant lot adjacent to the telephone office. A podium and public address system were placed on the flatbed making it an improbable stage. The public address system was powered through a long extension cord running into the side door of the telephone office. Dignitaries climbed make-shift stairs and sat in folding chairs on the truck bed. Crowds filled the vacant lot and adjacent streets. It was a proud day.

I was working just inside the telephone office while all this was going on. I sat on a seat connected to a rolling ladder, six or seven feet up. I was connecting wires at the main distributing frame. In those days, all connections were soldered. My soldering iron was plugged into a wall receptacle below me. The public address extension cord was plugged into another receptacle by the door.

The governor had a wonderful speech. I borrowed from it myself in later years when I was in a position of leadership. The speech was entitled "Know your own strength". Most people don't know what they can do until they try. These citizens had accomplished something together, that they didn't think they could do.

Then why did I interrupt such a good speech? Well, I was twenty-two years old and couldn't resist a good laugh. An outside telephone repairman stepped into the door adjacent to me. He paused to adjust to the change of light after being out in the sun. In an unguarded moment, I looked down from my ladder seat and said, "Hey buddy, could you unplug my soldering iron for me?" He reached over and pulled the plug on the public address system extension cord.

The governor's speech went silent. Then there was loud murmuring, and the telephone man realized what he had done. He plugged the cord back in before anyone reached our door. The governor's speech resumed. The telephone man looked up at me and said, "You S.O.B." Then we both had a good laugh. In making this confession, I trust that all those in authority that day have long since retired.

The Texas Longhorns had beaten my beloved Oklahoma Sooners that year in football, but this Okee boy did unplug the governor.

When the Bell System initiated a college tuition and book reimbursement program for approved employees, I jumped at the chance. I could have had about the same program on the G. I. Bill, but I thought if the company approved me for the program, surely they would keep me close enough to attend classes.

I enrolled in night classes at Oklahoma City University. It was going to be a long road. I took nine hours per semester and six hours in the summer. Classes were from 6:00 p.m. until 10:00 p.m. two nights per week.

Western did keep me close to school most of the time. When I was assigned night work, I was allowed to work 10:30 p.m.. to 7:30 a.m. rather than 10:00 p.m. until 7:00 a.m.. I worked one job in Chickasha, Oklahoma about an hour and quarter from school. Then I worked in Tulsa which was a two hour plus drive to school. I commuted from home on Monday mornings to Tulsa, and then took off an hour early at 4:00 p.m. My dinner while driving to the 6:00 p.m. class in Oklahoma City consisted of an apple and chips. I stayed home Monday night and drove to Tulsa on Tuesday morning. I made up the hour on Tuesday evening and spent the night in Tulsa. I repeated the process on Wednesday and Thursday.

In November, 1958, I was told I was needed on a job in Harper, Kansas. That meant I couldn't attend classes, but the supervisor said that I was essential for the job. I was three quarters through the semester and I was unable to appreciate the compliment. I stopped classes and went to Harper. I did make enough noise that they transferred me to Oklahoma City in January for three days so I could take the final exams. I got some assignment instruction by telephone and studied hard enough that I made A's in all three of my classes.

I really appreciated Oklahoma City University. They made every effort to accommodate working adults. Math and English instructors realized that many of us had been out of high school a long time. They allowed some catch up and review time the first two or three weeks. The long gap between high school and college was not a problem in the business courses.

The contract between the union and Western Electric spelled out our pay scale precisely. There was a starting pay with periodic raises over the first three or four years. At that time a merit scale took over. After each annual review the company, at their sole discretion, could award a raise up to the merit top. Those raises were hard to come by.

In 1958, I had been on the merit scale six or seven years and was five cents an hour from the top. I was told that senior management allowed only one installer in our Western Oklahoma division to reach top. One installer was already there. I was the second highest paid. That revelation helped point me in another direction. I wanted to be paid what I was worth, not what a job was worth.

The Harper transfer caused me to drop the second semester. The January performance review gave me a second jolt. Although I was essential for that job in Harper, I wasn't good enough to get that last five cents per hour raise. I re-opened negotiations with a State Farm Insurance Manager. I decided to quit and try to become a State Farm agent.

I was mature enough to not quit immediately. I still had a family and a mortgage. I studied insurance, selling, marketing and how to run my own business. I also built a file of prospective clients.

When I left Western Electric, I was licensed, had a modest office set up and six hundred prospect cards with the expiration dates for home and auto insurance.

After it became known that I had resigned one of my supervisors said, "Elmer, I bet we could have kept you for a nickel, couldn't we?"

I replied, "You will never know will you?"

END SIGHT

Corporal Barney McGill was quite an
unusual guy.
His most obvious peculiarity was his left
glass eye.
The eye must have been uncomfortable for
him to wear,
because Barney took it out to sleep, leaving
the socket bare.

In the morning, he would take the eye out
of his pocket.
Put it in his mouth to warm and moisten,
then pop it in the socket.
On one chilly morning while Barney was
warming the eye,
Bill came up behind him, clapped him on
the back and said, "Hi!"

The blow so startled poor Barney that he
swallowed the eye,
sending Barney and Bill over to sick bay
on the fly.
The medic, after a laugh, told Barney
there's no need to worry.
"The eye will pass in due course, be
watchful but not to hurry."

The medic also gave Barney some pills to
help the process along.
"But if it doesn't pass by Monday, go to the
clinic to see what's wrong."
The guys in the barracks kidded poor Barney like
you wouldn't believe,
for all of the trips to the latrine and
inspections the eye to retrieve.

But Monday came and alas, the eye still
hadn't made its exit.
So Barney went over to the clinic to see if
a doctor could fix it.
A giggling receptionist sent Barney back to
a room in the rear,
where proctologist, Doctor I.C. Bottoms
would soon appear.

But first, a cute little nurse cleaned Barney
on the inside
while completely destroying his dignity
and pride.
Doctor Bottoms was a man of few words and had his
routine down pat.
He did his exam first and if talk was
needed, it came after that.

Barney peeled off his clothes and donned the famous
open back door gown.
He mounted the torture table, belly first
with his knees dangling down.
The table tilted Barney's face toward the
floor raising his posterior
making it easier for Doctor Bottoms to
view Barney's interior.

The doctor plunged in the scope and
pumped in a little air
so Barney's insides were clearly visible, all
shiny and bare.
Doctor Bottoms then peered into the scope
and what did he see?
"Heaven help me", he said, "This poor
wretch is looking back at me."

Doc came down from his stool, looked into
Barney's face and said, "Brother,
the very first thing we must do – is learn
to trust each other."

*P.S.   Well, Barney survived this adventure. Then some high falutin
friend took him to the opera. When the soprano hit that highest note
– Well that's just too gruesome to tell.*

STARTING A FAMILY

John was born in 1948, and Sheryl was born in 1951. We thought two children made a pretty good size family, but we forgot something. Teresa was born in 1961 and David in 1964. John and Sheryl say they were born to young parents who were so afraid of the responsibility that they were too strict. Then Teresa and David came along to totally different parents who spoiled them and treated them like grandchildren. There was also a big difference in household economics when the two sets of kids were born. But Evelyn and I loved them all equally.

Our first son, John Charles Mulhausen

John was shuffled from one school to another. In our nomadic life with Western Electric, John started school in Oklahoma City, then Enid, then McAlester and Lawton, then back to Oklahoma City again. We moved to Ada for his high school years. John was very bright and did well in spite of the moving. In Ada, he was almost too bright and came close to not graduating. After high school, he attended Central Oklahoma University, but he already knew more then the instructors there. After a couple of years as a brick layer helper, and a Navy tour in Viet Nam and Cambodia, John decided that education was a pretty good idea.

John went to the University of Oklahoma but dropped out four hours short of a degree. He moved to Texas.

In 1977, Evelyn and I lived in Columbia, Missouri where I served as an Agency Director for State Farm Insurance. I had been assigned to chair our summer Regional Management Conference. I took Evelyn with me on a trip to the Lake of the Ozarks to negotiate the conference facilities and make some plans

We were having dinner at the Four Seasons Resort when we were paged for a telephone call. It was John announcing that he and Jeanne Panza had just gotten married in Austin. Although we hated not participating in their wedding, we were delighted. We knew Jeanne. She had a wonderful family in Oklahoma City and was an Oklahoma University graduate.

At State Farm Insurance nepotism is not a bad word. In fact, nepotism is celebrated. Our C.E.O. is a third generation chief executive. Agents and employees encourage their children to join State Farm. After we moved to Dallas and after our grandson, John Dylan Mulhausen, was born, we encouraged John to go to work for State Farm.

John got a job in the claims department, but in Oklahoma City rather than in Dallas. He wanted to distance himself from my influence or interference. John was his own man. He started on a clerical level rather than the professional level because he lacked the four hours for a degree. He quickly completed those four hours and graduated. He was promoted and worked every level before going into management. He and Jeanne live in Tulsa. John manages one claims unit in Oklahoma City and another unit in Tulsa.

HAPPY ANNIVERSARY JOHN AND JEANNE

Some things just go together
like a bottle and cork.
A cup needs a saucer
and a knife goes with a fork.

That's like John and Jeanne
together all these years as one.
We celebrate their anniversary and
their bond in both sickness or fun.

Happy Anniversary dear ones, may
your love continue to grow
with health, and happiness, knowing you
have each other whatever wind may blow.

All our love,
Dad and Jo Ann

It is hard to believe John started his career with State Farm Insurance thirty years ago. I'm proud of both John and Jeanne. Jeanne is an artist. She designed this book cover and designed the illustrations. She got help from my talented grand daughters Sarah and Mary Mulhausen.

John Dylan, who we call Johnny to differentiate from his Dad, lives in Seattle. He is an engineer for Microsoft. He loves his work, but his first love is music. He is just completing a leave of absence from Microsoft. He has been on a cross-country concert tour promoting his new C.D.

My first grandson, John D. or "Johnny" Mulhausen
was a computer whizz at a very young age.

My beautiful granddaughter, Sarah, is still taking classes in college and lives with the family in Tulsa. Mary Ruth, who just turned sixteen, is now in home schooling taking both college and high school subjects.

Sheryl was a beautiful baby. She walked and talked earlier than any of our other children. She attended Lafayette Elementary School in Oklahoma City. My State Farm office and our home were both within a city block of Lafayette.

Sheryl was nine when I took a promotion and moved to Ada, Oklahoma. While we lived in Ada, Sheryl went on an outing to Oklahoma City with our pastor's wife and children. On that trip, their car was rear-ended by another car. Sheryl had severe back pain and it always seemed to return when she had any stress. That was my first awareness of Sheryl having health or emotional problems, that she has been plagued with ever since.

Sheryl Mulhausen

At that time Popa Crow was also having serious health problems in Oklahoma City. Evelyn wanted to be close to her father and Sheryl hated her school in Ada. Although Ada was more central to my district and I liked the town, we moved to Shawnee. I stayed within my district and we were only forty-five minutes from Popa and Nana Crow. I received a severe reprimand from Paul Todd, my agency vice-president, for moving to the very corner of my district without asking. That was the only chewing out I ever received in my thirty-four year career with State Farm. I didn't tell Paul, but I didn't ask because I didn't want to disobey if he said no. I still performed my job but my family came first.

Shawnee was a wonderful place to live, but it didn't seem to help Sheryl. She had more problems. She married a son from one of our finest church families. They had a nice church wedding. The young couple went away to college, back to Ada of all places. Their marriage didn't last long, and Sheryl came back home. Sheryl worked as my secretary for a while.

Evelyn opened a dress shop, and Sheryl really enjoyed working with her. When I accepted a promotion to Columbia, Missouri, Sheryl didn't move with us. She had developed a relationship with a young man named Damon Downing. We were active in the Shawnee community theatre, which is where Sheryl met Damon. We left Sheryl in charge of the dress shop, and moved to Columbia.

In a couple of months, Sheryl and Damon married, and Damon took a job in West Texas. We were unable to sell the dress shop, so we shipped the stock to Columbia and opened Carrie's Fashions in Columbia.

The West Texas job didn't pan out, so Damon and Sheryl moved to Columbia and then to Dallas where Damon directed a Christian Dinner Theatre. We had to make a couple of emergency trips to Dallas as Sheryl continued to have health problems. Sheryl was such a beautiful, intelligent girl, and her problems are the heart breaks of my life.

Dominique was Sheryl's first baby girl. She was a delightful, beautiful baby and held the special position as our first grandchild. Patrick and Danielle followed. They were equally delightful. I have wonderful memories of my grandchildren growing up. We dearly loved all of them.

We were living in Plano, Texas when Sheryl and Damon's marriage finally ended. Dominique stayed with her mother. Patrick and Danielle bounced back and forth between Damon and Sheryl.

Sheryl went to work for State Farm in the Dallas Regional office. She started as a clerk in the life insurance operations department. She worked and studied hard. She earned the FLMI professional designation (Fellow, Life Management Institute). State Farm sent her to Boston for the conferment exercises. Evelyn and I went along and were very proud. The company promoted her to underwriter.

In the life insurance business, FLMI is a professional designation for home office employees. C.L.U. (Charter Life Underwriter) is a professional designation for insurance agents. After earning the FLMI, Sheryl started studies toward the C.L.U. designation. Both of these programs are in ten parts and each normally takes five years to complete.

I took special interest because I am also a C.L.U. I promised her two things. First, we agreed to join her and take the children on the conferment trip and secondly she would be given a chance to compete for a State Farm Agency. When she completed the program, the company paid her expense and also Dominique's expense to the conferment in San Diego. Evelyn and I picked up the expense for Patrick and Danielle. We had a delightful vacation to Disney Land, Universal Studios and the beaches. Danielle celebrated her ninth birthday at Disney Land. We also enjoyed the annual C.L.U. meeting and conferment exercises.

When I asked Agency Managers to consider Sheryl as a candidate for agency, I intended for her to go through the complete selection process and compete with other candidates for appointment. I think that process enhanced the odds of success for the candidate, the company and the manager.

A manager that I had recruited into management put her on a fast track and appointed her in Plano. He did this out of loyalty to me, but I would have been more pleased if she had competed for the appointment. She struggled for two years with illness, family responsibilities and finances. The agency experience didn't work out and the company hired her back into the regional office.

Sheryl did well back in the office and reached the position of senior underwriter after moving to the Austin Regional Office. Meanwhile, her illness was diagnosed as fibromialgia. She worked ten years with the disease, but finally took disability retirement. She also qualified for Social Security Disability.

Fibromialgia causes great pain, fatigue, depression and a diminished immune system. Uncontrollable nausea first caused Sheryl to leave her job. Before returning to work, she contracted pneumonia. She then suffered depression and never returned to work.

Sheryl's oldest daughter, Dominique, has had some of her own traumatic experiences, and she too is in the process of qualifying for disability. Sheryl and Dominique live together in Lewisville, Texas. It breaks my heart that these two beautiful and intelligent women live under such unhappy circumstances.

Our third child, Teresa, now lives in Plano, Texas with husband, Troy Federspiel, son Shaun, 17 and daughter, Emily, 15. Their oldest son, Jeff lives in Lewisville, Texas with his wife, Kathleen. Kathleen has a son Alex Becceri by a previous marriage. He is a real sharp nine year old and I'm honored that he considers me as his great grandfather. Of course all the grand kids and Alex simply refer to me as Popa.

Jeffrey and Kathleen have a beautiful toddler, Amelie, who is my first great grandchild by birth. She and the family were here for Thanksgiving, and she has learned to call me Popa also. She really steals my heart.

Teresa was born in Ada, Oklahoma in 1961. Evelyn and I had moved to Ada from Oklahoma City when State Farm appointed me Agency

Manager for Southeast Oklahoma. Of course, she shook up the household. We hadn't had a baby around for nine years. She was a delightful child, the center of attention and spoiled by all of us, especially by brother, John.

We moved to Shawnee, Oklahoma where she started to school. I can't recall Teresa ever causing a problem when we lived in Ada or Shawnee.

I accepted a promotion from State Farm January 1st, 1974. We moved to Columbia, Missouri. Evelyn had questioned the move because she liked Shawnee and hated cold weather. I told her we were moving only one layer of states north. Well, a record setting storm hit Columbia the very first week we were there. Businesses and schools closed because of the twenty inch snowfall. Our subdivision was built around three small spring fed lakes. Those lakes froze and all the children were ice skating. Teresa broke her ankle right away.

Of course, I was at work. Evelyn and the neighborhood children loaded her onto a sled. They finally got her up the hill and to our home. Evelyn accused me of moving her to Alaska. That was a beginning of Evelyn's unhappiness with living in Missouri, even though we had only two severe winters out of the five winters there.

Maybe it was starting school life in a cast or maybe it was my frequent absences, but we began to have a few problems with Teresa in Columbia. My office was in the Missouri-Kansas Regional office in Columbia, but my division was the greater St. Louis area. All of my agents and managers were there, so I was in St. Louis two or three nights a week.

On one occasion we agreed to let Teresa have a party for a dozen or so of her school friends. We had a full basement recreation area which provided a good place for the party.

A school fad, unknown to us at that time, turned into a problem. If there was a party anywhere, it buzzed around school and everyone considered themselves invited. As the evening progressed, more and more youngsters showed up for the party. We discovered later that Teresa didn't know all of them. Some boys were going outside then coming back in. After a while I told them that if they left, they couldn't come back. This turned into a physical confrontation. Then it got rowdy downstairs. I went down to check. Instead of a dozen, there were at least thirty. Someone had smuggled alcohol in and some older boys had roughed up David.

I dismissed the party. We called the parents of the children we knew. Of course, Teresa was in tears. I had embarrassed her and ruined her socially at school.

That event was a parental lesson. After that, any party would be by written invitation. We would have a guest list and be introduced to each guest entering our home. No others would be admitted. Evelyn and I would more closely monitor activities.

Most people attributed Teresa's behavior as normal adolescence to teen behavior. Teresa had always been so good that any change was disturbing to us. All in all, she was a bright and loving daughter.

Teresa started driving at age sixteen, and that was a whole new experience. John and Sheryl went through their teen driving years with no tickets or accidents that we know of. Teresa had three accidents the first year she drove. I was in the insurance business, and that sure disturbed me. When she learned her lesson, she learned it well. She hasn't had an accident in the following thirty years.

We moved to Plano, Texas in May of 1978. Teresa graduated from Plano Senior High School, and then married Troy Federspiel. Troy served a hitch in the army. After his enlistment, Troy worked full time for the Texas National Guard, and was called into active duty in the Desert Storm War.

Jeffrey and Shawn were born before Troy was called into active duty. When he returned from Iraq, it was a major family happening. All of the family went to Fort Hood and waited in a gym until Troy's flight arrived. Teresa, Jeff and Shaun all had welcome home signs. It was a joyous reunion. Emily was born the next year.

Teresa did not work outside her home until all three children were in school. To supplement Troy's earnings, she cared for other children along with her own. She loved all of them. She was a wonderful mom and caregiver.

As Jeff, Shaun and Emily grew up; their family life centered around youth sports. They all played whatever sport was in season. They were associated with a budding organization called Plano Sports Authority (P.S.A.) Teresa and Troy volunteered as coaches, officials, schedules directors and committee members as the organization grew.

When all the children were in school, Teresa accepted full time employment with that organization which continued to grow. P.S.A. is now a huge non-profit with a facility that includes a real ice hockey rink, fourteen basketball courts and administrative offices. During the course of a year 2.5 million people play or view sports in the building, and they serve 45,000 youth. As each session rolls around, P.S.A. builds the team rosters and leagues, assigns coaches, schedules games and officials for each game. Teresa is the administrative Director. I'm proud of her and the work P.S.A does.

Troy is a quality control engineer for an electronics firm. He stays involved with P.S.A. in various capacities. Shaun also works part-time for P.S.A. He officiates games and works in concessions. Shaun will graduate from Plano East Senior High School this coming spring. He is a very patriotic young man and plans to go into the army upon graduation.

Shaun has played youth sports from the time he was four years old in soccer. He played whatever was in season until he began to concentrate on football. He was competing for a varsity position last year when he sustained a calf injury and gave up football.

Emily is our remaining athlete. She has played everything, but has narrowed her activity to ice hockey. At first she had to play with the boys because very few girls play ice hockey. She then joined a girls club team associated with USA Hockey. They still have to compete with boys in local and state tournaments, but compete in girl's tournaments in the United States and Canada several times a year. Her current team is the 'Texas Attack,' sixteen year old girl's division.

I am amazed by how good they are. My pride in her is heightened by the fact that she is diabetic and wears an insulin pump. She has attended Olympic and college camp and hopes to earn a scholarship. Of course, she will have to go to the North, because there is no women's college hockey in Texas.

I'm very proud of Teresa, Troy and all their children.

Shaun, Troy, Emily and Teresa Federspiel, 2007

Happy Birthday Emily

Happy Birthday Emily, our favorite hockey star.
We don't see you a lot when you travel near and far.
But we want you to know we love you
and we are proud of all you do.

Hope your birthday is happy and full of cheer
and you enjoy a healthy and successful year.

All our love,
Papa and Grandma Jo

My hockey star granddaughter Emily Federspiel

*We found this in Teresa's Junior High notebook,
and kept it over the years.*

THE LOST FLOWER

I see the lost flower growing in the grass.
I just can't seem to reach it.
The only hope for my happiness is that
one lonely flower growing in the grass.
I'm getting closer to it.
If my leap gives out I'll crawl.
It will take time for me to make it,
but I'm not a quitter.
Some day, that last flower in the world
will be mine.
Unless someone else finds it and needs it more.

Teresa Lu Mulhausen

Jay David Mulhausen came to bless our household in Ada, Oklahoma in September, 1964. I'm sure God sent David to shake Evelyn and me out of any complacency we might develop. There was no rest around David. He was perpetual motion, fearless, strong willed and an accident going somewhere to happen. All the family loved him, dearly.

David always wanted to be older than he was and participated in whatever the older children were doing. When he was two years old, he would hold up four fingers and say he was four, because Teresa was four. We moved to Shawnee when David was two then to Columbia, Missouri when he was nine. We knew all the emergency room personnel on a first name basis in both cities.

We built a new home in Shawnee on two acres. We bought the smallest Honda motor bike for the kids, but David monopolized it. He ran full throttle all over the place. We had a couple of loads of dirt hauled to the back yard for landscaping. The dirt piles became his motocross course. He drove up the front side then flew off the back side. When we were finally able to spread the dirt, David was mad at us for tearing up his playground.

David did and still does love to fish. We had a small lake stocked with bass, sunfish and catfish adjacent to our lot. David became a skilled fisherman at an early age. When we moved to Columbia, we also had neighborhood lakes. He spent hours exploring and fishing those lakes.

We took David with us on a company trip to Canada, and he took his rod and reel on the flight. While we were in meetings in Montreal, David took public transportation to go fishing. In Quebec City, I drove him out north of town to a river. After Evelyn and I completed our activities, I drove back out to get him. He did the same on trips to Florida and to White Sulphur Springs, West Virginia.

When David left home, I lost my last regular fishing companion and sold our little fishing boat. David now lives in Ft. Lauderdale, Florida which provides him with a great number of fishing choices. He has also taken up duck hunting. When I visited him, he took me into some of the local water ways, to the keys and out into the everglades. Still the daredevil, he drove his john boat full speed down a narrow shallow airboat trail to get to the canal we planned to fish. We had to keep the john boat on a plane or get stuck. He said that if we met another boat, you keep full throttle until you meet them, veer slightly right as you brush the other boat and bounce into the edge of the saw-grass, then back down into the shallow trail. We survived.

The bass fishing was good in the canal, but I was distracted by the alligators. The small alligators were diving to avoid us, but the big twelve foot grand-daddies didn't seem to be afraid of anything. They stayed on the banks sunning and hopefully snoozing as we passed by

David and I also had a wonderful trip to Alaska in 2000. We saw the sights and caught a lot of king salmon on the Kenai and Kasilof rivers.

In 1978, we transferred from Missouri to the Dallas regional office so that my office and my assigned territory were in the same city. We bought a home in Plano, Texas. David's school problems continued. He just didn't like to go to school. Unlike me, David was a skilled craftsman. He liked working with his hands. He studied mechanics and was a skilled auto mechanic, but didn't want to make that his vocation. He did repair and renovations to our home and did a good job. I bought a house that he renovated for sale, but that didn't make any real money. For a while, David was self-employed repairing insured damages. He also installed alarm systems.

Then David found his niche. He heard there was a need for workers on broadcast towers. Daredevil David applied. Though he had no experience, that tower company bought David a one way ticket to California. He reported to a 1200 foot tower on a mountain near Kilroy, California. To test his nerve and initiate him, they instructed David to straddle an antenna. A cable pulled the antenna to near the top where a couple of crew members waited. Before mounting the antenna, they kicked the antenna away from the tower and started it swinging like a pendulum 1200 feet above the tower base and umpteen hundred feet over the valley below. David laughed about the trick and was accepted into the crew.

He worked on towers all over the country and for several companies until he reached management. He became operations manager for Tiner Communications of Ft. Lauderdale. The boy that hated school studied enough management and engineering to be earning a six figure income.

David was now climbing only occasionally to inspect or trouble shoot or make estimates for selling. One day he decided he didn't want to climb or travel any more. He didn't want any more stress. He quit.

David then became an apprentice marine electrician. He studied hard and is now working on some of the world's most luxurious yachts as a journeyman marine electrician. He isn't making as much money, but he earns a good living. He doesn't take his job home with him every night. He has time for a life. He owns his home and has time to hunt and fish. He is happy.

David has had three soured relationships and he is now a confirmed bachelor. As I write, I'm looking forward to David's annual Christmas visit. I just called one of David's old high school buddies, Joel Schmieg. I invited Joel to come visit while David is here. I admire Joel for his character and his many self-taught skills. He is also a confirmed bachelor and has been self-employed all his life, choosing to not ever sacrifice quality working for someone else. When I lived in Plano, Joel helped me with repair problems several times.

When Joel bought a home in a rural area near McKinney, Texas, he joined the volunteer Fire Department. He became interested in the technology of fire fighting and fire fighting tools. He is now the Fire Marshall and Assistant Chief. Joel's latest invention is called the "aggressor." It is a high quality piercing nozzle. It is swung-like an ax to penetrate car hoods, dumpsters or other enclosed compartments. After piercing, the nozzle directs a high velocity spray inside closed areas. www.americanfiretools.com

WILLIE WASN'T A BOY SCOUT *

Willie and Belle met at the senior center dance.
From their very first eye contact, it looked like romance.

Oh Belle, her personality was a delight,
and her figure was curvaceous.
Her eyes were bright.
Her smile was – well flirtatious.

Willie's poor lonely heart fell like Niagara.
Though the spirit was eager,
the action was meager.
Cause Willie forgot the Viagra.

A Nomadic Life

A couple of months after marrying Evelyn, Western Electric Company transferred me to Lubbock, Texas. Evelyn gave me about a week to find a room, and then she came out on the bus. She said we didn't get married to live apart.

We couldn't find an apartment so we rented a sleeping room in a private home. We shared a bath with another roomer who was a fellow employee from Oklahoma City. We fixed a few meals on a hot plate. But basically, we ate out and snacked.

We were in Lubbock about ten or eleven weeks, but that was just the beginning of a nomadic life. Some of my fellow workers had permanent transfers to other cities, but I was able to keep my base in Oklahoma, City. I went where ever the company needed me. A per diem was paid when working away from our base. We always kept our expenses below the per diem so we actually made a little extra money for the inconvenience. Of course when working at home, I always worked another part-time job or went to school.

After Lubbock, we equipped ourselves to live in a small apartment. I went by myself and rented rooms in private homes on short jobs close enough to be home every weekend, but my family went with me on longer jobs.

In addition to Lubbock, we lived in Borger, Longview and Dallas, Texas; Little Rock, Arkansas; Enid, McAlester, Lawton, Shawnee, Idabel and Woodward, Oklahoma. The kids even attended school in Enid, McAlester and Lawton. I went on jobs without Evelyn to St. Louis, Missouri, Carthage and Ft. Worth, Texas; Kay City, Fairview, Elk City, Ponca City, Ada, Guthrie, Tulsa, Duncan, Chickasha, Wapanucka, Sand Springs, Pauls Valley, Durant, Holdenville, Norman, Henrietta and Okmulgee, Oklahoma and Harper, Kansas. I am sure I have forgotten some places. We were young and resilient and I don't remember it being that hard.

We still tried to maintain a home and church home in Oklahoma, City. Just as soon as I turned twenty-one in 1949, we bought a little two bedroom frame G.I. house. It cost $7,700. The G. I. loan was at 4% with payments of $47.00 per month. It was our castle. We had some "gimme" furniture. We bought furniture one stick at a time and appliances as we could handle it. Until we could afford a washing machine, Evelyn did the washing by hand. Until we could afford a dryer, she hung the laundry on a clothesline.

I had a weekly deduction from my pay check to the credit union. Part repaid the loan and part went to savings. When we saved half of the cost of what we wanted to buy, we bought it. We financed the other half and usually didn't have to change the amount of the deduction. If I stayed in Oklahoma City for any length of time, I usually got a part-time job to supplement my earnings. Later on, I went to school at night and could not hold a part-time job.

That little house at the end of Melrose Lane was the first of three homes in Oklahoma City. By the time I resigned from Western Electric and while I was an agent for State Farm, we lived on S. W. 45th Street. I have a lot of fond memories of living in that home. We were just one block from the elementary school and two blocks from my office. We had great neighbors. Evelyn and I sponsored high school age young people at church, although we were not much older than they were. We had a lot of social events with them and with our adult friends. It was a great time of life. Oh, to be thirty again!

John, Teresa and Sheryl Mulhausen, Ada, OK, 1962

In 1961, we moved to Ada, Oklahoma where I became manager of Southeast Oklahoma for State Farm. We bought a new house in Ada. It was our first house that had central air conditioning and heating. We enjoyed that! We also enjoyed adding two more children, Teresa and David, to the household.

In Ada, we actually owned three different homes. We didn't move because we wanted to. Our moves were financial moves to capture some equity or lower payments. I had received a promotion. I was a manager, but for the first time in our marriage, we didn't have control of our finances. When I earned next to nothing, we had a firm budget and stayed on it. It was simple. Don't spend more than you earn. When I became an agent it was tough but I was in control. I increased my income by personally making more sales. Evelyn also went to work for a while.

Now as a manager, my income was dependent on the sales of others in an economically depressed area. My district actually lost ten thousand in population over a ten-year period. Managers paid their own business and promotional expenses. Back then, we participated with the company in financing new agents. I terminated one agent for fidelity reasons and had to pay what he had taken. The agents assigned to me just did not produce enough to pay my business and personal expenses. It takes time to recruit quality people, train them and help them develop profitable agencies. So, in my first years as a manager, I robbed Peter to pay Paul. I juggled houses and mortgages and other loans.

Evelyn and I had very few serious disagreements in our fifty years. In Ada however, we had some emotional disagreements over using funds in the business or in the household. It took three years to start breaking even, and five years to breathe easily. Thank God, we overcame some tense times and emerged with good credit and our marriage intact.

We were getting over the financial hump when we moved to Shawnee. We lived in three homes there, too. We rented a home before buying an old antebellum, two-story house. That old house was in a row of classics from by gone days. North Broadway was where the town's well-heeled lived in the old days. We had fun in that old house. We then built our dream home in a new sub-division at the edge of town. We had two acres on a lake. My daughter Sheryl did most of the designing and did a good job.

We lived in our dream house only a year before I accepted a job into executive management in Columbia, Missouri. It seems I had developed a pattern. By the time I reached a living income at Western Electric I quit and went into the insurance business. By the time I was making a profit as an agent, I went into management where I really struggled. When I had it made as a manager, I fell for yet another "promotion." That was January, 1974.

We did get over being nomads. We were in Columbia four and one-half years in one house. Then, we moved to Plano, Texas. The real estate market was hopping there in 1978. Evelyn made two trips to look at houses. There were too many to pick from and they went up in price from one day to the next. I had to start on my new assignment and Evelyn went back to Columbia. I bought a house she hadn't seen. I thought I made a good deal and it was vacant so we could move in right away. I thought she would choose another place within a year or so but we lived there twenty years until she died. I lived there three more years, until Jo Ann and I moved to Lake Whitney.

Evelyn and I had been married about two years and still did not own a car. We had gotten by making deals for rides with fellow workers, relatives and fellow church members. While working in Oklahoma City, I usually walked the seven blocks to a bus stop and rode a bus to work.

Evelyn's Dad, Popa Crow had an old 1939 LaSalle Cadillac that he wanted us to have. He offered to sell it to us for $10.00 down and $10.00 per month for ten months. I took him up on the deal but worked the $100 into our credit union rotation. The old car served our needs for about a year, but caught on fire one Sunday morning in the church parking lot. Luckily a friend had a fire extinguisher in the trunk of his car. He drove up just as the fire started and no real damage was done. The incident did add a little heat to the Sunday services.

I didn't trust that old LaSalle on the road and I did need a car for out of town jobs. So, I bought a better used car. In fact, I bought two used cars before I was ready to buy a new one.

In 1954, we took our first family road vacation. We drove our 1950 Mercury to Washington. We also took Mother as far as Quincy, Washington where we visited my sister Orissa and her husband Al Schultz. Then my family drove on to Everett, Washington to visit my Dad. We had a good time including a tour of Yellow Stone National Park. We did have some car trouble including a vapor lock climbing Monarch Pass in Colorado. The car died about two-thirds of the way to the top. The highway then was a two lane black top. We enjoyed the thrill of a dead stick, gravity turn around, so we could roll back down hill and start the car. We found a store where we wrapped the fuel pump and carburetor in cold rags. After a cool off, we went back over the pass and got a new fuel pump in Montrose. We needed a new car.

I started working a new car into our budget. My banker told me to shop for the right car. After negotiating my bargain, write a personal check then call him with the details. I could come in a few days later and sign the paperwork. I knew how much my payments would be for each $100 financed. That's a little different from the way bankers work today.

We found a 1954 Ford 4-door sedan. It was a six-cylinder stick shift with overdrive. It had two tone pea green and cream paint. We loved it.

I negotiated the price of about $2,600. After negotiating the trade-in, the salesman turned me over to the credit manager. I told them, I am just going to write you a check. They looked at Evelyn and I and the kids and seemed quite surprised. They took the check. Now, I was too proud to call my banker in front of them. While they made the car ready, I went around the corner to a pay phone. Pay phone calls were a dime in 1954.

When our new car was ready, our happy family drove off. John was six years old and even more excited than the rest of us. He asked, "Daddy, how much did you pay for our car?" I told him, "A hot check and a dime".

I didn't know that John would tell everybody that Dad bought a new car with a hot check and a dime. He told our pastor, his teachers, and our neighbors. I took a lot of ribbing about that.

I cherish the memory of how proud and thankful we were. I regret becoming so jaded that such events became commonplace. I pray that I have returned to a point in life where I can express thanks for every good thing.

That car we loved so much was totaled in 1960 by a tornado in Oklahoma City. Evelyn, John and Sheryl were in the car. They were scared nearly to death but not injured. I was experiencing my first catastrophe as an insurance agent. I gained a whole new perspective as I saw my sales turn into lifesavers for my clients.

We didn't become a two-car family until 1961. I was traveling around my district on business, and I finally had to buy an old clunker so Evelyn would have something to drive when I was away. That travel in the summer time also convinced me to buy my first air-conditioned car. I had always considered an automatic transmission to be sissy, but in 1963 I bought an automatic transmission. I doubt if I could use a stick shift today. It was in the late 80's before Evelyn tired of inheriting my business cars and insisted that I buy her a new car, too. Our wheels changed over thirty-five years.

When I became an agency director, State Farm furnished me with a car. When I retired in 1993, I quickly missed three things; a secretary, an expense account and a company car.

Grandson, Jeffrey Federspiel, admires Uncle David's new wheels.
Plano, TX 1981

THE VOWELL FAMILY

In the late fifties, Evelyn and I sponsored high school young people at Prairie Queen Baptist Church in Oklahoma City. The name of the church came from a school in the area. I don't know why, but the church changed its name to Southwood Baptist after we had left.

One of our favorite young ladies brought a young man to a party at our home. C. W. Vowell later joined our church and our group of young people. He was a bit rowdy, but seemed like a nice young man. If Carol Blancett liked him, that was a good endorsement.

One evening Carol and two of our other young ladies visited Evelyn and me. They told us that C. W. had been orphaned. He lived on his own in a rented room. He worked two jobs, went to high school and played on the high school football team. He was a devout Christian.

The girls asked if we would let C. W. come live with us. We were overwhelmed. Our home was modest. Our family of four already filled our bedrooms. I had just started my insurance business, and I was struggling. Evelyn was ready to agree. I had to ponder all the possible ramifications, but I knew God sent those girls to make the request.

C. W. immediately became family. He lived with us for only a short time, but he was a blessing. After C. W. and Carol graduated from high school, we moved to Ada, Oklahoma where I assumed my new job as manager for southeastern Oklahoma. C. W. moved to the home of another family in our church. He lived with Bob and Ina Mae Dixon until he and Carol graduated from the University of Oklahoma. C. W. and Carol married shortly after graduation.

C. W. worked for Phillips Petroleum for a short while, and then had a long career as an engineer for NASA. Carol had a long, satisfying career as a teacher. They lived many years in Alvin, Texas, but now live in Friendswood, Texas. When C. W. retired from NASA he became a consultant with the Japanese Space Agency and a liaison with NASA. He is now working part-time on that job.

C. W. and Carol have two sons. Chad is a little older than Corby. Chad, an outdoorsman graduated with a forestry degree from Stephen F. Austin University. He is now an environmental engineer. Corby graduated from Baylor then obtained a law degree from the University of Houston. Corby's law practice specializes in Intellectual Property cases. He and Julie live in Pearland, Texas. In addition to being mother to Courtney and Brandon, Julie teaches school.

I love and respect C. W. and Carol for a great number of reasons. I really admire them for their success as true Christian parents.

UNCLE NEWT

Uncle Newt and Aunt Jen had a beautiful home
on a quiet street.
The lawn was lush and colorful gardens
made it complete.
Even in his advanced years, Uncle Newt
worked long and hard,
to perpetually maintain the neighborhood's
most beautiful yard.

He planted, sprayed, mowed and trimmed,
at an amazing pace.
He seemed to enjoy it, and pride
kept a smile on his face.
Uncle Newt was a sight to behold in
his dirty, sweaty shirt,
dirty overalls, worn out straw hat and
arms covered with dirt.

One morning while he worked in a flower
bed quite content,
a blue haired little lady drove up to his
curb with ill intent.
She lowered a window and yelled with a
commanding voice,
"Hey Boy ! Come here." Uncle Newt complied like
he had no other choice.

"How much is this lady paying you?"
was her rude query.
Uncle Newt paused a minute before
answering his adversary.
Impatient for an answer, she said, "Come
work for me.
I'll pay you two dollars an hour more
than she does – agree?"

Uncle Newt replied with a twinkle
in his eye and a smile.
"The problem is, this lady lets me
sleep with her once and a while."
Uncle Newt chuckled to himself
as the Cadillac sped away.
He went back to his flowers and really
enjoyed the rest of the day.

Going Into the Insurance Business

I had a friend whose Mother, Alice Douglass, represented State Farm Insurance. She had a very small, one-person office and also sold some real estate. The company had some part-time agents at the time, but was working hard to develop a full time, professional agency force. Evelyn worked for Alice occasionally when Alice had to get away. Once in 1954, Alice had a family emergency and Evelyn ran her office for a couple of weeks. She knew nothing about the business and called on the District Manager, Ed Carter, for frequent help.

One Sunday after church we ran into Mr. and Mrs. Carter at a restaurant. Mr. Carter asked me for an appointment the next week to discuss the possibility of me becoming an agent. I was intrigued, but after a couple of discussions, I decided I didn't have the education, funds or the gumption to quit my job and start a business. We had just gotten to the point of having a decent home, car and furniture. We were paying our bills. I was not ready in 1954.

I did keep that career possibility in mind. In 1958, Western Electric angered me by making it impossible for me to continue my college studies at night. My anger intensified when they did not increase my pay to the top of their merit scale. I contacted Mr. Carter. We started negotiations in January, and I became a full time State Farm Insurance Agent June 1, 1959. I converted a room in my home into an office. When talking to a prospect, I referred to it as my studio office. In reality, it was no more than two chairs, a used desk and an empty used file cabinet.

Evelyn's parents had a fit when they learned I was quitting my good job to go into the insurance business. They thought I had lost my ever-loving mind. Even so, my first sale was to Popa Crow. He was a tough, skinflint miser. Although he was known to drink sometimes, he had a bare bones liability policy on his car with a "non-drinker" company. On the application, he had sworn he never took a drink. Their premium was lower than mine, and in those days, State Farm charged a membership fee to new applicants.

Several family members were gathered in their house. I took Popa to the kitchen and sat him down. I gave him my very best and complete sales talk. I explained all the advantages of State Farm and explained the coverage in detail. I proposed changing his 5-10-5 state mandated liability limits to 10-20-10. He said that liability is just for the other guy.

I countered that payments to the other guy would be on his behalf and only what he legally and personally owed. If he hit a bus and did $10,000 damage, his current policy would pay $5,000 and leave the other $5,000 for him to pay personally.

I also added emergency road service, medical payments and un-insured motorist coverage. My premium and membership doubled his current renewal premium. After a lot of cursing and raving, he bought. He wanted his grandchildren to eat.

Popa went back into the living room still cursing. He told the family gathering, "If Elmer takes that long to sell every policy, those kids are going to starve to death".

When I started selling insurance, Evelyn got a job to supplement our income. We enlisted our niece, Betty Jo Booker (now Luttrell) to watch John and Sheryl and answer the telephone. She was only a teen, but very responsible. One evening, I picked the kids up from school, or store or something. I took them somewhere with me and delayed their return home by thirty or forty minutes. Their absence scared Betty Jo. When I drove up with the kids, she expressed her anger for not letting her know. I was amazed by her vocabulary and the unique names she called me.

Of course, I was wrong. She was conscientious and rightfully concerned. She had every right to be angry with me. I've always thought the world of Betty Jo.

I had accumulated about six hundred x-dates before leaving Western Electric. We call it a renewal when it is time for our customer to pay a renewal premium. When that time arrives for our prospect, we call at an expiration date (x-date). That is when we try to offer them a better buy. Well, I needed to start selling some insurance. Those six hundred x-dates were not enough. With no customer on the books, I didn't have service work. My x-dates did not yield enough day time sales interviews, so I had to get more x-dates.

In my first ninety days I traversed the streets in surrounding neighborhoods. I knocked on doors. I introduced myself, gave them brochures and asked when their insurance expired. When no one answered the door, I hung literature on the door. Every couple of hours I went home to see if anyone called – no one called – I went back to the street.

Sometimes, I took John and Sheryl to the shopping center for an hour. They distributed flyers to people. I kept an eye on them and looked for men sitting in their cars waiting for their wives. I walked up to their cars and found most were bored and receptive to talking. Once I hired a service to distribute flyers. I stopped that when a friend of mine found about two thousand of them in a storm drain.

State Farm has come a long way since then and is now a household word. Then, when I said I was with State Farm, many people thought I was a guard at the reformatory or the state mental hospital.

I filed x-date cards by the month. About forty-five days in advance, I arranged the file by the week. I mailed the prospect some literature and a personal note asking for the opportunity to compare. If people didn't call me, I called them in a couple of weeks to get an appointment. On evenings, when I didn't have sales calls or appointment making calls, I did more x-dating by telephone. Evelyn was eager to help any way she could, but she wouldn't make cold calls. I discovered that it was too time consuming for me to call friends and relatives, so Evelyn called them. She would chat a while, then ask for the x-date. I could be more productive making cold calls.

It was a numbers game. Talk to a hundred people and get fifty x-dates, that granted fifteen sales appointments, and that yielded five sales of people who were eligible. It was tough, but got me started. It didn't take long to learn it was more profitable to make someone a client than to just sell them a policy.

While knocking on doors one day, I met a lady whose husband had recently died. She operated a small beauty shop in her home and did have some coverage questions which I answered. I helped her with some other problems with social security, changing the mortgage and so forth. She had me go through her lock box of documents and policies. Her husband had been in oil field service work and had a stack of cheap, worthless accident policies. He had died from a heart attack. They did have a mortgage life insurance policy.

She had already turned in a claim but hadn't yet been paid. That company wanted her to take a physical. They were going to sell her a policy as part of the claim settlement. I called their hand on that deceptive ploy and helped her collect the claim.

I also found another small whole life policy from a good company. Mrs. Cash told me that they hadn't paid premiums on it for two or three years and it lapsed. Whole life insurance builds cash values. If you discontinue premiums, you have the option to take your cash or payments, or to take a smaller paid up policy. If you do neither, the cash value buys extended term coverage for the face value. Sure enough that policy was on extended term. It was only three thousand dollars, but I became a hero when she collected that three grand.

I wrote all of Mrs. Cash's property insurance, her cars and a life insurance policy. I learned a lot while performing the service. The most valuable thing I learned is the value of having a booster to send you business. Women talk in a beauty shop. I sure profited by Mrs. Cash bragging on her agent.

I hand delivered policies and promised top notch service. I reviewed all coverage for those who would allow the time. I asked my clients to refer friends to me. I was amazed by the lack of organization of important papers. People were keeping policies that had expired twenty years ago. I threw those away and made a record of their coverage. Sometimes there were overlaps. Sometimes there were glaring omissions. One day I got a call from a lady who wanted to compare car insurance. She was referred by Mrs. Poteet. I went to her home and gave my best presentation to her and her husband. They looked a little baffled. I was just a few dollars more than their Farmer's premium. I asked what other questions they had. She said, "Mrs. Poteet told me that you would come over and tell us what to throw away, what to keep and what to change".

I answered, "Yes I do that, but it's a service I usually give after I have a line of insurance. I can go ahead if you want me to". They didn't need to be sold. They were ready to do whatever I recommended. I wrote three cars and their home. More importantly, I earned a client who would in turn recommend others to me.

At the end of my first ninety days, I no longer had time to cold x-date. All my time was taken with service and sales calls. I continued to review coverage and asked for referrals. When I started, fifty x-dates yielded about five sales. Now fifty referrals would yield forty sales. At that time, most State Farm sales were for auto insurance. My manager commended me for having a greater balance of home, business, auto and life insurance.

In September, I moved from my home to an office in downtown Oklahoma City. State Farm had a wonderful lady with an office in a downtown office building. Every one loved Mrs. Loring, but she was nearing ninety years old. She had trouble moving around with a cane and was losing her sight. My manager used me to help persuade Mrs. Loring to retire. They made a deal for me to assume her remaining lease and buy her office furniture.

My task was to organize her book of business so it could be divided to three new agents. One of the other new agents joined me in the office. Her records were a mess. We finally developed files for all her policyholders, and I got my third of her business.

When that lease was up, I rented a small office over the Jones Drug store at S.W. 44th and Walker. I was back in the neighborhood where I started, only two blocks from my home. I was still so hungry that I had an extension of my office telephone in my bedroom. My business continued to grow. Evelyn quit her job to help me, but that didn't work. As much as we loved each other, she couldn't take orders from me.

I hired my first help and had great difficulty in finding time to train her and still get out of the office for sales calls. Modern agents do almost all of their business in the office. Then I was like old doctors. I made house calls.

I was still just striving to survive when my manager said the company wanted to discuss management with me. I couldn't believe it. Agents were supposed to have a degree. That requirement was frequently overlooked when candidates had strong business, management or sales experience. I had no degree and just approaching two years in the business. They must really need a manager somewhere.

I agreed to participate in a "Look at Management" seminar in Dallas in April, 1961. All the other nine or ten participants were more experienced and more successful than me. My manager pointed out that I may not have a big agency, but my new sales were in the top one percent of the company's agents. I was building my agency along the lines that the company wanted new agents to build.

Our legendary Regional Vice-President, Earle B. Johnson led the seminar. Later, he became the chief agency officer of State Farm and the chairman of State Farm Life Insurance Company. Earle told us he needed seven outstanding men to help grow a great regional organization. He was very motivational and persuasive. My ego overpowered my common sense. I traded my agency to become the manager for Southeast Oklahoma on July 1, 1961.

HERBIE'S FINAL ANSWER

Hark back to days of yesteryear when traveling salesmen
rode into town on the train,
to sell their wares, then retire to our little hotel
for the nights refrain.

The typical hotel of that age had stairs up to a long hall
with rooms on each side,
and a bathroom at the end. The lobby downstairs was
the social place where games and jokes abide.

Each room was equipped with a wardrobe, a mirror,
a chair, a bed and a rug.
A pan and pitcher and a repository reverently dubbed
"the thunder mug."

One regular guest was named Herbie, a compulsive
fastidious, remote from the rest.
He made rigorous inspections of his room, demanding
corrections, always a pest.

Bob, the owner, was a fun loving soul enjoying most
of those passing his way.
But, Herbie was becoming too much, so Bob planned
a joke; the pest to repay.

On Herbie's next visit, Bob and the salesmen implemented,
their plan so kooky.
They took a new pot to Herbie's room, poured cider in it,
and crumbled up a cookie.

The gang waited in the lobby as Herbie went
upstairs to his accommodation.
Then Herbie ran back down screaming at Bob
to come and assess the abomination.

The salesmen followed them upstairs cramming into the
room and laughing at the furor.
Herbie continued to rant and rave as he pointed at
the pot and expressed his horror.

Bob picked up the pot and tortured Herbie even more
as he swirled it around.
Then with a laugh and a wink, Bob raised the pot
to his lips and drank it down.

Bob then wickedly advised, "It's only some cider
and cookies, though tastier than most."
Herbie was dumb founded, his face was as white as if he
had seen a ghost.

Herbie paused for a long time trying his best to
understand this strange ingredient.
He finally replied in his high pitched voice,
"if I'd known that I wouldn'a peed in it."

STATE FARM INSURANCE MANAGER

When I accepted the appointment to become manager for Southeastern Oklahoma in 1961, my then Deputy Regional Vice President, Buck Edgeworth, gave me a word of advice. He said, "Elmer, don't be surprised if these agents aren't interested in working as hard as you do." That was the understatement of the year. I also learned that all manager appointments were not created equal. An experienced, successful agent would not have taken my assignment. This opening was for a naïve, short timer like me.

My friend, Bill Gildner, became a manager in Arlington, Texas about the same time I started. Bill was an experienced, successful agent with an agency large enough to divide among several new agents. Bill recruited at home, where he was known. His new agents started with a base of business in a rapidly growing, economically strong area. Bill was an instant success. I'm not relating this to take anything from Bill. He deserved a better deal than me. He gave up more. He became one of the best managers in the company for many years. I relate this to illustrate my excuse for struggling for so long before having success.

When I traveled to the Dallas-Ft. Worth area, I was amazed at the mile after mile of quality new construction. I returned to my district where one new house a year might be built in some of the towns. I discovered immediately that my income wouldn't cover my business and my living expenses. In those days, managers paid all their own business expenses, and participated with the company in new agent financing. At one time, I had to repay the company for a trainee agent's fidelity problem.

The company was supportive and financed me as much as the contract allowed. My agency director was Marion Pearce. He expressed confidence in me, even loaned me money and co-signed a bank note for me. I appreciated that confidence, but hated owing money to my boss. I repaid every dime. Back in the sixties, many new managers went heavily in debt on the company's financial plan. The contracts were improved and right after I had paid off my debt, the company cancelled the debts of managers still owing.

Marion made up for any lack of expertise with enthusiasm, hard work and humor. I needed the humor in those days. We worked until midnight several times, and he bragged on every little bit of progress I made.

Agents assigned to me included Albert Wiley in Shawnee, Lloyd Jack in Ada, Norman Mills in Holdenville, and Virginia Marshall in Talihina. I had another part-time agent in Holdenville and one in Hugo. I had three failing trainee agents. One was in Shawnee, another in Durant and one in Antlers. I had a non-producing agent in Seminole. Mr. Johnson was a full-time agent in McAlester, but too ill to work. He passed away within a year after I started.

Albert Wiley was a former schoolteacher, coach and Navy Commander. He was a cancer survivor in poor health. He was like salt of the earth, a solid, quality agent. He was a supporter and advisor. He tried to keep me out of trouble. His wife Ruth was like a second mother to us.

Norman Mills was also a quality person and former school administrator. Norman doubted that there was enough market in Holdenville for him and another part-time agent. I talked the part-timer into retiring and convinced Norman to put all his efforts and resources into building an agency. Norman survived a heart attack in 1962, and went on to be an outstanding agent as well as good friend and advisor. His wife Nola taught school and was a true friend.

Lloyd Jack was a younger man that started three or four years previously. He thought it was a temporary job until his teaching job came open in the fall. Fortunately for me, Lloyd had decided each fall to stay in the insurance business. Lloyd had been an outstanding athlete in high school and was full of energy, enthusiasm and competitiveness. He needed and accepted a lot of direction and coaching. Effie shared his enthusiasm and was an asset to our team. Lloyd took a lot of my time, but he was worth it. He became an outstanding producer.

Mrs. Marshall worked from her home in Talahina. She had no office, sign or advertising. She didn't need it. Everyone in the area knew and loved Mrs. Marshall. She was a full-blooded Native American. She wrote only auto insurance. I taught her life insurance and got her licensed. She became a good life insurance producer. Once when she was confined in the Talihina Indian Hospital, she wrote life insurance on three of her doctors. I also taught her about property insurance, but she never wrote many homes. She wanted her sons to take over her business, but they were not interested. One was a successful rancher. The younger son graduated from West Point and wanted a career in the big city.

I had a non-producing agent in Seminole. It took a few years to talk him out of the business.

In those times, trainee agents were employees the first two years. After complying with training, production and service requirements, State Farm awarded a contract making them independent contractors. It didn't take me long to realize that the three trainee agents assigned to me were failing. I had the tough job of eliminating them and a huge job of recruiting if I was to succeed as a manager.

The trainee in Durant and the trainee in Antlers were just not qualified. After first attempts to salvage them, I realized that it wouldn't work. I sat down with the agent and his wife in Durant to explain that this career just wouldn't work out for them. They thanked me and resigned. The trainee in Antlers made it easier on me with a fidelity breach. He also resigned.

The trainee in Shawnee was an outstanding individual. He had intelligence, good character, and a great personality. He had commanded a platoon in the army, played football at the University of Oklahoma and coached high school football. I knew he could be successful. But every time I drove to Shawnee to work with him, he had problems for me to solve, questions on his study assignments and wanted to be drilled on his prospecting and sales presentations.

I finally realized he was using up our time together to avoid prospecting and sales calls. One day, upon arrival, I told him his questions and study assignments could wait. We were going x-dating. We drove to a nice neighborhood. I agreed to x-date the first four houses, and then we would alternate on two houses each. Then I would observe him for an hour. It wasn't rocket science. I introduced myself at the door, acknowledged that it would be unlikely that the prospect would need any insurance at the present time. I did want them to know the new agent in town, and handed them literature. I then asked if they would be interested in a better buy the next time they had a premium to pay. If so, we recorded all the information on a prospect card and thanked the people.

After those first four houses, I noticed that my trainee was sweating profusely and looked uncomfortable. I told him it was his turn, but instead we went to the curb and he tossed his cookies. He had been fearless in battle and on the football field, but he couldn't ask a stranger for his business. He readily resigned.

This was a good man. He went into school administration, studied for and received his doctorate degree. He became the assistant superintendent of schools in Oklahoma City.

I thought the State Farm Agency opportunity was so great that any qualified candidate could succeed. I learned that this job wasn't for everyone. It was hard, time-consuming work to find the right candidates. I had to spend enough time with them to discover all the red flags.

My part-time agent in Hugo owned and operated a service station. His wife provided most of the insurance service. She worked part-time selling advertising for the local newspaper. It really bothered me that people needing insurance service had to wait until she got off work or wait until he finished pumping gas or greasing a car.

I told these folks that State Farm needed a full-time, professional agent in Hugo. He or she could have first shot at the position. I offered financial assistance and training. He said he was interested, but would first have to sell his service station.

One day I drove into Hugo to go over some service questions. I discovered that my agent had bought a second station. We needed to sit down and talk, but he was too busy until closing time. I waited until both were off work. We took his greasy box of files to his home. We sat down at his dining room table. His wife brought coffee for all three of us.

As we started on the first file, a siren sounded. Both man and wife ran out the front door leaving me at the table. They were both volunteer firemen. It was about 7:00 p.m. I was a hundred miles of bad road from home. I said to myself, "Self, what are you doing here?"

I had totally wasted a half-day. I took a notepad from my brief case and wrote a resignation letter. The letter would be complete with my fireman, service station operator agent's signature. I took the greasy file box to my car; it would be easier servicing the business myself. When my friends returned home, I commended them for their community service, obtained a signature and asked for their help in finding a full-time agent.

My career as a manager was moving backwards rather than forward. I improved to one step forward and only two steps back, then to holding even, then eventually started moving forward.

The first trainee agent I recruited was almost a carbon copy of the one replaced in Shawnee. He had also played football at Oklahoma University. He played on the team with the longest winning streak in college football history. I had been an avid fan of Oklahoma University sports since childhood. Evelyn said I was so enamored by former players that I was blind to their faults. This one didn't do well enough to keep and didn't do bad enough to fire. That's the ones that are costly and heartbreaking. His failure really rocked my confidence.

This book isn't long enough to relate all my missteps. I did learn from mistakes, and I would rather dwell on successes. My first successful recruit was Bill Derichsweiler in McAlester. Bill was a well-respected hometown boy who had been assistant manager of the Goodyear store. He had been promoted to store manager in Ardmore. I was recruiting him for my opening in Durant when my agent in McAlester passed away. Bill was a natural to move into the McAlester agency. I was ready for a success story and I'm thankful for Bill giving it to me. Bill and his wife Val built the largest property and casualty agency in our district. He has retired and his son, Mark, is now agent in McAlester.

Norman and Lona Mills' son, Ed, had an interest in State Farm, but Norman wanted him to be an agent in Oklahoma City. He had no confidence in our markets in Southeastern Oklahoma. Ed lived in Oklahoma City, but was ready to return to the rural area. Ed filled the opening in Durant and became my first agent to win regional and national honors. When I accepted a promotion, Ed became the manager of the Southern portion of my district. Many years later, Ed moved as a manager to Dallas while I was agency director of that market.

I then recruited John Hudspeth in Shawnee. He was the third straight Oklahoma football player I had in Shawnee, but he had been a substitute rather than star. He had not been on a pedestal and didn't fear rejection. John and Jan moved home to Oklahoma from Farmington, N.M. John built a very nice business, and I was proud of him.

In Hugo, I recruited the local Army recruiter. I took some heat from our regional office because "Sarge" was considered too old. Back then, we were to target people twenty-five to thirty-five years old. I finally got approval and appointed Master Sgt. Albert Doane when he retired from the Army. Sarge became a successful agent and I didn't have to continue personal service for policyholders in the furthest three counties of my district. Sarge's widow Wanda and her family are still good friends.

Roger Scarborough was too young at twenty-three when I submitted appointment papers for him. He started part-time in Idabel and I moved him to full-time in two or three months. Roger was an amazing success and also a huge managerial challenge. Roger needed and demanded a lot of attention. It was over two hundred miles from my home in Shawnee to Idabel, so working with him required one or two over-nights. Roger was a challenge, but worth it.

Million dollar life insurance production is common place now, but in the mid-sixties that was quite an achievement for a multi-line agent. Roger was our region's first Million Dollar Producer. He also qualified for the President's Club which is the top fifty agents in the company in any line of insurance. At that time State Farm had about sixteen thousand agents, so the top fifty was a huge achievement.

I logged a lot of telephone time and wrote frequent motivational notes to Roger, but he was not satisfied if I wasn't in Idabel working with him. After receiving one note, he called and said I reminded him of something his wife had told him while he was in the Air Force. Roger had been stationed in Greenland and wrote his wife a steamy love letter. His wife told him, "Roger, you can't get me pregnant by mail".

I told him, "Roger, I don't want to get you pregnant".

In one meeting I would brag on Roger and lavish him with rewards. In the next meeting I might dismiss him for disrupting the meeting. One time Bill Derichsweiler told him, "Roger, shut up. You are like a big old catfish; all mouth and no ears".

All in all, I owe Roger a debt of gratitude. He contributed greatly to the success of our district and therefore to my personal success.

After I was promoted to Agency Director, Roger was promoted to manager in Tulsa. That didn't work out. Roger left State Farm for a while, but came back as an agent in Wichita Falls and served until he retired.

I appointed Bill Hall in Wilburton, where he built a successful business. Bill and Betty's son, David, became an agent and later moved into management.

My non-productive agent in Seminole finally resigned. I replaced him with Mike Jordan who built a quality business there. While Mike was completing his pre-contract work, I hired his wife Sondra to run the office. She did a good job and became a great help to Mike. A few years after I left the district, Mike became a manager. After a few years, he returned to personal production in Garland, Texas. He just recently retired from a large successful agency there.

I met Jim and Mona Clopton in Tulsa. They moved down to McAlester, and succeeded as the second agent there. We expanded into Madill where I appointed Benny Keith. After Mrs. Marshall retired, I appointed J. B. Fitzgerald to replace her in Talihina. He did a good job.

After my first three or four years as a manager, I began to see that we were not going to starve or go bankrupt. The job became fun. Our team was like one big family. We had many social get-togethers, always including the spouses and quite often included the kids.

We had lots of sales promotions. Some were successful, some were not. Some were creative, others were just dumb. We had a competitive spirit and began to take pride in the outfit. Ed Mills said, " There's nothing more fun than making an extra thousand dollars while trying to earn a five dollar prize."

In the mid-sixties, the company announced that we would have a national convention in Las Vegas. We always had a twelve to fourteen month period to qualify for invitations and travel expenses. We always kicked off promotions like that with a party, to explain the rules, prizes and score keeping. Evelyn made little red felt bags with some gold decorative stitching and a gold drawstring. We filled each bag with nickels as party favors for each wife. We called them mad bags. We couldn't imagine any one gambling more than one nickel at a time. We also had a first three-month contest to encourage a fast start. The winner received a hundred dollar bag of nickels. Lloyd Jack won that heavy bag.

Fast forward to twenty-five years later, I am an agency director in Dallas, and Ed Mills has also relocated to Dallas. He is one of my managers. I have announced my retirement and my last week of work will be in October 1993 at yet another Las Vegas Convention. Carolyn Mills still had that old faded red mad bag. While we were in Las Vegas, Ed gave that old bag back to me. But this time, it was full of five dollar gaming chips. The nickels had grown.

Going back to the sixties, a district in Houston had astounded us by writing a million dollars in life insurance in one month. Today, that doesn't sound like much, but in 1968, that was a momentous task. No Oklahoma or North Texas district had ever done it. I decided that we could. Now the bigger job was to convince the agents that we could really write a million in a month. That would be a tremendous confidence builder and create team pride.

Evelyn created our scoreboard. It started with a large framed poster board. The title at the top said "The Million Dollar Bouquet". Below that, she made a skeleton of flower plants from brown burlap glued to the poster board. I enlisted the help of our regional life manager, Jim O'Donnell. He agreed to hang this "bouquet" on the wall in the regional office. I furnished his underwriters with colorful paper daisies and postage stamp photos of each agent. As each application was received during the promotion, the underwriter placed a daisy on the poster board with the agent photo in the middle of the daisy. The paper daisy and picture was fastened to the burlap skeleton and the bouquet was built over the course of the month.

Million Dollar Bouquet with $1,334,372, Life Insurance, June, 1968

We had a big steak dinner at Pete's Place in McAlester to kick-off the promotion and we invited my agency director, Art Langeloh and Jim and their wives to join us. After dinner, I presented the plan to my agents and wives. We displayed the bouquet and daisies with pictures. Every agent that volunteered to try got their first free daisy on the bouquet. That helped them visualize what the bouquet would look like. Every agent had their picture on a paper daisy on the bouquet. Jim agreed to hang the pictures on the Regional office wall. Of course they accused me of smoking something illegal, but I could tell the team was buying in.

In my opening remarks, I planned to use the old stunt of driving a paper straw through a raw potato. I wanted to illustrate the power of total concentration and commitment. I almost blew it. Of course I practiced before hand, but when I tried it in front of the crowd, the straw didn't go through the potato. I tried again. The second straw didn't go through. Albert Wiley and his wife Ruth were sitting at a table next to me. He took my left arm and whispered, "Elmer, you are jerking your left hand. Hold it steady". The third time, I concentrated on holding the potato steady in my left hand and driving the straw through the potato with my right.

After dinner another agent told me, "That was a good illustration. If at first you don't succeed, try, try again".

Yes, we went over the goal. The fun, pride of team, the individual pride, the confidence built was fantastic. I paid for the promotion, but the Regional office paid for our celebration at Lake Texhoma State Park. Our Regional Vice President, Buck Edgeworth and Deputy Regional Vice President, Paul Todd, attended the family outing.

In 1971, our region split. State Farm opened a new regional office in Austin to serve South Texas. Our Vice President moved to that office. Robert Warren became our new Regional Vice President and that started a long personal friendship. Norvel Trask, a friend since 1960, became Deputy Regional Vice President over the agency force.

Norvel knew that at one time, I had applied for a managerial opening in Oklahoma City because I felt I could be more successful in a metro area. I had been passed over. Norvel and Bob Warren were not happy with our progress in Tulsa. They thought I might be able to improve that progress and at the same time improve my lot. We started negotiating a re-assignment, but it became apparent that making room for me would hurt other managers.

I came to the conclusion that my market might be poor, but I loved my agents and their families. I had paid my debts. I was making a good living and really enjoying my career. Why trade that? I stayed with my Southeast Oklahoma team.

At our Regional Fall Management Conference in 1971, Mr. Warren announced a new manager promotion for 1972. Managers reaching certain goals would be designated "Key Managers." The manager reaching the highest points would be designated "The Key Manager." With objectives changing to meet the times, that program became traditional and was still in effect when I retired in 1993. Every year in our Spring Manager's Conference, Key Managers came a day early for golf and recreation. The Key Manager was awarded a plaque, a Jack Nicholas blazer and had to make a speech.

When that program was announced, I thought I had a chance to compete for the top spot. I only had to beat forty-five managers, and it would be an honor to win that first year of our new regional alignment.

I shared that thought with my team, and many of them were excited about us shooting for the top If we won I agreed to take them and their wives on a trip to tour our brand new corporate headquarters in Bloomington, Illinois.

We had a tremendous year in 1972. Million dollar months became more common place. Three of our team members, Ed and Carolyn Mills, Lloyd and Effie Jack and Roger and Sarah Scarborough qualified for the company's new millionaire travel program. By having three, Evelyn and I got to go with them to Acapulco. In later years, most managers qualified for millionaire travel, but in 1972 only three managers in our region qualified. We were having fun and discovering the power of being focused on a goal.

When all the scores were tabulated at the end of the year, we tied with the G. W. Callaway district. I had long admired G. W. as a professional manager. He had a good group of agents in the plush North Dallas market. It had been a long hard road from the very bottom in 1961 to the top in 1972.

By the time I was able to line up a group tour to our home office, we hit upon an alternative that the agents liked even better. We had another National Convention scheduled for Las Vegas in September. The weekend before the convention, Oklahoma University was playing number one University of Southern California in the Los Angeles Coliseum. The agents agreed that we could utilize the company's travel expense money to Las Vegas. I would pay for the extra costs for a weekend in Los Angeles plus tickets and transportation to the game.

We flew to Los Angeles where I rented a car for each of the two couples. By a stroke of luck, our hotel near Universal Studio was the same hotel the team was using. We were able to meet and converse with some coaches and team members. It was Barry Switzer's first year as head coach. We took in Disney Land and other area attractions. It was a great football game ending in a seven-to-seven tie.

We drove the cars to Las Vegas and kept them through the convention until we flew home. It didn't cost me any more than I would have spent on a trip to Bloomington, Illinois.

S.E. Oklahoma State Farm Agency Team, 1973.

Sitting- Bill Hall/Wilburton, Roger Scarborough C.L.U. /Idabel,

J.B. Fitzgerald/Talihina, Bill Derichsweiler/McAlester, Benny Keith/ Madill, Ed Mills/Durant. Standing- Elmer Mulhausen/Manager, Albert Wiley/Shawnee, John Hudspeth/Shawnee, Albert Doane/Hugo, Jim Clopton/McAlester, Lloyd Jack/Ada, Mike Jordan/Seminole. (Norman Mills of Holdenville was unable to attend for the photo)

THE MATURE APPROACH *

Farmer Brown planned to buy a new bull to help his old bull, Hugh.
At first, this offended Hugh, then he took a philosophical view.
Hugh knew he might need a little help, as he was getting on in years.
Farmer Brown was good to him, why not calm his master's fears.

One sunny day, the energetic new bull arrived at the farm.
Hugh greeted him, showed him around and assured him of no harm.
"My name is Hugh", he said. The youngster said, "Paul's my name".
Hugh said, "I'm not leaving, but I can use a little help all the same."

They walked over and looked down at the pasture in all its beauty.
Hugh said, "Taking care of all those wonderful cows was their duty."
Young Paul jumped up and down, excited to the core.
He said, "Let's run down there right now and service three or four."

"Oh no", was Hugh's sage advice to the young bull, Paul.
"Let's just <u>walk</u> down there and service them all."

Becoming an Agency Director

Our Southwestern Region's 1973 Spring Management Conference was held at the Broadmore Hotel in Colorado Springs. Our special guests were Roger Thompkins, then Vice President Agency at Corporate Headquarters and Richard Stockton, Corporate Vice President and Chairman of State Farm Mutual Auto Insurance Company.

Our tradition at the time was to have two conferences for managers each year. Spouses were invited to the spring conference, usually held at a nice resort. Key Manager Qualifiers came in a day early for recreation. The schedule was lighter and the program tilted toward reporting on the previous year with recognition and rewards. The fall conference was more demanding with emphasis on planning for the next year.

As Key Manager for 1972, I had to make a speech at the 1973 Spring Conference. I can't recall a word I said, but no vegetables were thrown my way. Evelyn and I were seated with Mr. Stockton and his wife at the awards banquet. We also had lunch with Mr. Thomkins and his wife. I had met and liked Roger Thomkins previously, but had never met Mr. Stockton. He and his wife were very interesting. They had met and married in Egypt during World War II. He was a general in the Army and she was a Red Cross nurse. Evelyn and I enjoyed the honor and the conversations with them, but I began to suspect that my bosses and good friends were arranging exposure for a possible promotion.

The idea of promotion was flattering, but also disturbing. Just as I had gotten comfortable as a local agent, I went into management. I had a long, hard climb. Now I was comfortable and making some money as a manger. I had a new home in a town we liked. I loved the agents and their families. I enjoyed my work. Why change? It wasn't for money. The salary for an entry level executive wasn't as much as I was making. But the security of a salary, a company car, expenses paid and excellent benefits was also inviting. At that time, they also had a cost of living benefit that automatically increased salary with inflation. That was a big factor in 1973.

My first reaction was no, I'm happy. But in a few months I got a call from Don Dugan, Regional Vice President for the Missouri-Kansas region. Don asked that I just come up and meet him and his deputy, Max Lingafelter. I liked them both. They and their families were salt of the earth type people. The agency director for the St. Louis division was being promoted. There was an outstanding group of managers and agents in the division, making it an attractive opening.

Before long, Evelyn and I were invited to corporate headquarters in Bloomington, Illinois. Candidates for entry level executives were interviewed by senior management at corporate. That experience became known as "Riding the Donkey".

The night before we left for Bloomington, my neighboring manager, Bill Kent of Norman passed away.

Going to Bloomington meant missing Bill's funeral. We didn't learn of his death until we were leaving our home for the airport. Don Dugan and Max Lingafelter had made plans to meet with Evelyn and I at the St. Louis airport. I decided to back out of the trip, but when I called Don, I was told that they had already left Columbia for St. Louis. There were no cell phones in 1973, so we boarded our plane.

I did use Bill's death as an excuse not to make any commitments. Earle B. Johnson, our chief agency officer had been my Regional Vice President when I became a manager. Earle also knew Bill. Earle said, "Elmer don't make any decisions until you are home at your own desk and weigh every side of the issue".

Nothing specific had been offered, but I was supposed to act like I was applying for the job. One executive would "sell" the position. The next would tell me how hard it was. The next would seem only to be evaluating me. I was non-committal, but trying to decide what was best for my family.

After returning home, we did get a specific offer. I still vacillated. I wouldn't have had the patience Don Dugan had. I would have told me to go jump in the lake. Intellectually, I said no. Emotionally, I said yes. Within a year I had lost my mother, my step-father and a close friend. I had been executor of the estate. Both Evelyn and I had surgeries in 1973. I hadn't added an agent in a year. We had the stress of building a new home. I didn't have the productive gain anticipated and slipped to fourth in the Key Manager competition.

I was in the chairs to become president of the Oklahoma Life Underwriters Association. Moving to Missouri was an escape. I needed a different challenge to regain momentum in my career.

On January 1, 1974 I became Agency Director for the greater St. Louis area. We lived in Columbia where the Missouri-Kansas Regional office was located. My office was in Columbia, but my one hundred sixty-three agents and twelve managers were in the St. Louis area.

By the time I moved to Columbia, I already admired and trusted Regional V.P. Don Dugan and his deputy, Max Lingafelter. Eugene Meying was also deputy Regional Vice President responsible for the underwriting, service claims and support divisions. My fellow agency directors were Preston Goodwin, Charles St. John, Hans Hansen, and Tom Taylor. When Tom returned to Ohio, Joe Leal replaced him. We all reported to Max. All of us and the operations department heads had a great working relationship as well as social life in Columbia.

About seventy percent of the Agency Director's job involved the performance of the assigned division. Performance included growth, sales, profitable operations, level of service, business practices of agents and the appointment and training of new agents and managers. These responsibilities were carried out by working with our Agency Managers. I rarely worked with an agent except in conjunction with the manager.

About thirty percent of my work was staff assignments on regional projects, such as chairmanship of regional conferences, sales promotions, regional conventions, dean of agency schools, task forces, or any chore assigned by the Deputy Regional Vice President or Regional Vice President. We had regular staff meetings involving the heads of all departments and regular meetings with the other agency directors and our deputy. I served on one company-wide task force studying metropolitan loss problems.

The St. Louis division was one of the most productive in the company. Production was the fun part. I tried not to foul it up. The most challenging chores involved dispute resolution, infringements, service complaints, ethics, business practices and profitable underwriting. My first major move was to make it understood; I had zero tolerance for any breach of ethics. With the large number of people involved, it sometimes took some discussions on the definitions of good ethics.

As a manager, I had a rural district and I was responsible for whatever went on in my district. In St. Louis, the managers all overlapped each other. They weren't "district" managers, they were Agency Managers. Geographically adjacent agents probably had different managers, so I was involved with almost all infringements or disputes.

Our agents are independent contractors. So rather than "manage" them we "lead" them and "reasoned" with them. Considering the volume of business and the numbers of people involved, I as amazed that we had so few problems. I was very proud and fond of our agency force.

Overall, my work was very satisfying. However, there were some situations that caused stress even between good friends. There was a tradition called the "seed corn" principal. When the economics of a market justified it, we added managers. The realigning became easier if we grew when there was a retirement, promotion or resignation of a manager.

When there were no agents available for a new manager, we asked managers for contributions or "seed corn" for growing a new district. The obvious objection was that agents represented managerial income. Of course, we expected some resistance. The company had the authority to re-assign agents as needed whether the manager liked it or not. Most managers had been assigned agents when they started. Even so, I strived to get agreement and retain a good working relationship. I understood their concerns and was not upset if they got angry.

My reasoning points were (1) they were fortunate to be in a growing area rather than in a stale economy, (2) reducing numbers earned recruiting opportunities, (3) managers knew that new agents gave new energy to their teams, (4) they might reduce expenses and increase their own efficiency, (5) they might get rid of a personality conflict or other problem.

One day, I drove into St. Louis mulling over my strategy to get seed corn commitments for future growth. No cell phones in those days, so I stopped at a claims service center to use a telephone. I chatted briefly with the divisional claims superintendent. His biggest concern that day was convincing superintendents they could increase the number of claims reps supervised from an average of six to an average of eight. Some superintendents were resisting the increase of span of control from six to eight. My managers were resisting decreasing span of control from an average of fifteen to thirteen.

The difference in viewpoint was due to how they were paid. The claims superintendents were salaried. Managers were commissioned.

Not long after I began leading the St. Louis division, we discovered that growth wasn't our top priority. There was a company wide trend of large underwriting losses in big metropolitan areas. St. Louis was not exempt. Our top priority was to return to profitable operations. I learned all I could from every source possible including the agents and managers. We had fact finding meetings, honored agents who were profitable and did a lot of underwriting training.

It was easy to read eligibility rules for people applying for our preferred rate policies. It was much harder to determine "desirability" than "eligibility". Many agents instinctively recognized undesirable risks. Others learned.

In some metro areas, drastic steps were being taken. Underwriters were taking over some of the Agency Manager's duties. Some agencies were being laundered. I resisted those measures for our area. I felt that if Agency Managers were professional enough to recruit agents, train agents and lead them to success, these managers were also professional enough to lead us back to profit.

Our information technology people broke down all our profit and loss by region, state, city, county, zip code, division, manager and agent. It was also broken down by coverage and classification. We could compare quality of everything, everywhere and every body.

I rented hotel conference rooms in St. Louis. Our auto operations manager, underwriting superintendent and I scheduled half day conferences with each manager. The manager was instructed to study data for each agent in advance and come to the conference with recommendations for each agent. Then all four of us reviewed each agent and agreed to a joint recommendation. It was hard work. On some days we scheduled three half day conferences. Some managers couldn't complete all agents within the time frame and had to come back. I repeated the process with property and life departments.

After one difficult day in St. Louis, our auto division manager, underwriting superintendent and I decided to reward ourselves with a good dinner. We chose the Japanese Steak Restaurant on the top floor of an office building at West Park Plaza. We ascended in the glass elevator looking out over all the mall parking lots and the busy interchange of Page Freeway and Interstate 270. I asked the two men, "Isn't it amazing that we insure nearly one out of every four cars we see down there? I really appreciate all of them for making it possible for us to enjoy a nice dinner tonight."

The divisional manager said, "No wonder we have so many claims problems here."

The underwriter said, "No wonder we can't make any money in St. Louis."

I smiled and thought, "If we can't make a profit from a market like this, it's our own fault. Let's fix it."

Although those conferences were hard work, the follow-up with each agent was even more difficult. I assisted managers as needed to implement each program and to monitor progress. About a third of the agents were on some kind of program restricting their new business.

In Missouri, we could draw our own rating territory lines. We spent hours looking at zip code data and driving the city. We worked with home office actuaries to re-align some territories. Obviously, it costs more to insure a car parked on the street in a high crime area than one parked in a garage in a quiet subdivision.

We were very careful that no program discriminated along social, ethnic or religious lines. Even so, we could not have implemented the same programs in today's world. Then, I believed that a professional person had a right to do business with people they chose to work with and refuse people they didn't wish to work with. Now if a person meets the eligibility rules, they are never turned down. An eligible, but undesirable risk can click in on the computer. They are bound and assigned to an agent.

Thank goodness that in my day we had the benefit of an agent's judgment. They knew that accountants were better risks than topless dancers. They were also aware of countless other factors that make up quality business.

At any rate, our managers became skilled underwriting managers. Our division became profitable again, without having to eliminate any of the manager's jurisdictions. We also grew and prospered.

Although Evelyn was basically unhappy living in Columbia, we did have some good times. We had a great social life with the other staff members and their spouses. They were really great people starting at the top with Don and Mary Dugan and Max and Norma Lingafelter. We had been in Columbia about a year when our deputy, Max Lingafelter died of cancer. Everybody loved Max and that was a terrible blow.

Max was an all around super person and universally loved. He was a health and exercise enthusiast and appeared to be in top physical condition when he became ill. It was a terrible shock when he died within seven weeks of getting sick.

We had planned a party for Teresa and her girlfriends the morning before Max's Saturday afternoon funeral. We didn't relish having the party that day, but we didn't want to cancel it either.

I can't recall how it was damaged now, but we had an upholstered chair in our living room with a broken, front left leg. While contemplating repair or replacement, I placed an upright brick under the corner of the chair. The brick was hidden by the skirt and was just the right height to make the chair relatively stable. The brick was serving well enough to aid and abet my procrastination.

At that point in life, David was about as mischievous as any junior high school boy that you can imagine. He thought it would be very funny to remove that brick from under the chair so his sister's girlfriends would tilt forward when they sat down.

The night before the funeral, Gerald Robinson called and asked if I could pick him up at the airport the next day. Gerald was an executive assistant at corporate headquarters at the time. He was flying his own plane to the funeral and was bringing three more from Bloomington. I told him I would be at the airport.

Before Gerald arrived at the airport, I saw State Farm's corporate plane land. Gerald wasn't on it, but a delegation of senior officers from corporate led by Earle B. Johnson deplaned. Earl, the senior agency officer and chairman of State Farm Life Insurance Company assumed that I had come to pick him up. I explained that I would be happy to give him a ride, but I was there to meet Gerald.

I asked for a minute to make a call for help. I called to alert Evelyn. I asked her to call our Regional Vice President for directions and my fellow agency directors for cars. In the meantime, other funeral attendees were arriving including Gerald. To thicken the plot, the church postponed the funeral an hour, because of a wedding. The visitors needed somewhere to go while waiting for the funeral.

Generally, all protocol would have been handled by the Regional Vice President, but Don Dugan was very close to Max. It was like Don and Mary had lost a son. When Evelyn called, the Dugans were not home. They had gone to be with Norma Lingafelter. We wouldn't disturb them there. Evelyn said, "Bring them to our house".

I brought Earle and his party home with me. Rather than take their passengers to their homes, all my buddies brought everybody to our place. Our relatively modest home hadn't quite recovered from a school girl party, but it was quickly full of more people than we had chairs in the living and dining rooms. Many went to our basement recreation room. Somehow, Evelyn managed to come up with some sandwiches, cookies and drinks.

When I walked into our living room, I noticed that the three legged chair was on tilt. I quickly sat in it to hold it steady and keep any visitors from sitting in it. About then, Mr. Johnson walked up and said, "Elmer do you have any coffee?"

I jumped up to get the coffee. When I returned, the top officer of the State Farm Agency Force was sitting in the three-legged chair. When I handed him the coffee, he tipped forward. I apologized profusely and told him the whole story about the chair. Someone behind me laughed, but I don't remember Mr. Johnson laughing.

Agency Director Tom Taylor and his wife Judy raised registered German Shepherds. The other agency directors and I ragged Tom quite often about carrying those dogs in the company car. Every Monday before his business travel, Tom had our administrative services people vacuum all the dog hair out of his car. Unfortunately, Tom's car was pressed into taxi service on Saturday before the Monday morning vacuum job.

Nothing was funny that Saturday. We had just lost Max. Thirty-three years have now passed and I can't recall everything. Two things though are indelible in my memory. I'll never forget Earle Johnson pitching forward in that three-legged chair. And, I'll never forget walking behind another senior officer at the cemetery. He wore a beautiful black suit. The sunshine reflected brightly off all of the dog hair matted all over his suit.

I guess after thirty-three years, I can have a chuckle now.

Elmer and Evelyn Mulhausen in 1975

Max was replaced by Glenn Dorsett. We enjoyed the Dorsetts while they lived in Columbia. The same job became vacant in Florida so

Glenn moved back to his native state. He was promoted to Regional Vice President in Northern California a few years later.

Native Missourian Calvin Roebuck and his wife, Lydia, then came to replace Glenn. I served three deputies while in Columbia and enjoyed a great professional and social relationship with all of them. All of my colleagues and their wives were great friends also. Cal eventually became Regional Vice President in the Ohio Region where he retired. We just received a card that Cal and Lydia had moved back to Columbia.

We were also fond of our managers and wives. We could have had a much better social relationship with them if we had lived in St. Louis rather than Columbia.

Evelyn did enjoy spending a week with me in St. Louis each December. We made the rounds of several of the manager's Christmas parties. We usually hosted our managers and wives to an "After New Years" party because the December calendar became so crowded

One year when I chaired the Spring Management Conference, Evelyn decided we needed something special for the wives. In the dark ages of the early seventies, we had no women managers. Evelyn had a dress shop in Columbia and good contacts in the fashion industry. Our agency staff agreed to have a sales promotion for managers in the months preceding the conference. All the managers in the region could win certificates for lady's clothes. Suppliers actually set up a temporary fashion store at the Lake of the Ozarks resort so the ladies could select their awards.

Several of the ladies volunteered to serve as runway models for a fashion show at our banquet. Five attractive wives of my St. Louis managers also agreed to do a dance show. One of them knew a dance teacher. Evelyn went to St. Louis to meet with the teacher and volunteer dancers. They learned the can-can. They were terrible at first, but by the time of our conference they were good. They put on a great banquet show in their can-can costumes.

Oh yes, we did take care of some business at the conference, and the guys got in some golf.

I was very proud of my St. Louis division. I worked very hard, and we had an outstanding group of agents and managers. When I arrived, Daryl Hilbert and John Hoffmeister were still in their new manager development programs. Max McGowan, Joe Freund and Doug Auzat were fairly new managers in the building stage. Jack Prade, Tom Montgomery, Jerry Turk, Jack Brase and Russell Beebe were veteran managers. Ray "Scotty" Winscott was a veteran manager who related well to both the veterans and the new upstarts. He was very helpful in our development into a management team.

John Brase was a legendary pioneer manager. He and his son, Jack, worked together. In those years, retirement was mandatory at age sixty-five. John didn't want to retire. I didn't want him to retire, but he had to. What a waste! He had more energy than any of us. That rule was changed by law later on. Tom Montgomery passed away and we sadly mourned his loss. Doug Auzat was promoted to Agency Director in Southern California. Russell Beebee elected to return to personal production.

Our priorities had changed from growth to profitable operations in St. Louis, so we replaced those four lost managers with only four others. It was not necessary to increase the number of managers.

George Bequette was an agency director for a short time. He decided he didn't like that role and moved back to our division as a manager. Ray Cassidy had been an agent in our division that we promoted to manager in Southeastern Missouri. We brought Ray back to St. Louis to fill one of the openings.

We appointed two new managers. Conrad Denault was from Kansas City and Ken Gunter from Springfield. During that time, we promoted agent Rich Montgomery to manager in rural Missouri. He was deceased Manager Tom Montgomery's son. Rich eventually became Regional Vice President of the region.

Working with this great group of people was very satisfying. But, family was more important. Every time the furnace broke or the kids were in trouble, I was in St. Louis. Evelyn's father was critically ill in Oklahoma City. She was unhappy in Columbia.

I heard about an Agency Manager opening in Garland, Texas. This Dallas suburb was a lucrative market. I asked Cal Roebuck and Don Dugan for permission to apply for that opening. Their response was that they were recommending me for promotion. They would be disappointed to see me go the other way on the corporate ladder. Of course I was flattered. I had a lot of respect for both of them, so I delayed my appeal.

In the State Farm agency organization, rank didn't make that much difference. There was no disrespect in moving from director to manager or to local agent. Many times earnings opportunities were inverse to rank. I may have earned more money in my career if I had kept my local agency in Oklahoma City. I'll never know, but I have no regrets. I loved every position I held. Average manager earnings were more than average agent's earnings, but top agents earned more than top managers. The same principal held true between managers and directors.

Satisfaction in the job was more important. I wanted to be where I could make the greatest contribution. Promotion for me would have been to Executive Assistant (E.A.) in corporate. That is supposed to be a temporary job as part of the president's office. E. A. had the same executive rank as directors, but was in preparation to become deputy regional vice-president. They traveled out to the regional offices conveying corporate programs to regional vice-presidents and taking regional concerns back to the president's office.

My friend, Glenn Dorsett, Deputy Regional Vice President of the Florida region heard through the grapevine that I planned to move. He called and un-officially suggested that I move to Miami to take the South Florida Agency Director (A.D.) opening. I would only have to travel to meetings. They had some specialized problems down there and were under the corporate "eye." Doing a good job there would be a guaranteed promotion. I thanked him but neither Evelyn nor I wanted to move to Miami.

If I had stayed on the corporate ladder, my real objective would have been to become a regional vice-president. That meant a promotion to corporate headquarters for a traveling job, then another move to who knows where to be a Deputy Regional Vice President. Then if my ambition was reached, another move to who knows where to become a Regional Vice President; I decided to stick to my original decision. I wanted to live where I worked and any move would be to my home region. By then, the Garland opening had been filled. However, my old friends R.V.P Robert Warren and D.R.V.P. Norvel Trask welcomed me to Dallas as an agency director. Mr. Warren said he would keep me in the Dallas division until David graduated so I wouldn't have to travel. In requesting the move, I was effectively telling corporate that I wasn't interested in a promotion.

We moved to Dallas in May, 1978. We left some great friends in the Missouri-Kansas Region and rejoined some great, old friends in the Southwestern Region.

Valuing Diversity *

The dude peered into the smoke filled lounge,
his eyes piercing the nicotine and tar.
Not many patrons on this mid-week night,
but there is a lady alone at the bar.

He quietly entered the establishment
and carefully assessed the scene.
Then he selected a place four seats down,
ordered a beer and tried to look serene.

But as the dude gazed down the bar at the lady,
he realized his lust was chronic.
So he told the bartender he would like
to buy the lady's next gin and tonic.

"That's fine," came the bartender's reply,
"but it's only fair to tell you sir,
the lady is a lesbian." "That's okay,
I would still like to buy the drink for her."

She acknowledged the drink with a thank you,
smile and an embarrassed glance,
quickening the dude's pulse rate, and
making him think he had a chance.

The beer was cold and the music seductive,
as the lady finished her drink.
So the dude ordered her another one,
and gave the bartender a knowing wink.

The puzzled bartender responded with a glare,
that would make most men quiver.
"Man, I told you she is a lesbian," but the
dude waved him on, the drink to deliver.

It seems there is no fool like the man
who falsely assumes
after his brains have drained down
into his Fruit of the Looms.

When the unlikely two were finishing
that second drink, it was time to decide.
So the dude, moving with the music
smoothly took the seat by her side.

She said, "It was so nice of you sir,
to buy the drink. I thank you."
"Oh, my pleasure. Let's enjoy
each other's company with another drink or two."

"But sir, I must tell you. I am a lesbian,
I want to be fair."
"Honey, that doesn't bother me in the least,
I really don't care."

Bring this sweet thing another gin and
tonic. Bring me another beer.
We are going to have a great time with
conversation, laughter and cheer."

He waived to the bartender and demonstrated
that he didn't give a hoot.
Then he turned to her, "By the way, honey, how's
everything over there in Beirut?"

Rejoining Old Friends in Dallas

One of the old friends I rejoined in the Southwestern Region was Del Anderson. Del was my last Agency Director before I left for Missouri. I first met Del at the first Management Conference I attended in September, 1961. I was a new manager and Del was a new agency director moving down from Indiana. He became my director in 1972 after other assignments in the Region. While I was in Missouri, Del returned to the Agency Manager role in Dallas.

He had been my director. Now I was his director, and we still remained good friends. This was quite common at State Farm. While serving as an agency director, I supervised five former agency directors and I count all of them as friends.

Del was a former track star at Pittsburg University. He played tennis and golf and remained athletic and trim well into his eighties. Even after his retirement, Evelyn and I remained friends with Del and his sweet wife, Dorothy. Del is remembered mostly for pep talks promoting the power of enthusiasm.

A few years ago, Del had a stroke. While rehabilitating, he fell and broke a leg. He developed a problem swallowing and now is fed with a stomach tube. He misses his beloved martinis. He is home with Dorothy but has twenty-four hour nursing care. He is looking forward to his 89th birthday this spring. I call him from time to time. Last week I told him that he sounded better on the phone. He replied that his New Year's resolution was to improve his enthusiasm and he guessed that he had. Well, he certainly helped mine.

Other managers in my new division were old friends from the days I was a manager in Oklahoma. They included Fred Driscoll, Troy Daniel, Galen Caddell, Thayer Sharp, Earl Jordon, and G. W. Callaway. I had met G. W. when he instructed in my 1960 trainee school in Mineral Wells. He and I tied, in the 1972 Key Manager Competition. It was great getting back with those guys.

Ernie Jennings was a development manager. He wasn't happy in the role, and we found a nice local agency for him. Lee Maxwell was an up and coming manager who had been appointed in Dallas while I was in Missouri. Lee was promoted to Agency Director within a couple of years and retired as a corporate vice president in charge of agency administration. Fred Sell transferred from Oklahoma City to replace Lee Maxwell.

I had known Charles England while he was a trainee agent. I had taught in one of his schools. Charley had been promoted from manager to agency director while I was in Missouri. He didn't like that role and was fortunate to get his old district back.

Re-alignment took Galen Caddell and the Sherman area out of our division and gave us Grand Prairie and Manager Don Seymour.

Eventually Southwestern had its loss and other problems, but the priority in 1978 was growth. Our agency force had fallen behind the fantastic economic growth in the area. My first task was to recruit managers and for managers to recruit new agents. We did not have a pool of manager prospects at that time, so it was hard work. I determined that I wouldn't let growth pressure compromise the quality of my manager selection.

In my first seven-year hitch in Dallas, I appointed Bob Weathers, Al Wagner, Phil Head, and Duane Baccus, and collaborated in the appointment of Patrick Warren. Pat was appointed just as I was re-assigned to the Fort Worth division. I'm very proud of this group. They did a good job. Al, Phil and Pat were all promoted to agency director. Al is currently vice president agency in Dallas, and Pat is vice president agency in Ohio.

In Fort Worth I joined even more old friends like Ken Littlefield and Bill Hennington. Bill Gildner had become a manager in Arlington the same time I did in Oklahoma.

Gordon Brown of Wichita Falls and Clifford Floeck of Abilene were also old friends. I met Clifford when we were in trainee agent school at Mineral Wells in 1960. We had quite a battle in the sales contest that followed school. Frank Massey had been appointed while I was in Missouri. He was a solid manager in Denton.

John Pattillo had been an agency director in South Texas. He had become a refugee from travel like me. He was doing an excellent job as a manager in Fort Worth. Dan Sweeney had also been appointed while I was in Missouri. He was doing an outstanding job and was promoted to agency director.

At various times the Texas Panhandle was part of our Fort Worth division. I enjoyed working with Andrea Metcalf, E. C. Roark and Bob Skerrat in Amarillo and the Panhandle.

Bill Hennington went back into personal production after suffering some health problems. Ken Littlefield retired. We replaced them with newly appointed Managers Rick Wilson, Art Brucks and Scott Fletcher. Old friend and veteran manager, Jack Torbert, moved to Fort Worth from Oklahoma. They all did a great job. Rick and Scott were eventually promoted to agent executives. Art did one of the best jobs with what he had of any of my manager appointees.

We not only grew in North Texas through those years, but we grew exponentially. More importantly, people grew. They grew professionally and financially. I have lost count of the number of trainee agents we appointed, but I am proud of them. As I look back over the years, I take great satisfaction in my tiny contribution to so many people's careers.

By the time I was re-assigned back to the Dallas Division, the marketplace had changed. The weather, the justice system and changed political climate moved to the forefront. We had caught up on growth. Now we were trying to manage growth with various controversial production restrictions.

In the management roster, we lost G. W. Callaway, Del Anderson and Fred Discoll to retirement, and Fred Sell to personal production. Al Wagner and Phil Head were promoted to agency director. Dan Smith and Lathan Garnett had been appointed as new managers while I was in Fort Worth. My former agent and friend, Ed Mills moved from Oklahoma to join our division in Dallas.

I appointed new managers Sharon McAuley, John Murray and Rendi Black. By the time I appointed John and Rendi, the market had really become restrictive, but they still did a good job. Sharon was promoted to agency director and has since retired as a corporate vice president.

I took a lot of pride in my new managers, but enjoyed working with the veterans too. At an Agency Director Conference one year, a very young agency director was talking about his problems and disdain for older managers. We were in a small discussion workshop, so I took an opposing view. I told him and the others that his assumption that age was an automatic disability was offensive to me. I couldn't help but brag on my veteran managers who had won our region's top key manager award while we were working together. I was just as proud of G. W. Callaway, Bill Gildner, John Pattillo and Cliff Floeck as I was of my new manager's successes. Those guys earned it with year after year of consistent quality work.

I did receive a lot of recognition for the number of my people who were promoted into the executive ranks. Because State Farm agents have such a huge potential for financial success, there was and still is a danger of the organization becoming "bottom heavy." As an Agency Director, I felt a strong responsibility to seek out high quality people who could find satisfaction in leadership and take on wider responsibilities.

I took pride in the managers I recruited. I also took pride in those I mentored for promotion. As a manager, I recruited three trainee agents who became managers. One of those became an agency director. In my nineteen years as an agency director, I appointed and/or mentored sixteen managers who were promoted with six of those reaching vice presidential ranks. Manager Bob Weathers and one or two more turned down promotions. That's satisfying.

It was in the early seventies that we started getting some enlightenment on the value of diversity. We hadn't been discriminating against women or minorities; well not on purpose any way. When a manager recruited for a new agent, he looked for the same description as the last successful agent. The last success was a white, married college graduate, thirty years old, with two kids, a sales personality, self-starter, with a little savings who wanted to earn what he was worth rather than what a job was worth. Oh yes, he had a helpful, supportive wife.

When we finally began to recruit successful women, their most common lament was that they didn't have a helpful, supportive wife.

Women and minorities were not lined up at our doors. Other candidates were not lined up either. Recruiting was hard work. Managers had to look for successful people to "sell" into the agency career. Most candidates were referrals from our agents or other centers of influence who knew the value of the opportunity. After selling someone into becoming interested, then we had to determine if the career was a good fit. We had to have multiple candidates to choose from and select the best of those. Managers had to learn when to sell and when to buy.

Very few of the women or minorities thought they would like the career. They feared they wouldn't succeed. They had no role models in our agency force. In St. Louis we were able to recruit some qualified minorities before convincing any women. In those days, it was necessary for a new agent to work evenings to succeed. Many husbands didn't want their wives working those hours or investing money in the business. Some manager's wives were jealous of their husband working that closely with new female agents.

I asked Evelyn if she would have been jealous if I had appointed a female trainee agent when I was a manager. She said yes. She then explained that she had been jealous of every trainee, male or female. She had been jealous of all the time, effort and attention to help that trainee succeed. The relationship between manager and trainee agent (in those days) was intense and sometimes emotional.

In St. Louis, Agency Manager Doug Auzat and I convinced a young claims representative named Tom Weatherspoon to become an agent. Tom and his wife Jackie didn't express all their fears and discomfort of being on an all white team until years later. Doug was promoted to agency director while Tom was still a trainee, so I spent more time with Tom than other trainees. I also spent a lot of time with Tom's new manager, Conrad Denault. Tom worked hard to succeed and helped us better understand how to recruit and train minority candidates. He eventually reached the position of vice-president agency.

In Dallas, my first Agency Manager appointee was Bob Weathers. Annette Fleming, now Annette Stone, had been Bob's office manager when Bob had a large successful local agency. Annette wanted to become an agent and she had a number of qualities that made her a good candidate. She had been a manager in a small company. She had contracted with agents to train office personnel. She had also worked for manager Del Anderson training new trainee agents on basics in the office. She had much to offer, but she didn't have a degree.

Since Bob was my first manager to train in Dallas, I had to teach him that his success depended on the quality of recruiting and selection. If a manager had only one candidate for an opening, he had a decision to make. If he had two, he had a choice, but three or more candidates offered a selection. I tried to require my managers to have a selection. I required Bob to have two "paper eligible" candidates to compare with Annette. If she was the best, we could appoint her with confidence. Quality of recruits, more than anything else, determined a manager's success.

Annette was the best in Bob's selection process. She was appointed and was highly successful.

A few years later, Annette told me that she thought I had been against her becoming an agent. She thought I threw a lot of road blocks in her way. I agreed that I had. I threw a lot of road blocks in the way of all candidates, male or female. A tough selection process helped assure the candidate's success, the manager's success and success of our company.

In fact, I admired Annette and saw some of myself in her. I pulled for her to nose out Bob's others "paper qualified" prospects. She was surprised when I told her that I didn't have a degree either. She built a large, successful agency. Bob was a very successful manager. They are both retired now.

We asked our first successful female and minority agents to help us get better at recruiting others like them. I'm grateful that they did.

One time, I was dean of a trainee agent school in Dallas. It was traditional to have a sales promotion following each school. Spontaneous challenges or team contests were always fun and productive. At the end of the school, I tried to lead the class into some challenges of forming some teams. I was doing a poor job of it.

I later learned that I said something that was interpreted as a racial insult to one of the students. I was devastated. This was a lady in my division that I had appointed. I admired her. I was fond of her and her husband. He was an attorney and later elected judge. I had supported them when their son had a diving accident and was paralyzed.

She was an attractive, cultured, likable individual with a master's degree. She was struggling in her business because of her son's disability. It hurt me personally that I had said something she took as racist.

After several requests, she agreed to talk to me. I met her at her office in Arlington at closing time on Saturday. I told her I didn't understand what I had said that insulted her, but I apologized. She explained what she understood me to say and why it bothered her. She also explained that an outside speaker at a divisional sales rally earlier in the year had offended her and other minorities. We had a good discussion and I learned. I think she accepted that I had no racial agenda.

I offered to take her to lunch but she insisted on taking me instead. She took me to a traditional, south Ft. Worth soul food place. As she hoped, I had the only white face in the place. She wanted me to have that experience.

As time went on, we had a number of highly successful women and minorities. They helped us learn and referred us to still more prospective agents.

Shalyn Clark is a highly successful agent in Hurst, Texas. Her manager at the time, Dan Sweeney, had a saying. "A person should feel like they have been hugged when they walk into a State Farm Insurance office." The warmth and enthusiasm of Shalyn and her office staff really make you feel that way.

When Al Clark, the top agent in our region married Shalyn, it caused quite a stir. They operated their separate agencies, Al in Arlington and Shalyn in Hurst. They each rank near the top of all the sixteen to seventeen thousand agents in the company each year. A few years ago, Al ranked number one and Shalyn number two. That's nearly an impossible numerical event.

Before retiring, I was able to appoint two women as Agency Managers. Sharon Bourassa was appointed a trainee agent in Lancaster, Texas by Agency Manager Del Anderson. When he retired four years later, she was a natural replacement. She became a very successful manager.

Sharon got married before being promoted to agency director. Sharon McAuley retired recently as a corporate vice-president in charge of all recruiting in the company.

Rendi Black was my great grand-daughter. I had recruited Ed Mills who became a manager and recruited Ed Long. When Ed Long became a manager, he recruited Rendi in Claremore, Oklahoma. I had a number of great grand-children who became successful.

Rendi had left her successful agency to become a training coordinator in the Oklahoma-Kansas Regional office in Tulsa. I recruited her to become a manager in Dallas in 1992. Unfortunately, we had some serious political and loss problems about that time. She got to Dallas in time to hear my announcement that we were discontinuing new auto insurance sales.

That restriction was lifted and she overcame other obstacles to succeed. She was promoted after I retired. I talked to her on the telephone a few weeks ago. She is back in Tulsa as vice-president agency. Her pre-school daughters are now becoming young adults— my how time flies.

Now with so many highly successful women and minorities, it seems ridiculous that it was such a challenge to recruit the first ones. They are at every executive level. Discrimination claims now are from white males.

RAGS TO RICHES

The rich old men visited in their oak
paneled club room,
reviewing their great deeds and sending
cigar smoke up in a plume.

Someone raised a question about
how they came into money.
Joe, the Ford dealer, said he had been so
poor it wasn't even funny.

"I didn't have two quarters to rub together
when I came to town.
Now, I'm in debt five million dollars and
spreading it all around."

Roscoe, the banker, ordered another drink
and despite their couth,
these men began arguing about who
was the poorest in their youth.

Roscoe said, "Some people think I had an
inheritance, money for life.
Truth is, we were very poor and I've
earned mine with hard work and strife."

"I'm telling you, we were so poor in those
deep, East Texas pines,
that my folks couldn't afford travel to
the unemployment lines."

"The only health plan back then was to clean
out your system each spring.
All the neighbors took strong laxative the same
day, and made it a fling."

"But, it was such a bad year for us
in nineteen thirty-three,
my folks couldn't afford to buy
the black draught tea."

"But family health was such an important
factor in my parent's worries,
they did the job anyway by telling us
their scariest ghost stories."

Elroy, the oil man, complemented Roscoe on
his great personal success.
Then he said, "I know you were poor but
our family had even less."

"In southern Oklahoma, I think it
was about nineteen thirty-four,
I tell you man, the old bad
wolf was at our door."

"We weren't concerned with health plans, styles
or political deceit.
The only thing on our minds
was getting something to eat."

"All our crops were destroyed by drought,
pests and disease.
The only exception was those tough, hard,
purple field peas."

"So momma gave we kids a bowl of those
peas for breakfast each day.
They were hard, tough and tasteless, but
kept starvation at bay."

"For lunch, we drank a big cold
glass of water from the well.
Then for supper, we had to be
content to – just swell."

Jill picked up Roscoe's empty glass. She was
the club's best on the wait staff.
She looked around the room, waiting
for someone to laugh.

But quiet prevailed, and Jill went back
to the kitchen for a little sip.
And she began to better understand
Roscoe's quarter tip.

Insurance Education and Training

During my thirty-four year State Farm career, agency training evolved but many basics remained the same. We always had pre-contract training administered by the manager as part of the selection process. Early training consisted of study and field assignments with the manager. Formal classroom training always consisted of pre-school study, a week of classroom, and then a field period practicing what was learned. The field period was really a sales contest.

Over time the names of schools and the number of schools changed. When I became an agent, we were a part of the Kansas State Agency located in Topeka. Our auto and property insurance was serviced in Dallas. Our life insurance was serviced in Lincoln, Nebraska.

My first school was on the campus of Oklahoma State University in February 1960. Agents and managers were there from all over Kansas and Oklahoma. Several significant things happened. First, my manager, Ed Carter, was sent home. I learned later that he was being terminated for causes unrelated to the school. Secondly, I learned that I was supposed to have completed some study exercises before coming to school. Thirdly, I met a lot of people that would be important to me for many years to come.

Norvel Trask was a successful agent from Bartlesville, Oklahoma. He was in a home office program preparing him to become a manager. One assignment was to attend and help in a trainee agent school. Norvel took me under his wing. Later, I knew Norvel as a fellow manager and still later as my Deputy Regional Vice-President.

Max Lingafelter was a manager in Wichita, Kansas. Later in my career, he was my deputy regional vice-president in Missouri. Frank Green was a fellow trainee from Tulsa. Our friendship continues to this day. We served together as agency directors in the Southwestern Region. We are both retired now.

Dean Corder was a manager in Western Kansas. He applied for the opening to replace Ed Carter so he could be in a better market. He became my manager and we enjoyed a great relationship.

Between my first and second school, there was a big management re-organization. The Kansas State Agency was phased out. All agency and all auto, property and life insurance operations were merged into the Southwestern Regional office with one regional vice-president. That included Oklahoma, Texas and New Mexico. Kansas agency went into the new Missouri-Kansas Region. As the company grew, new regions were formed. When I retired, our region consisted of North and West Texas.

My second school was held at the old Baker Hotel in Mineral Wells, Texas. It was about the same format. Again I met people from Texas and New Mexico who would be friends for many years.

After I became a manager, trainees had a different contract for two years. Successful completion of two years and the training programs earned them an independent contractor contract. The numbers of schools increased and were held at the regional office. A training department coordinated administration. An agency director was assigned as dean of each agency school. Individual classes were taught by operations specialists and managers attending with their agents.

Corporate had a manager development program when I became a manager. Either I didn't qualify or the timing was off, but I didn't attend. Our region did have a series of training classes for newer managers. These classes were taught by the agency directors.

I also participated in a two-week industry course taught by the Life Insurance Agency Management Association (LIAMA). That organization later changed to Life Insurance Marketing Research Association (LIMRA).

The company had a formal manager development program by the time I became an agency director. This included two schools at corporate headquarters and field assignments to be completed with the agency directors. New managers had a development contract which provided financial assistance during the training period. Upon completion, they received a career manager contract. The program had come a long way from 1961 when I started, especially financially.

Industry courses were available on a voluntary basis and the company reimbursed course expenses. Maybe it was because my college came to an end before I earned a degree, but I had a burning desire to learn all I could about my business. What the company taught wasn't enough. I wanted to know about the whole industry.

Insurance Institute of America sponsors vocational level courses for property and causality insurance. The basic course is in three semesters simply referred to as courses A, B and C. In 1963 a fine independent agent taught that course in Shawnee, Oklahoma. I lived in Ada at the time, about an hour and quarter drive. The two-hour class was at 7 a.m. every Monday morning. That year I started each week on the run.

Agent Albert Wiley attended and completed the course with me. I was recognized as having the highest grade in the nation on Part C. I was also in the top five for all three parts. The top five were asked to write an essay on insurance as a career. The writer of the best essay won the Hardy Award. The title of my essay was Opportunity, Security and Satisfaction. I thought it was pretty good, but it wasn't good enough.

The industry vocational level for life insurance sales was LUTC (Life Underwriter Training Council). It was also a three-part course to earn the designation of LUTC fellow. I took that course in Ada with three of my agents and all earned the LUTCF.

The American College of Life Underwriters confers the C.L.U. designation which is the professional designation in the life insurance business. When I started the program in 1966, it was a five part, five-year course. It became a ten-semester course by the time I completed it in 1971. No classes were in driving distance, so I completed that program with self-study. I did drive to Baton Rouge, Louisiana for a three-day cram course before my part 10 test.

State Farm gave Evelyn and me a nice trip to Chicago for the conferment exercises.

The American Institute for Property and Liability Underwriters confers the C.P.C.U. professional designation for the property and casualty end of the business. I started self-study on that program in 1972 and completed it in 1977. The company gave Evelyn and me a nice trip to San Francisco for the conferment.

I almost gave up on the C.P.C.U. designation. In 1976, I had a difficult time getting into a study routine. I was putting a lot of extra hours into my job. There were some family stresses. Evelyn's dad had been very sick in Oklahoma City, the kids had some problems and my excuses went on and on. Study in the evening was putting me to sleep fast.

The annual tests were always in early June. In January when I marked my calendar for the Part 4 test, I had basically given up. When I received my test ticket in the mail I paid little attention. I stuffed it in my wallet, because I doubted that I would take the test.

Evelyn got a call from Oklahoma City on the day the kid's school year ended. Her dad was in intensive care, so she and the kids flew to Oklahoma City. It was three weeks before the test. I would have uninterrupted study time at home and in the hotel in St. Louis. I re-doubled my efforts to prepare.

As test time drew near, I switched from evening study to early morning study. I had become skilled at scanning text books and chapter summaries. I could detect good, potential test questions, so I dictated key points and definitions. Then I listened to tapes in down times, like driving and shaving. I even went fishing with the dictation recorder clipped to my belt and a plug in my ear.

I studied until two a.m. the night before the scheduled test. The next morning I slept late, showered, and exercised to get my adrenalines flowing. I then drove to the University of Missouri for the 1 p.m. test. When I arrived at the test room, no one was around. The place was deserted. I re-checked my test ticket. I was at the right building and room.

As I looked at the ticket closer, I discovered that the test had been yesterday. I had marked the wrong date on my calendar back in January. The test is given only once a year at the same time nationwide.

I was devastated. I didn't tell anybody. I couldn't bear to discuss it. I had to punish myself in some way for such a stupid mistake. So I signed up for both parts 4 and 5 for 1977. I became a little more disciplined and studied hard on Part 5. I did a crash review on Part 4 the two weeks preceding the tests.

The C.P.C.U. tests are four hour essay tests. I had to write as fast as possible to complete all the questions in the allotted time. To my chagrin, both tests were scheduled on the same day. Part 4 was at 8 a.m. and Part 5 was at 1 p.m. I knew that I couldn't write for eight hours, so I signed up to write Part 4 then type part 5. I really couldn't type, but I hunted and I pecked for four hours and successfully completed the test.

State Farm Incentive Travel

Around 1970, State Farm's Chief Agency Officer, Earle B. Johnson wagered that travel incentives were very motivating for a sales force. They were expensive, but very effective. Our leading agents began to travel the world, and sales performance increased dramatically. Production levels, agents had considered out of reach, became common place.

The travel promotions were not only cost-effective; they also produced positive side effects. World travel adds a bit of confidence and sophistication to a sales force. Exposure to senior management at the destination was also motivational. Travel with the managers and fellow agents developed team spirit. Most agents just didn't want to be left behind. The list of benefits was endless, but on the bottom line, our people were having fun making more money and becoming even more loyal.

At first, only agents, managers and home office executives went on the trips. Then regional vice-presidents were invited and provided motivational companionship. As the program grew larger, our travel people needed help. Agency directors and Deputy regional vice-presidents were invited along to help. I think we added some value to the trip. It was always a bit of a chore getting people checked in at the airport and seats assigned on the charter. It was an even bigger chore getting everyone home. Upon arrival, we stayed at the airport until everyone cleared customs and claimed their luggage.

We were at the travel site to hear of any problems or complaints like an agent's wife reporting her prescription medicine stolen in Spain. We had an agent mugged at the Disney World Hotel. The report came in that a naked drunk was in the hallway. After further investigation, we discovered that someone came into his room through a first floor window while he was taking a bath.

When our agent hollered at the intruder, they struggled for his wallet. The intruder hit our victim on the head with some weapon and turned the hot water on full force. The agent ran into the hallway and was locked out. The intruder left via the window leaving the water running. When we got into the room, the agent's wallet was floating around in the overflowing hot water. He went to the hospital for a burn and head injury, but we saved his identification from the flooded room. Money in his wallet was gone.

One dreaded job was being in charge of the charter. On one of our early trips, our charter was an old Boeing 707. Later on we got newer wide body jets, but the old 707 was long and thin like a winged cigar with four engines. It had one long aisle. Most people tried to sleep on the overnight across the Atlantic. However, some couldn't or just preferred to visit with friends. The bar was all the way back in the tail, and a crowd gathered back there.

I was trying to sleep when an attendant woke me. She said, "Mr. Mulhausen, there are so many people crowded into the bar area, we can't move around to do our work. Can you help thin them out?"

Well agents are not employees. They are independent contractors. These were our top agents. Some might be tipsy. As I walked to the back, I wondered how I might order them to clear the area. As I reached the crowd in the aisle, the first agent had on a cute little canvass golf hat. I said "George, let me borrow your hat"

He complied, but asked why. I told him I was starting a pot. Put $5.00 in the hat and pick a number. Whoever guesses how many people it takes in the tail of the airplane to cause a spin down into the Atlantic, wins the pot. I told the story all the way to the bar. I didn't collect any money but did get some laughs. As I started back to my seat the aisle was clear.

We enjoyed incentive trips to London, Acapulco, Hawaii, Vienna, Munich, a Caribbean Cruise, Disney World, Montreal, Quebec City, Rome, Spain and Paris. We also had National Conventions in New Orleans, Las Vegas, Dallas, Atlanta, San Francisco, Denver and San Antonio.

Evelyn welcomed to Maui

It was tough dirty work but someone had to do it. A lot of our friends spent a lot of money shopping for souvenirs on trips. Evelyn and I decided that we would keep our budget under control by limiting personal souvenirs to travel spoons and Christmas tree ornaments. I did cheat and buy a silk tie in Florence one time. We wound up with spoons from each country visited and all fifty states.

While in Spain in 1978, we took a day trip to see the Rock of Gibraltar and tour Tangier, Morocco. We had a nice tour of the city. We saw snake charmers and belly dancers. The old ancient city, the Casbah, is in the middle of the modern city. You enter the Casbah through twenty-six foot thick walls. You go in a group with a Moroccan tour guide, because the narrow, winding streets are like a maize. You fear getting lost. There are no vehicles. Our walking tour, of course, wound up at a place to shop for souvenirs.

This store had some big ticket items and skillful sales people. Our guide and salesmen were all dressed in traditional Moroccan headdress and robes. A very clever salesman who spoke excellent English latched onto Evelyn and me. He showed us everything including the history and pedigree of hand-made rugs costing upwards of five figures. A lot of rugs were being bought to be shipped back to the United States. Our salesman said he would take Evelyn in exchange for a $15,000 rug. He said he would add a camel to the deal and I asked for two camels. We had a lot of fun, but wound up just buying our five-dollar spoon.

Our host then asked us where we lived in the United States. We were raised in Oklahoma, but lived in Missouri and had committed to move to Texas. I didn't figure he would know about Oklahoma or Missouri, so I asked, "Do you know where Texas is?"

He replied, "Oh, hell yes! I graduated from the University of Oklahoma".

Sales organizations do well when they are having fun. We have great memories of meetings and celebrations at fun places like the mansion at South Fork Ranch which was featured in the television series "Dallas."

In my Dallas division, we wound up one successful sales promotion with a barbeque and boot scooting country dance. The Johnny High Review is a long time tradition in the Dallas/Ft. Worth area. Johnny puts on a show every Saturday night in an Arlington theatre. He has a collection of performers, some former stars and some still looking for their lucky break. There are some wonderful musicians who love to entertain just for the joy of entertaining.

I was able to hire Johnny, his band and two or three singers to come to our Plano dance for just a thousand dollars. One little nine-year-old girl stole the show. She just blew us away. We enjoyed meeting her and visiting with the parents of Lee Ann Rimes. Even then, she knew she would be a star some day.

DOUBLE STANDARD

While recalling the past as a matter of course
and remembering the young officer in the Air Force
whose career was spotless and future looked bright,
until an affair with a subordinate came to light.

Unacceptable behavior, the Court-Martial ruled.
They threw her out of the Air Force though the affair had cooled.
She was dishonored and fired, proving my honest belief
that she infringed on a privilege reserved for the Commander and Chief.

INSURANCE INDUSTRY ORGANIZATIONS

I always tried to maintain an awareness of trends in our industry as well as in our own company. It pays to know what your competition is thinking and doing. When we moved to Ada, Oklahoma, there was a local Life Underwriters Association. I joined it and supported the organization. The National Association of Life Underwriters is now known as the National Association of Insurance and Financial Advisors (NAIFA). It seems that we salesmen always preferred to call ourselves underwriters or advisors rather than sales people.

The purpose of the organization is to professionalize the sales people and the insurance sales process. The organization also sponsors training, self-policing ethical conduct and work toward favorable legislation. I encouraged my agents to participate. Bill Derichsweiler worked to get a chapter organized in McAlester. Albert Wiley, John Hudspeth and I helped revive the association in Shawnee. Lloyd Jack and I worked to keep the association alive in Ada. The numbers in the small towns made it difficult, but it was worth the effort.

One mission in my career was to resist the commoditization of our products and promote professional relationships between our agents and their clients. We made progress in many instances but our products now are largely treated like commodities. I told my agents that insurance sales might not be a profession, but you can be a professional doing it.

In Oklahoma, our state association held an annual sales congress in conjunction with our annual business meeting. Some of the top sales people in the nation spoke in the program. When I became a state officer, I encouraged attendance and also took an agent or two with me for some of the social activity the evening before the congress. I felt there was value in rubbing elbows with the top sales people in the state and country.

As on officer I also had contact with regulators and other officials. I was able to escape to Missouri before my time to serve as president, but our Insurance Commissioner made me an honorary Deputy Insurance

Commissioner. Joe B. Hunt was the prototype, old time politician, and colorful stories of his career abound. He told a group that Elmer's move to Missouri raised the average I.Q. in both states by ten points.

As an agency director, I was no longer eligible for the agent's association but was an associate member. I encouraged my agents and managers to participate. In Missouri, Manager Scotty Winscott held association presidency for St. Louis and then a Missouri state presidency, Max McGowen was also influential and held office.

In Dallas, Herb Buschmann, Larry McHargue, David Smith, and Dan Smith were leaders in both the life underwriters and the C.L.U. Society. Larry, Herb and Dan became president of the Dallas association. After I retired, Dan became president of the Texas association. I talked to Dan Smith recently and he is still active on the national level of NAIFA. I think he is a regional chair of the Political Action Committee.

As an agency director, I belonged to the General Agents and Managers Association, the C.P.C.U. Society and the C.L.U. Society. L.I.M.R.A., or the Life Insurance Marketing and Research Association, was an association of companies rather than individuals. I think I gained a little better feel for our business by attending a few national meetings of all of these organizations, though I didn't have time for heavy involvement with any one of them.

Because I had selected so many managers that had been promoted, I was asked to be a presenter in the 1991 National L.I.M.R.A. Conference in Dallas. I was asked to make a presentation on selecting managers. My co-presenter was a L.I.M.R.A. staff scientist, who had developed a psychological profile test for manager selection. L.I.M.R.A. was marketing this test to companies. We used a L.I.M.R.A. aptitude test in agent selection, but I don't think we ever bought their management test.

In St. Louis, all the industry organizations would collaborate for a meeting called I-Day. This once a year function had speeches, workshops, recognition and a trade fair where companies selling to the industry rented booths. Several cities do this.

One year I was asked to present a program on Errors and Omissions Insurance at the El Paso, Texas *I-Day meeting*. I was honored to talk about why agents and claims representatives needed this coverage. I also reviewed a few case histories. You know what an expert is, don't you? That's someone a long way from home in a suit and carrying a brief case. That was me in El Paso.

AGENCY EXECUTIVE STAFF IN DALLAS

My Agency Manager friends were not the only friends I rejoined when we returned to Dallas in 1978. My colleagues, the other agency directors were also old friends. I had known Frank Green since we were both trainee agents. We met in my first agency school in 1960 at Stillwater, Oklahoma. I had known Cliff Galaway almost as long. He had been a manager in Oklahoma City and had been one of my closest friends.

Art Langeloh had been a veteran manager in the Chicago area, when he came to our region as an agency director. Art had been my director for a while when I was a manager in Oklahoma. Then there was Duane Tillinghast. Tilly was one of the most colorful characters in State Farm. He had been a manager in Michigan before joining the agency department at corporate headquarters. Before coming to Dallas, Tilly had been assistant vice president in charge of conventions and travel. He taught the rest of us a lot about planning large meetings.

Tilly lived life in the fast lane. He was big, loud, and boisterous. He was the first guy you noticed when you walked into a room full of people. He was a fun guy to serve on a staff with. Unfortunately, Tilly's heart couldn't keep up with his pace and he had a couple of attacks. Tilly came to the office one Monday morning saying he had fired his doctor. We asked why? The doctor had told him, "Mr. Tillinghast, if you won't stop smoking, get yourself another doctor."

Tilly got another doctor. The day of Tilly's funeral was one of the saddest days in the Southwestern Region.

Art Langeloh also took medical retirement. Long time friend John Westmoreland joined our staff. John had become an agent while I was still an agent in Oklahoma City. He was also a fun guy to work with, and was promoted. He was the Deputy Regional Vice President of the Oklahoma-Kansas Region when he retired.

Rob Ruth joined us from Missouri, then Eddy Chew and Doyce Walker from Oklahoma and Don Alford from East Texas. Don actually started in Oklahoma and was my grandson in agency. Don was also a horse race crony.

The regions were realigned in 1985 when Oklahoma and Kansas became a region with a new office in Tulsa. Doyce was fortunate enough to get his old team in Clinton back. We lost Cliff, Frank and Eddy to the new region. One of my managers, Al Wagner, was promoted. Al is now Vice President Agency in Dallas. Another of my manager team, Phil Head had promoted to the South Texas region. When our region gave up Oklahoma, we became the North Texas Region and picked up West Texas and some of the South Texas Region. When that re-alignment took place, Phil came home. Phil was also a horse racing crony and still owns horses.

Irene White came up from South Texas. Two more of my former managers also joined us on our agency director staff, Dan Sweeney and Sharon McAuley. I've listed a lot of people but no more than six of us served in the region at the same time. They were all good friends and I enjoyed serving with them.

Only Phil and Rob are still serving as agency executives. Dan Sweeney tired of management and was able to get a nice local agency. Others retired or were promoted. Don Alford passed away this last year. He was a great friend.

I am also thankful for and appreciate all the support people I worked with over the years. My first secretary in Missouri, Helen Douglas, gave me more training than any other one person. She had been secretary to agency directors before me, and was a huge asset in getting me oriented in a new job. The same was true when I moved to Dallas. Eleanor Payne, Barbara Thomas and Jane Stone were invaluable. Several others like Linda Vest and Executive Secretary, Monete Vinson, were very helpful. Debbie Ferrell was so special that my boss stole her from me. I was happy for her promotion but really missed her.

I was lost when Jo Ann Griffin moved back to Missouri. When I retired, I was working with Patricia Robertson. Pat was and is a class act.

Working with the deputy regional vice president in charge of operations was also important for agency directors. We worked with them as part of the region's executive staff. Cooperation between agency, the underwriters and claims forces make State Farm special. I enjoyed working with Eugene Meyung, Bob McSween, Drew Hamilton, and Dick Shellito. They were all good friends.

My longest and closest relationship was with Norvel Trash and Bob Warren. I always had the deepest respect for both of them. I didn't always agree with them, but after expressing my opinion, I supported their decision. I trusted their leadership.

Family get together in Plano, TX 1992

Front kneeling: Jeff Federspiel, Teresa Federspiel holding Emily Federspiel, Shaun Federspiel, Jeanne Mulhausen holding Mary Ruth Mulhausen and Sarah Mulhausen by her side, Patrick Downing and Dominique Downing. Back row standing: Danielle Downing, Troy Federspiel, David Mulhausen, Evelyn, Elmer, John, John D (Johnny) and Sheryl Mulhausen.

Bob Warren and Norvel Trask created a real sense of brotherhood in the region's Agency Manager group. It was like a club that people wanted to be a part of. There was a sense of belonging and a motivational morale that will probably never be duplicated.

Over those years in the Dallas regional office, I became known as the agency director that hated golfers. Of course that isn't true. Practically all my friends were golfers. I didn't play golf because I have a personality defect. I don't like to lose. I like to do things where I have at least an even chance of winning. At the age when most people start playing golf, I was working hard to make ends meet. I always worked long hours, and didn't want to take additional time away from my family. When I did start to play, I was a beginner and terrible. I became an oxymoron, an insurance man and sales manager that didn't play golf.

One year, I was assigned chairmanship of the spring management conference at the Shangri Las Resort on Grand Lake in Oklahoma. Our key managers were invited a day early for recreation and a banquet. We paid for rooms and meals but we did not pay the manager's golf green fees. When I tried to block off tee times for our key managers, the golf pro wouldn't do it unless the green fees were billed to State Farm. I have never liked creating a situation where we had to collect from the managers, and the golf pro had an eight hundred number for reserving tee times.

I wrote the key managers that they should form their foursomes and call the eight- hundred-number to reserve their tee times.

As I reviewed plans for the conference in the Agency Staff Meeting, Norvel asked if I had set the key managers tee times. I said no and explained the reason. I distributed my letter to the key managers.

Norvel said, "Oh, Oh! It will be all messed up. They are accustomed to our having the tee times all set up."

That's when I said, "It isn't that I hate golf. It's just the damn golfers that I hate. Are you telling me that they don't have sense enough to dial an eight-hundred-number and reserve a tee time? Who is going to wet nurse the tennis players? Who will pin the diapers on the people going fishing? Who will bottle feed the shoppers and sight seers?"

Of course, Mr. Warren and Mr. Trask are golfers as are all the other staff members. At first they were shocked. Then everyone started laughing. I don't remember how we resolved it, but I couldn't live down the tag, "The A.D. who hates golfers."

Bob Jeffus was my Regional Vice President when I retired. When Bob Warren retired, we were glad that Bob Jeffus was promoted to replace him. I had known Bob Jeffus since he was a trainee agent in 1969 in Houston. Bob Warren was tremendously popular with all the agency force and employees in the region. He was a tough act to follow.

Building our company had been great fun. We were transitioning from that fun to all the problems of running a huge company. The justice system, politics and the weather heaped problems upon problems. Add the pain of my daughter, Sheryl not succeeding in agency and my last couple of years were not as much fun as previous years. It was time to retire.

Bob Jeffus and I had some unpleasant moments, but he is a good man. He has since retired and we remain friends.

In all my years with State Farm, I was never asked or expected to misrepresent anything, cheat or short change anybody. We never plotted against anybody. We expected anything said, or heard, to be true.

When I was working, I took that principle for granted. Now as I look back, I think our basic honesty was quite remarkable. I am very thankful for that.

AGENCY REORGANIZATION

After I retired, the company re-organized agency leadership. The agency director job and the Agency Manager jobs were eliminated. Agency field offices took their place. Each office was lead by an agency field executive and assisted by a consultant and a specialist.

Thayer Sharp, Troy Daniel and Ed Mills took enhanced retirement packages. Charley England, Don Seymour, Bob Weathers and Dan Smith were able to get nice local agencies. Pat Warren, John Murray, Rendi Black, Lathan Garnett and Earl Jordan were promoted to agency field executives. Pat Warren is now a vice president agency in Ohio and Rendi Black an agency vice president in Tulsa.

Thirteen managers were retired all in one day when the re-organization took place. It seemed like a huge waste of talent to me. One of the retired circulated the following "tongue in cheek" bulletin.

> To: THE MAGNIFICENT THIRTEEN
>
> RE: NEW RETIREMENT POLICY *
>
> As a result of the reduction in money budgeted for agency purposes, we are going to cut down our number of personnel.
>
> Under the plan, older employees will go on early retirement, thus permitting the retention of younger people who represent our future plans.
>
> Therefore, a program to phase out older personnel by the end of the current fiscal year via early retirement will be placed into effect immediately. The program shall be known as RAPE. (Retire Aged Personnel Early).
>
> Employees who are raped will be given the opportunity to secure other jobs within the system, provided that while they are being raped, they request a review of their employment

records before actual retirement takes place. This phase of the operation is called SCREW. (Survey of Capabilities of Retired Early Workers).

All employees who have been raped or screwed may also apply for trial review: this will be called SHAFT. (Study by Higher Authority Following Termination).

Program policy dictates that employees may be raped once, screwed twice, but may get the shaft as many times as the company deems appropriate.....

HORSE RACING

The first horse race I remember was at Sunland Park in New Mexico right across the state line from El Paso. We were in El Paso for a company function, and I went to the horse races with a group. It was exciting, but I really didn't know what was going on. Two or three of us pooled our funds to place a two dollar bet. That was around 1970. I was still raising my family and the budget didn't have any wagering room.

After we returned to Texas in 1978, we went on a company outing to Hot Springs, Arkansas. We went to the races at Oaklawn Park. Louisiana Downs near Shreveport, Louisiana was also a destination for some sales promotion pay offs. Then, Remington Park opened in Oklahoma City. All those were about right for weekend get-a-ways. I gradually began to really enjoy the beauty of the horses, the excitement and challenge of handicapping.

I studied some of the history of the sport and a couple of books on handicapping. I went to handicapping seminars. By the mid-eighties, I was a full-fledged fan.

My first real horse race cronies were Don Alford and Phil Head. They had both been horse owners. Phil and a partner still own a mare that produces a racing foal every year. In fact, one of those off springs set a new six furlong record for Lone Star Park.

In 1992, Evelyn and I went to the Arkansas Derby in Hot Springs. Betty Vamvakos is the State Farm agent in Farmersville in Don Alford's agency division. We were meeting the Alfords in Hot Springs. Betty rode up there with Don and Gayla Alford since her husband, Pete, was already in Hot Springs. Pete was already retired, and he had made arrangements for a box for the Arkansas Derby. Getting a box on Derby Day at Oak Lawn Park was quite a feat. I was impressed.

I met Pete for the first time when we all got together at our hotel. That meeting was the beginning of our traveling to races together for the past sixteen years. Pete and I and sometimes Don and Phil traveled to twelve Kentucky Derbies. We also traveled to about a dozen World Championships (Breeders Cups) at various tracks all over the country.

I gave it up as too big a hassle and too expensive. Pete still goes. He added the Preakness Stakes and the Belmont Stakes to his itinerary. Pete called me last week to see if I wanted to go to the Derby and Preakness this year. I declined. He said he was slowing down, too. He had dropped the Belmont from his schedule.

We still get together at Lone Star Park at Grand Prairie occasionally. I might try to get to Oaklawn Park in Hot Springs this spring.

I still follow the sport nationally. The top jockeys and horses are athletic heroes just like the football, baseball and basketball stars many people idolize.

After Texans watched horse racing tax dollars and tourism dollars flow out of the state for fifty years, they finally legalized racing again. Pete, Charles England and I supported that legislation.

Charles England was a manager in my division and a good friend. Around 1991, Charley asked if he could run for mayor of Grand Prairie. A group had asked him to run and pledged their support. Charles went on to say it was only a figure-head position and wouldn't take much of his time.

Charlie was also a good friend of our Regional Vice President, Bob Warren. I figured that Bob Warren had already given his permission but sent him to see me. I told Charlie that if he would cut the B.S. about the job not taking much time, I was all for him if Mr. Warren approved.

Charlie had a tough campaign but won the mayoral race in 1992. Since then, he has had only token opposition. I talked to Charlie last week and he said he didn't have an opponent in 2008. Obviously, the citizens of Grand Prairie think he has done a good job for them over the past sixteen years.

Since State Farm's management re-organization, Charlie has been an agent in Grand Prairie. His son, Kirk, is also an agent. Kirk entered politics two years ago and was elected to the state legislature.

Obviously, Charlie has done a lot for his hometown, but his fight to get Lone Star Park built is my reason for writing about him. It was a long, hard battle, but Lone Star is a facility to be proud of. Charlie and Lone Star management then began a quest to host the Breeders' Cup Championship at Grand Prairie. I was with them at several Breeders' Cup cities. They worked long and hard making presentations to the Breeders' Cup hierarchy on behalf of Lone Star and the City of Grand Prairie.

They were successful in bringing the Breeders' Cup thoroughbred World Championship to Grand Prairie in 2004. We have a wonderful track at Grand Prairie and I am anxious for the 2008 season to open in April. I've learned not to worship the horses, but horse racing is one of the loves of my life.

One time in Hot Springs, Pete and I caught a taxi from our hotel to the track. We asked the driver for a tip. He had none. We asked if he ever got tips from the barns. He said that maybe one time each season, they would get a call so the working folks could get paid. After that, every time a fifty to one horse with no apparent chance wins a race, Pete and I refer to that as the taxi cab race.

In all my years going to the races, I have had four insider tips. I ignored two on long shots that won. I bet on two of the tips and won. I bet on one and lost.

In reality, no one can predict the outcome of a race with any certainty. My goal in preparation before the race is to rank the "probabilities." I give each horse a numerical rank. At the time of the race, I adjust for scratches, weather conditions and appearance of the horse. I'm not good enough to pick a winner by looking, but I do eliminate some horses by the way they look. I then compare my probabilities to the betting odds. A good wager presents itself when the best probability has decent odds.

Betting favorites win about one third of the time. If my number one horse has odds of 2/1 or less, it is a bad bet. A $2 win bet at 2/1 odds pays $6 when winning. ($4 plus return of $2) If only 1/3 of favorites win, that means you bet three times for that one win. (3 x $2 = $6). If my favorite is less than 5/2 in an average field of seven or eight horses, I look for a better probability to odds ratio.

Betting on random long shots is also a loser. But betting on long shots with decent probabilities can be profitable. Kentucky Derby history is full of examples. In 1992, Pine Bluff beat Lil Etee in the 1 1/8 mile Arkansas Derby. Lil Etee was gaining at the end of the race. The Kentucky Derby is run at 1 ¼ miles with a tough early pace. At 17 to 1, Lil Etee was an attractive long shot in the Kentucky Derby and won.

In 1995, I liked a west coast horse named Jumron. I had already placed my wager. Three young ladies sitting in front of us were asking everyone for tips on a good long shot. I reviewed the tote board and there was Thunder Gulch at 24 to 1. His last race at the Blue Grass Stakes was terrible, but up until then he had been spectacular. I told the girls and ran to the windows, barely getting my bet down on time. I bet $4 to win, place and show. That $12 bet paid me $247. The young ladies thought I was a wise old man.

In 2003, Empire Maker looked unbeatable. I made my bet then watched the odds fall to 5/2. He had just beaten Funnycide at the Wood Memorial, but only by a neck. Funnycide was at 13 to 1 in that sixteen horse field. I went back to the windows and placed a $4 win, place and show on Funnycide too. Funnycide won. Empire Maker was second. I enjoyed collecting $116.80.

I won't bore you with all the bad bets I have made. My horse playing is for recreation and not a vocation. I lose sometimes by making too many silly, little exotic bets because they are fun. There are some races that should be skipped, but I'm there for recreation and I play those races, too.

My favorite horse racing trip was to the 1999 Breeders Cup in Florida. Not only did I get to visit with my son, David, but Pete and I enjoyed three good days at Gulf Stream Park. I won everyday. In fact, I won a superfecta each day including one on the Breeders' Cup Sprint. On Breeders' Cup Day, I picked five winners out of the eight championship divisions. I didn't pick the winner of the Classic Division but did win on two long shots placed second and third. That's the story in the poem "Lost Colt Finally Found".

I covered all my travel expenses plus a healthy profit.

VIVA DERBY

Oh how I love the horses.
I love to see them run.
A day at Lone Star Park
is my idea of Spring time fun.

I've followed the horses from Remington.
Belmont and Gulfstream, too.
Then on West to Santa Anita and
Hollywood near the ocean blue.

But, the greatest thrill comes on
the first Saturday in May.
They run for the roses at Churchill,
and I'm off to Kentucky to play.

They call it derby fever and I
always get a bad case.
I spend hours studying and handicapping.
Who will win that race?

Trainer, jockey, race distance,
form, works, fitness and class?
I'll study every thing available,
I'll question everything that comes to pass.

While some just pick the
cutest name or bet a magic number,
Or wager the expert's tip
or something even dumber.

While they merrily sip their Juleps,
and dress so elegantly,
I'm still studying; determined
to lose my money intelligently.

RETIREMENT

Evelyn and I got off to a fast start on our retirement in October, 1993. Since, I was always goal-oriented; we set a goal and made plans. We both loved travel but didn't care for any more foreign travel. We decided to visit every state that we hadn't already visited.

But that could wait until we finished our first trip. Our destination was the Santa Anita horse racing track in Arcadia, California. We were going to the 1993 Breeders' Cup. For the uninitiated, the Breeders' Cup is thoroughbred horse racing's version of the World Series or Super Bowl. It's held at the end of October or first of November every year. Champions in several different divisions are crowned.

We decided to drive and plan several interesting stops along the way like Santa Fe, Colorado San Juan Mountains, Mesa Verde National Park, Lake Powel and the north rim of the Grand Canyon. We took in Bryce and Zion National Parks before Las Vegas. We met my horse racing cronies, Don Alford and Pete Vamvakos at our hotel in Pasadena. They had flown out to California.

On Friday before the championships on Saturday, Evelyn bought a two-dollar exacta box in race five on horses seven and eleven. They were both long shots; such long shots that her four-dollar ticket paid $1,187. Pete and Don raved about how anyone could be so dumb to bet on such unlikely horses. They finally shut up when Evelyn agreed to buy dinner.

It was that kind of meet. A French horse that no one had heard of named Arcongue was entered in the classic. The horse's career had been ruined by chronic back trouble. Jockey Jerry Bailey had never seen the horse before meeting in the paddock before the race. This "nobody" was entered against the best horses in the world for a four-million dollar purse. When Arcongue won that race a two-dollar win ticket paid $269.20, a Breeders' Cup record. I heard later that a chiropractor had adjusted the horse's back. That's the only real big race the horse ever won.

On our way home, we met my cousin, Harry Mixer and his wife, Pat in Laughlin, Nevada for a few days. We spent a couple of days in Sedona, Arizona before heading on home. We had a great first retirement trip.

We had many more good trips. First, we went to Myrtle Beach to wrap up South Carolina. To complete New England, we flew to Hartford and rented a car. We toured New England during leaf peeping season. We really enjoyed the Christmas Farm Inn in Lincoln, New Hampshire.

To pick up our missing mid-western states, we headed north one summer. Our high points were the Mackinac Bridge into upper Michigan, fishing a few days in Wisconsin, International Falls Minnesota, and Deadwood, South Dakota.

We had only one state to go, Alaska. The most popular way to visit has become the Alaskan Cruise through the inside passage. After we listed everything we wanted to do and a little research, we decided to plan our own tour.

We flew to Anchorage and rented a car. We drove for sixteen days doing what we wanted to do. We included a fly out to Glacier Bay. We satisfied our cruising needs on the Alaska Ferry and small craft cruises in Glacier Bay and Prince William Sound.

Mapping had told me how big Alaska is, especially if you include part of the Yukon Territory. But you can't realize how vast it is until you drive those bad roads. We saw both brown and black bear, a wolf, caribou, doll sheep, elk, moose, hump back whales, sea otters, seals, sea lions, eagles, terns, puffins and countless other species. I caught a thirty-two pound king salmon. We didn't see any mountain goats, killer whales or beluga whales. We really enjoyed visiting our fiftieth state.

Evelyn and I enjoyed five years of retirement together. She developed a love for video poker machines. She probably liked them too much, but she didn't criticize my love of horse racing so I didn't criticize her video poker madness. She had her own household expense account, so

I didn't audit her wins and losses. I just helped celebrate her jackpots which were frequent.

We discovered the Harrah's Hotel in downtown Vicksburg, Mississippi when it was brand new. It was a small tasteful hotel and casino on the Yazoo River. The casino was the friendliest I have ever been in. Everyone was on a first name basis. We never spent a dime there. Everything was comped. If we were celebrating a birthday or anniversary, we always found a champaign and goody basket in our room. We preferred Vicksburg to Las Vegas.

I don't know who operates the place now, but I heard Harrah's sold it. Jo Ann and I haven't been to a casino in five years and really don't miss it.

Evelyn dearly loved our grandchildren. I do too, but she spoiled them to a fault. When they were little, we had "Camp Nannie" every summer. All the grandkids would come for a week and literally camp out in our house. Our swimming pool got a good workout as did the rest of the house. They played games, listened to music, created plays and made some great videos. Those are great memories.

Evelyn shared my love of the horse races up to a point. Her handicapping consisted of betting on every horse ridden by Pat Day, horses with cute names, and if a race had at least eleven horses, she bet a 7-11 exacta box. Amazingly she did pretty good with that scientific approach. She went with me to one Kentucky Derby and one Breeders Cup, but didn't go back, She didn't like the expense, the hassle and the huge crowds.

I had Dallas Cowboy season tickets for several years. She went with me to some games, but really didn't care for it. When my name was drawn to be eligible for Super Bowl tickets, she couldn't make up her mind. Finally, she liked the idea of going with friends to Vicksburg, the ladies staying at Harrah's and the guys going on to the Super Bowl in Atlanta. I lined up Ed Mills to go then he had emergency surgery and could not go.

Although people were paying eight hundred dollars a ticket in Atlanta, I was having trouble finding someone to go on short notice. I talked to Agent Randy Shockey and he wanted to go, but there wasn't time for his wife to line up child care. She graciously told Randy to go on. We spent the first evening at Harrah's in Vicksburg. We left Evelyn there for two nights while Randy and I went to Atlanta to watch the Cowboys beat Buffalo. When we got back to Vicksburg, Evelyn was still having a good time at Harrah's.

LOSING EVELYN

Our daughter, Sheryl, lived at Round Rock, Texas in 1998 and worked at the State Farm Regional office in Austin. Sheryl's fibromyalgia was making it difficult for her to maintain her home. She planned to sell the house and move to an apartment. Evelyn went to Round Rock to help Sheryl get the house ready for the market.

One morning I received a call from Sheryl at 4 a.m. Evelyn had gotten real sick and gone to the emergency room at Round Rock Hospital. I left immediately to go down there. As I passed through Waco, I got a call on my cell phone. Evelyn had been transferred to a large hospital in Austin. Sheryl gave me directions.

When I walked in the hospital door, Sheryl's family and a brain surgeon were waiting on me. Evelyn had a ruptured aneurysm in her brain and a consequent stroke. I signed papers for surgery.

We were told that the surgery had mended the aneurysm. We had one of those weeks in the I.C.U. waiting room measured by the ten minute visiting period every two hours. Only two people could visit at a time. We rented a nearby room and slept in shifts. The family gathered from Tulsa, Florida, Round Rock and Plano. The Vowells came up from Houston.

Evelyn got better. After a couple of days she could visit lucidly. Her voice was slurred but we could understand her. The doctor said that her voice would clear up, but she would always have a weakness on the left side of her body. That is if there was no contamination left on her brain. If there was contamination, she wouldn't make it. I had gotten pretty rusty on my praying, but I learned all over again.

Toward the end of the week, Evelyn started going down hill again. We were informed that she was terminal. They kept her on life support while each of us had an opportunity to spend some final time with her.

I always knew I loved her, but I didn't realize how much until that moment. We had planned for me to precede her. We had no plan for her preceding me. I was lost.

MARY'S AND SARAH'S BIRTHDAY

John and Jeanne's girls have birthdays on adjacent days. In nineteen ninety-nine after Evelyn died and before I married Jo Ann, Sarah had her sixteenth birthday and Mary Ruth had her eighth. I drove up from Plano, Texas and John's family drove down from Tulsa for a celebration in Oklahoma City. This made it possible for them to also visit Jeanne's parents who lived in Oklahoma City. I made reservations in Silks Restaurant at Remington Park. We celebrated the birthdays, had a nice dinner, and watched the horse races.

Their birthday poems follow. I will have to confess that I almost duplicated Sarah's poem for Grandson Shaun Federspiel when he turned sixteen. In fact, I have duplicated several lines as the grandkids have turned sixteen, eighteen, and twenty-one.

Mary was attending Country Day private school in Tulsa at the time. I had been quite impressed with the school on a previous visit. It just dawned on me as I wrote this, that Mary turned sixteen this year and I didn't write her a preachy poem. I must be mellowing out. To be truthful, I have just about stopped writing poems for greeting cards for fear of repeating myself.

Now the girls are 16 and 24
Jeanne, John D (Johnny) Sarah, Mary and John Mulhausen

BIRTHDAY CARD TO MARY

Like a lady bug keeping the garden neat,
Mary's bright smile makes the day so sweet.
She's growing up so fast, it makes my head spin.
So the back of my neck is ahead of my chin.

I sure like Mary's real neat school.
With all the great kids and animals, it's cool.
Two gerbils, llamas and a fox on mount,
all help Mary learn to read, write and count.

We went to the races to celebrate and I told her
she's getting prettier and prettier and one year older.
So Mom, Dad, Johnny, Sarah and Popa too,
raise our glasses and say, "Mary, Happy Birthday to you".

Even the horses who prance and run
join in Mary's birthday fun.
Mary even picked some horses that won out right.
Again, I say, Happy Birthday, I love you with all my might.

Love, Popa

Keys on Your Sixteenth Birthday

Happy Birthday dear Sarah: This is a wonderful time to share.
Reaching the sixteenth is a great milestone. I love you and care.
Girls turning sixteen want keys to cars, that's loud and clear.
But, I'm writing this message about other keys this year.

Keys will come in due course when it should be so.
But there are other keys to life you should know.
Of course there are many keys that come to mind,
but these special four, I trust you will find.

Love, enthusiasm, self-esteem and learning,
are keys to serenity and happiness worth earning.
Know down deep you are unconditionally loved so true
by so many, including God, family and us, too.

Loving others is also a very important key.
But loving yourself comes first, you see.
Be proud and confident in who you are.
Then loving and helping others will be par.

Believe in yourself and all your qualities innate.
Then with confidence and assurance to others relate.
Enthusiasm for life is also a valuable key
to finding beauty others just can't see.

Finding light in darkness, turning error to hit,
finding opportunities in problems with courage and grit.
Finding laughter in distress, finding color in gray…
yes, Sarah, enthusiasm turns labor to play.

Find excitement in learning. Be curious forever.
That's an important key to happiness in every endeavor.
And may it not be too long before you get keys to wheels.
But remember, these keys to life are already a deal.

Love, Popa

THE QUESTERS

As young adults, Evelyn and I worked hard in our local churches. We belonged to Walker Avenue Baptist and Prairie Queen Baptist Churches in Oklahoma City. We rarely missed a service and filled whatever roles of service assigned to us. We even sponsored high school aged young people even though we were not much older than they were.

We moved to Ada and joined a new Baptist Church near us. That church needed lots of help, and we filled every role we could. We were beginning to burn out by the time we moved to Shawnee. We joined a larger Baptist church there and worshiped regularly, but avoided leadership roles.

We were beginning to become uncomfortable with intolerance. Rising into church political and financial leadership had been dis-enchanting. We had been over-whelmed by a couple of scandals and instances of hypocrisy. I was too naïve to realize that pastors and deacons are human too and subject to all the same temptations as all of us.

Those are facts, but not excuses. There is no good excuse for drifting away from Christian service and worship. By the time we moved to Missouri, that's exactly what we did. We still believed, but we put God on the shelf. I hear people say they can worship privately and live a Christian life without going to church. That's true but not likely. I said the same thing many times. For us private worship suffered if we were not having regular corporate worship. We needed an organization through which we could serve God and mankind. We needed the strength of association with others of like-mind.

By the time Evelyn died, we professed to loving God, but we were not living it. When she died, we didn't even have a church home. Luckily we had our nephew, Terry Wilson, a Baptist Minister, preach the funeral. I have never doubted Evelyn's faith or salvation, but her death was a wake-up call.

The weeks following Evelyn's death are a blur in my memory. But after a time, a good friend, Beverly Sharp, told me that a grief seminar in her church had been helpful for her. Her husband, Thayer, had been one of my managers and a good friend. He died a couple of years before Evelyn. I attended that seminar at Custer Road United Methodist Church, and it was very helpful.

That church had an outstanding singles ministry. The group planned a dance at the Los Rios Country Club in Plano, and Beverly invited me. She introduced me to her fellow Sunday school classmates. The class was named The Questers. While Beverly and I were dancing, the D.J. played a song that was used in Thayer's funeral. We sat down. When we started to dance again, they played "Wind Beneath My Wings" which was used in both Thayer's and Evelyn's funerals. We sat and talked about our former spouses for the rest of the evening.

I knew I should be in church, so I joined the Questers, and later joined the church. I have never known such an outstanding support group. Most all the Questers had families over the years but now were all alone. We had a great Bible class with Agnes Bianco teaching. Leon Combs was president. Secretary Judy Edwards kept us organized. Bob Sillimon was chief jester and story-teller.

The Questers always sat together in the worship service, and many of us went to lunch together after church. We had one official social every month, and then some of us got together for something nearly every week. For a period, Linda Pack, Agnes, Vic Hall, Duane Schue and I met at a dance place.

When I met Jo Ann, our first date was a Quester function. We went to Nancy Chase's home for covered dishes, then to Swan Court to dance. As Jo Ann and I got to know each other, she joined the Quester class and joined the church.

It's hard to believe that wonderful class and support group doesn't exist now. There had been a couple of weddings before I joined the class. Then Jo Ann and I got married. It wasn't long before Judy Edwards and Bob Stroud married. Nancy Chase married Roger Frederick and Jan Gregg married Alan Strickland. The class began to fold when the teacher, Agnes Bianco married the then class president, Duane Schue. Some members moved to other classes and some moved away. The class ceased to function as a singles class.

When Jo Ann and I got married, I was president of the class. They wanted us to stay with the class until the end of the Sunday school year, and then we moved to a class called the Positive Thinkers. They were a great group, but there will never be another support group like the Questers. When we visit Plano, we try to see friends like Holly Linskie, Jane Kietzer, Jo Ann Barbee, Inez Dublin, Haverly Hedges, Artelissa Kile, Dolores Saari, Muriel Watkins, Medie Cashon and Grace Tipton. I know I'm overlooking someone, but we love them too.

My sister, Betty Ruth, had her period of life outside of the church, but returned to Christian service before I did. She is a devout Baptist. Over several years when we visited or talked on the telephone, she always closed by saying, "Elmer, you know you need to be back in church serving the Lord. I'm praying for you."

I always thanked her. When I finally did re-join the church, I called her. I said, "Betty, I have good news and bad news. The good news is that your prayers have been answered. I have joined the church."

She said, "Wonderful! What is the bad news?"

I answered, "I've joined a Methodist Church."

There was a long pause, and then she said, "Well, that's alright."

WE ARE THE QUESTERS

We have had family around us most of our life.
Now we find ourselves home alone; no husband, no wife.
But as the autumn of our years come to pass,
God has given us each other, our Questers class.

We are the Questers.

Whether in prayer and worship or at a party or show,
we support each other wherever we go.
Life is a gift from our Heavenly Father and we'll do our best
to both serve Him and have fun. That is our quest.

We are the Questers.

AGNES

We the Questers Class – to Agnes our
teacher much preferred
We wish to express our love and thanks
for blessings incurred.

Your lessons from the heart are apt,
sincere and thought provoking
taken from the Bible, and great books
with discussion and even joking.

You are sweet, beautiful and caring,
and we are in one accord.
You are what the doctor ordered
and we are never bored.

Each Sunday, we come to class
full of anticipation.
And our lives become richer, so please
accept this token of our Appreciation.

Irregardless of all theological theory
Cannons, titles or liturgy,
my religion boils down to be
the relationship between God and me.

MY SPIRITUAL JOURNEY

I was raised in a strict, puritanical religious atmosphere. Anything considered fun by the world at large was deemed to be sin. I came to know God personally at a very early age in a Nazarene revival meeting. I knew I had done wrong. I asked for forgiveness. I understood that Jesus had paid a price for my sin and by God's grace I was forgiven. I determined to live right.

The evangelist didn't get any numbers credit that night, because I didn't make any public profession. Even though I was just a child, I do believe I became a Christian at that time. It was a couple of years later that I made a public profession and was baptized in a Baptist Church.

Growing up, I had periods of rebellion to my church's teachings. After marrying Evelyn and when John was born, I made up my mind to serve in my church and live a Christian life. To enhance our relationship with God, we studied the Bible both independently and with groups. As we came to know and associate with a variety of people, we began to question some of our religious roots.

We met good, devout people who had a glass of wine or cocktail at dinner. We knew good, spiritual people who even liked to dance. We knew people who regularly attended their church, shared what they had with the less fortunate and worked for the betterment of their communities, but would actually wager on a horse race.

As I searched the Bible, I began to conclude that the church I was raised in spent a lot of energy making up sins just like the Pharisees did at the time Jesus walked the earth. We slowly began to develop our own beliefs and tolerances.

I have good friends who condemn any drinking of alcohol. Who can criticize them if they have had loved ones killed or maimed by a drunken driver? Alcohol abuse has caused all kinds of destruction to relationships, families, careers and fortunes. I respect abstinence, but the Bible does not prohibit a drink of wine. My Savior made wine for a wedding celebration.

The Bible condemns the abuse of alcohol and drunkenness. Alcoholics are sick. They shouldn't drink alcohol, just like a friend who is allergic to peanuts shouldn't eat peanuts. Just as I shouldn't abuse food, I shouldn't abuse alcohol. I enjoy a glass of wine or a beer three or four times a week. I believe the entire Bible including Ecclesiastes 3:12 and 13.

Many Christian friends criticize my love of horse racing. I asked one friend, a golfer why he objected to horse racing. He said it was because of gambling. Well, I think there is more money wagered every week on golf than there is on horses. Where in the Bible is gambling pronounced a sin? I have a hard enough time trying to avoid sins specifically prohibited in the Bible without making up new ones.

Of course, many Christians condemn gambling because they feel it has a negative effect on society. I agree that abusing gambling can be sinful. Participating in illegal gambling is wrong. Gambling with money, you don't have is wrong. When I was raising my children, it would have been sinful for me to gamble. Every penny was called for in my budget. Compulsive gambling is sick, and wrong.

But as people reach a point in life when they can spend on personal recreation, some play golf, some ski, some travel and some buy fancy boats or vehicles. I play the horses and spend no more than a friend going on a deep sea fishing expedition. I budget within a personal recreation frame work.

If I over-do my horse playing as I have done at times, that's abuse. If my friend spends money he can't afford to go elk hunting, that's also abuse.

My personal code for having reason and balance is to spend no more on personal recreation than I am willing to contribute to my church and other worthy causes. I don't impose that belief on others, but that helps me keep a balance.

Actually true religion is not about avoiding certain conduct, but is all about our personal relationship to God. Anything we possess or anything we do that comes between us and God is idolatry. The Bible has plenty to say about idolatry.

I have to confess that I have spent too much of my life outside of the will of God. I'm very thankful that God has forgiven me, not because of my goodness, but because Jesus paid the price for my sins on the cross and I have asked for that forgiveness.

A great hymn by George Beverly Shea expresses my feelings— *"There's the wonder of sunset at evening, the wonder as sunrise I see; but the wonder of wonders that thrills my soul is the wonder that God loves me."*

OUR HEAVENLY FATHER

For all we have, for all we are,
for fresh air, blue skies, for every star,
for every blessing of this past year,
for this food, For every friend that's here;

Lord, for all this, we give thanks and exaltation.
Please bless this food and bless our celebration,
as we give up the old year and ring in the new.
revive our goals, our spirits and faith in you.

Happy New Year

I was in Florida on a motor trip when J. W. Booker died in Oklahoma City. I didn't make it back for the funeral. He was not only my brother-in-law, but a best friend.

HELEN AND JAY

I honor the memory of my super in-laws, Helen and Jay.
They both meant so much to me with favors I could never repay.
Helen was the older sister of Evelyn, my child bride.
And Jay, Helen's husband was like a big brother by my side.

We married in their home in nineteen forty-seven.
Oh, we were such children, but thought we were in heaven.
Things were pretty tight for us in those early years.
But Helen and Jay provided dinners, shows and other cheers.

They were examples of married love for us to see.
And we also observed parenting as it should be.
Jay was the classic milkman starting in the horse and wagon days.
He became the city's top milk salesman with service and friendly ways.

Later he became independent and bought his own milk truck.
For thirty-five years nursed it, cursed it and spent a buck
to keep it running several hundred thousand miles
while serving his customers with cold milk and warm smiles.

Helen and Jay and our families, such great times we had.
Boating, camping, skiing and fishing both good and bad,
always with lots of laughs, jokes and good food.
They kept plenty of toys to keep the children in a good mood.

Jay's hearty laugh was always quick, loud and bold,
no matter how bad the jokes were that I told.
First Helen, then Jay, have gone on to a better place.
They are missed and remembered with a love that won't erase.

Three lovely daughters with their own grace and love they don't hide.
Grandchildren and great grand-children extend their legacy with pride.
So with love, honor and respect in every way,
my heart joins with theirs in loving memory of Helen and Jay.

Every time one of my children or grandchildren has a birthday, I'm over-whelmed by the years that have passed. Danielle Downing turned 18 after Evelyn died and before I married Jo Ann. This piece was handwritten in a card with a picture of puppies. Danielle is now married to Trey Brooks and lives in Lewisville, Texas.

HAPPY 18TH DEAR DANI

Even puppies grow up as time passes by.
But Dani eighteen! That makes this old man sigh.
Please accept these congratulations I'm sending,
wishing good cheer and happiness unending.

The responsibilities of adulthood can get heavy
But finish school, get a good job, and be in the gravy.

I love you very much and pray for the best for you.
And whatever happens, know God loves you too.
Be confident and proud with your head held high.
You are eighteen and ready to look the world in the eye.

So happy birthday, dear Dani, this special year,
I pray it will bring fulfillment, happiness and cheer.

All my love, Popa

*Granddaughters, Danielle "Danny" Downing Brooks
and Dominique "Niki" Downing Barnhouse*

Virgil McNary was in my senior high school class. We were also in the Marine Corps together. We made connections while both of us lived in the Dallas area some forty years later. Virgil talked me into playing senior softball in the spring of 1998. We were both seventy years old. He had played for the Farmers Branch Codgers for several years.

Sadly, Virgil passed away two years ago.

SENIOR SOFTBALL

We just couldn't imagine such a thing
when Virgil urged us to play senior softball.
Though I disavowed any athletic prowess,
he had Coach Leo give me a call.
I protested that I was seventy years old
and Leo said, "I'm seventy-two."
The rules sounded comfy enough,
slow pitch and someone can run for you.

No stealing, forces at bases rather than tags,
no sliding and two extra on defense.
So I agreed to practice with the guys
as it all began to make sense.
When Leo couldn't quite reach a fly ball
no matter how hard he ran,
Then yelled, "I would have gotten it when
I was seventy," I joined the clan.

While you declined, I joined the Richardson
Road Runners in the Senior Metro League,
to share camaraderie, laughs,
sweat and summertime fatigue.
That was three years ago when you
thought I was absolutely crazy.
But you have missed out on a lot
of fun just because you are lazy.

Have you ever seen an eighty-six year old
codger run down your fly ball?
Or excitedly argue, and then laughed
about a close third base call?
Or heard the chorus from our bench
"Ump, are you sure he went all the way around?"
After Chuck swung and missed with
such force he nearly fell down.

Or thrilled at watching Beach
blast one through the gap,
as Dominic loudly exhorts him to run harder
and complete the four base lap?
Have you been called to a conference
by our pitcher, a real deep thinker?
Saying "we better watch this next batter;
he's a low ball hitter and a high ball drinker."

Or have you shared the disappointment when
your opponent wins in the last inning?
Then hear our old sage Gerald say,
"guys we are really winning."
Slowly we agree, as we hear the
wise one further assert,
"guys, it really is a beautiful morning
and no one got hurt."

The two most important rules in
Senior Softball ever acclaimed
are, first don't get hurt and secondly, don't get blamed.
Then under a shade tree, Ted serves up the sodas.
A breeze helps good humor restore.
Good-natured kidding resumes and even our
Manager Bill can't remember the score.

MEETING JO ANN

By football season in 1999, I was leading an active social life. I was getting away to some races. I had Dallas Cowboy season tickets; participated in Questers Class social activities, played senior softball, and attended other occasional parties. The male-female ratio was good for socially active senior men. Oddly, male Questers who liked to dance out numbered the ladies who danced.

When I attended a football watching party one Sunday afternoon, I was on the lookout for someone to invite to the next Questers dance party. Neither the lady I took to the party nor did I have any interest in furthering our relationship. We were both active in meeting and visiting with new friends. After surveying all the ladies, I decided that the brown-eyed, red-headed chick catering the food was the classiest lady there. I visited with her and asked for her card. The card read, "Texas Chili Biscuit Factory, Jo Ann Albright."

I called Jo Ann the next day. She said she couldn't remember meeting me the night before. That was a real ego booster. I told her about our Sunday school class and our social activities. I invited her to go with me to a covered dish supper at Nancy Chase's home. After gathering there, we all planned to go to the Swan Court and dance. Jo Ann agreed to go.

I wrote Jo Ann a little poem comparing her and her culinary expertise to Martha Stewart. That was a little corny, but it did break the ice when I picked her up at her home. I've heard a lot of people talk about the horrors of dating after having been married for many years. I actually enjoyed it. Yes, it was challenging but also adventurous. There are so many different personalities in the world.

I couldn't imagine ever getting married again. I loved all the ladies in our Quester Class. They were such good friends; I had decided not to date any of them. Only two things can happen. You break up or go on to a serious relationship and maybe marriage. I liked all of them too much to risk that.

After Jo Ann got over the shock of this odd ball giving her a poem on a first date, we drove to Nancy's house. She enjoyed meeting my friends and they enjoyed meeting her. She fit right in.

We went to Swan Court and all got seated. Jo Ann and I danced one time before she noticed she had a message on her cell phone. Her sixteen year-old son Charlie, was on the way to the emergency room. That ended our first date. I took Jo Ann to the hospital where she met Charlie and daughter, Laura. Jo Ann wouldn't let me stay around to help. That was a great start on a relationship.

The next day I talked to my daughter, Teresa on the telephone. Since we both lived in Plano, she had been looking after me since Evelyn's death. Now she was getting mixed feelings about her seventy-one year old father's social life. She asked about my evening and I told her what had happened. She said, "Dad --- what were you doing with a woman young enough to have a sixteen year-old son?"

I answered, "I was dating her. I was with a lady ten years younger when I met Jo Ann."

I'm ashamed to admit that the availability and interest of women from forty to seventy did tweak my ego. You know, I'm not tall, dark and handsome. I'm short, dumpy and gray.

I called Jo Ann to inquire about Charlie. He was alright. They thought he had broken his wrist, but he only sprained it. Jo Ann agreed to go out to dinner with me. After a few more dates, including our church singles' Halloween Party, Jo Ann joined our Questers Sunday School Class and our church.

Before long, we found ourselves dating each other exclusively. We were amazed how our beliefs and values matched up almost perfectly. Our relationship grew.

MISSING COLT FINALLY FOUND

It's May, nineteen ninety four.
Don, Phil, Pete and I were in Kentucky.
Taking in the Derby and really
hoping we would get lucky.
There was a nice filly and
mare stakes race on the under card.
A classy mare named Santa Catalina
stood out and I bet her hard.

The Daily Racing Form revealed that
in the past she had really cruised,
but her stodgy performance
today left me bruised.
No big deal, I've made mistakes
before and I'll make more.
But, the review in the Louisville newspapers
made me angry to the core.

Santa Catalina was in foal as
she raced that day, so I learned.
She had been bred to A.P. Indy.
I read the story and burned.
Although I had studied the racing form
and program through and through,
there was no information provided
in either to give me a clue.

With all that history and stats,
there is no category for a pregnant mare.
I complained to the Racing Form and
the track, but they didn't care.
And now my cronies tease me
almost more than I can bear
for betting and losing on
that pregnant mare.

In subsequent years of handicapping
races I searched in vain
for that secret offspring that
had caused my pain.
Then, while preparing for the Breeders'
Cup in nineteen ninety nine,
it was exciting to come
across this revealing line.

Four year old colt –
Golden Missile was the name;
A.P. Indy the sire, and Santa Catalina the dam,
yes, he's the same.
This is the colt I've been looking
for and he must pay.
His racing record didn't justify,
but he's entered in the Classic anyway.

The last time the Breeders' Cup was
run here at Gulfstream Park
in nineteen ninety two, we watched
Golden Missile's sire make his mark.
Yes, A.P. Indy won the classic
that year and all its glory.
That's before he met Santa Catalina
and started this story.

All year in ninety-nine, upsets had
ruled the classic division.
Behrens was the classic betting favorite,
making it an easy decision
to forget handicapping this race,
and bet on a long shot;
like Golden Missile,
because that colt owed me a lot.

Golden Missile was going off at
seventy-five to one - what a play.
It was bright and breezy at
Gulfstream and this is my lucky day.
Bud Royale was twenty-seven to one,
another great value, I know.
To spread my chances, I bet them,
both-win, place and show.
Bud Royale's full brother Tiz Now
would win the next two classics in a row.

Suddenly, fourteen of the world's finest
thoroughbreds speed around the track.
They thunder into the second turn,
then stretch for the finish not looking back.
Down the stretch three long shots are neck and
neck but Cat Thief came in first.
Pat Day was riding, and I didn't bet him?
Am I still cursed?

But all's not lost; Bud Royale and
Golden Missile are nose to nose.
Close behind the winner,
they both try to close.
Bud Royale placed second,
paying thirty three dollars counting show.
And golden missile paid thirty dollars,
twenty cents to show.

I didn't pick the long shot winner,
but my spirits were bright.
It took five years, but my secret colt
finally made it right.

HAPPY MOTHER'S DAY
QUESTER MOTHERS

On this special day, please
accept our congratulations
for your devotion and all
of love's manifestations.
The handiwork of your sacrifice
Will continue through the ages
as your teachings and your
influence play out on life's pages.

Today, I honor my own mother.
Her memory is dear.
Her sacrifices made it possible
for me to be here.
Her teachings, example and
unconditional affection
gave my life meaning
and positive direction.

And I see that specialness in
each of you, just now.
So please accept this taken of
our respect and take your bow.

HAPPY BIRTHDAY DUANE SCHUE*

To Chief Quester and good friend Duane,
Happy Birthday cheers.
But we don't believe that you have
lived seventy five years.

Because you run every day with all
that vigor,
then dash out nearly every night
quick on the trigger.

Testosterone, gin sing, Viagra and
all that stuff,
might be okay whenever you
get old enough.

Just keep smiling, thinking young. Keep the
twinkle in your eye
And we will attest that the calendar
and records lie.

All our love,
Elmer and Jo Ann

JO ANN

This book would be a lot more interesting if it were about Jo Ann rather than me. When she first told me about herself, I thought what kind of line is this gal feeding me? I learned that it was all true.

When Jo Ann was a month old, her mother abandoned the family to run off with a terrible man. Her father, Joe Dodd, was a cook by trade. Knowing that he couldn't care for Jo Ann and her older three siblings by himself, he placed them in the Lena Pope Home in Fort Worth, TX. He worked at the home as a cook for almost three years in order to be close to his children.

After leaving the Lena Pope Home, Jo Ann's father went to work as a short order cook at Toddle House. Until about age 8, her father regularly took Jo Ann out for visits. During these visits Jo Ann remembers hanging out all day at his work and watching in awe as he filled the short orders from multiple waitresses. Jo Ann's lifelong passion for cooking stems from those experiences.

Jo Ann was nine months old when she was crippled as a result of her feet and legs being severely burned by scalding hot water. While helping to organize a party for the children at the Lena Pope Home, a Fort Worth high school girl, Tommie Albright, took a special interest in Jo Ann. From the age of one to three years old, Jo Ann spent a great deal of time visiting with Tommie and her parents, Jerry and Marian Albright. It was due to the Albright's intervention on Jo Ann's behalf that the Ft. Worth Cook Children's Hospital and Dr. Louis Patterson donated their services to provide Jo Ann with a series of plastic surgeries which allowed her to regain normal use of her burned legs.

As was the custom of children living in the Lena Pope Home, Jo Ann had learned to call all the women caretakers in her life "Mommy". When she visited the Albrights and would call out for "Mommy", they would have to ask her which Mommy, "Mommy Tommie?" or Mommy Marian?" One of the memorial memories the Albright's have of Jo Ann was when she was the three year old flower girl participating in Tommie's wedding with Morris Reinhardt. After doing her part as flower girl, instead of going to sit with Mommy Marian as she was supposed to, she disrupted the wedding ceremony by going back to the alter and pulling the eighteen year old bride's dress out and lovingly announcing to all-- "Oh Mommy, you look so pretty". Needless to say, this caused quite a stir to many in the church who did not know of Jo Ann's relationship to the family. To make matters worse, Jo Ann grabbed the preacher's legs and threw a screaming and biting temper tantrum while being forcefully removed from the scene.

It was after the wedding scene that Tommie's maiden Aunt, Ouida Albright, decided that she should be the one to take on the job of "taming" Jo Ann. Miss Albright was a powerful woman and the matriarch of the family although she was single. She had the designation of being the first female Certified Public Accountant (C.P.A.) in the state of Texas and was second in command in a large paving and construction company.

Since parental rights had never been legally severed, Jo Ann wasn't eligible for adoption. However, on weekends when neither of her parents wanted her for visits, Jo Ann was allowed to visit with Miss Albright. When Jo Ann was five years old she and her older siblings were transferred to the Tarrant County Orphanage. Because of the terrible conditions at the orphanage and Jo Ann's special health needs, Miss Albright used her clout to get Jo Ann transferred back to the Lena Pope Home. When Jo Ann was eight years old Miss Albright arranged for her to live in a Catholic convent with nuns. When Jo Ann was ten and Miss Albright had hired full-time help to care for her invalid mother, the courts allowed Jo Ann to begin living with Miss Albright. Jo Ann went from being an abused orphan to a little rich girl who thought Nieman Marcus was the only place to buy clothes.

Finally, when Jo Ann was fourteen years old, Miss Albright became the first single woman allowed to adopt a child in the state of Texas. Jo Ann was privileged to attend Camp Waldemar, an exclusive summer camp, and graduate from a prestigious prep boarding school in Scottsdale, Arizona. She attended T.C.U., the University of Texas at Austin and the University of Houston. By the age of twenty, she survived two major cancer surgeries. Even more painful, she survived breaking up with her high school love.

Jo Ann became a stock broker in Houston before women were allowed to be stock brokers. She moved into drilling and oil production investments and became independently wealthy while still in her twenties.

Jo Ann married into a prominent, wealthy banking family in El Paso. While there, she owned a regional shopping center and a multi-national travel agency. She adopted her husband's two girls, Laura and Avery Hammond. Jo Ann and her husband adopted an infant, Charlie Hammond together.

The oil, real estate and banking crash of the mid eighties impacted the Hammond family. When her husband's family's bank stock went to near worthless, her husband with the conspiratorial help of "others" perpetrated a fraud on Jo Ann that resulted in multimillion dollars losses to her separate estate and the need for her to defend herself from illegitimate I.RS. tax claims against her for two million dollars. Jo Ann's financial world and her marriage came crashing down. She and Charles Hammond divorced.

Jo Ann spent the next eight years in court suing for recovery and defending herself against the I.R.S. She won against the I.R.S, but didn't recover any of her losses. The time demands on her during the eight years of litigation made it impossible for Jo Ann to commit to any meaningful work. She lived during these years by selling her jewelry, antiques and other valuables.

When Jo Ann moved to the Dallas area, about the only assets she had left was $4 million in Net Operating Losses (N.O.L.'s) awarded by the I.R.S. She wouldn't have to pay any income taxes until those expired. Electronic Data Systems (E.D.S.) in Plano, TX employed Jo Ann to manage some large loan portfolios. That job ended when E.D.S. moved her department to Pennsylvania. Fortunately for me, Jo Ann wasn't willing to move to Pennsylvania.

Jo Ann is a gourmet cook. She loves cooking and entertaining. When I met Jo Ann she was marketing her Texas Chili Biscuits and catering to support her family.

Even with the drastic financial fall, Jo Ann was undaunted. She was full of enthusiasm, confidence and a positive attitude. Even with hard times, she was always ready to help someone else. If she has a fault it is that she believes she can do anything.

She had that dare devil attitude from a young age. A drug problem in her high school surfaced when she was in boarding school. The administration was reluctant to discipline some children of very wealthy parents. Jo Ann was senior president and her boyfriend, Don Nelson, was president of the student body. They led a student drive to make their school drug free.

She played tennis, snow skied, and water skied. She flew airplanes and was both a scuba and sky diver. She survived cancer twice and volunteered for everything. In El Paso, Jo Ann led the fundraising for a state of the art rehabilitation center for physically disabled children. After successful construction, she served as president to assure the success of the operation.

One morning when Jo Ann was living in El Paso, she woke up with a powerful urge to locate her birth father. Jo Ann had not had contact with her birth family since Miss Albright had adopted her at age fourteen. Jo Ann started her search by trying to find her sister Glenda. She knew Glenda had been classified as mentally retarded and sent to a state school. When Jo Ann called the state school at Mexia, TX the social worker told her, "I can't believe I'm talking to you. We have been trying to locate you."

It turned out that her father was sick and in the hospital. He had been living with Jo Ann's older sister, but the sister died while Joe was in the hospital. Social workers were trying to find someone to care for Joe. They located Glenda, but didn't think she was competent to care for Joe.

Jo Ann immediately flew her father and her sister Glenda to El Paso to live with her. Her father was in very poor health and she had him for only a short while. Glenda is sill part of our lives. Jo Ann never found her older brother.

Glenda is not retarded, however, because she spent so much of her life being treated like she was, she is dependent on Jo Ann for help in many areas. She is a hard worker and for many years worked two jobs by choice. Mornings she worked at the school cafeteria wherever Charlie was going to school so he wouldn't have to worry about forgetting his lunch money, and afternoons at Albertson's Super Market. Since she never learned to drive, finding jobs that are within walking distance to home has been a limitation.

When I met Jo Ann, her household included Glenda and her son Charlie Hammond. Adult daughters, Avery and Laura lived nearby.

Recently, I looked through Jo Ann's yearbook for her senior year at Judson High School. This exclusive boarding school had students from all over the world. Jo Ann is the star of the yearbook. She's senior class president and all-everything. Her boyfriend Don Nelson is king of everything. He was an athletic star and being recruited to play football by several of the top college programs in the nation.

I wondered how a 'nobody' like me wound up with this vibrant, beautiful girl pictured throughout the yearbook.

Jo Ann Albright
Miss Judson, Senior Class President

No In Between

Can a business or an organization
just stay even over-time?
It seems almost impossible to do.
We either descend or we climb.

We move forward or we slip back.
If we don't make a profit, we lose.
Staying even just isn't an option.
So which way do we choose?

We hide our light under a bushel,
or we can let it shine.
We must reach out and grow,
or we will decline.

Surely we choose to move forward,
rather than prepare for a wake.
If not, the only question
is, how long will it take?

New York Congressman Rick Lazio mailed me a request for a contribution when he ran for the Senate versus Hillary Clinton. I didn't send him any money, but I just couldn't waste that stamped self-addressed envelope lying on my dining room table. So I wrote him a poem. He didn't use it and lost the race.

CARPETBAG

Hillary told us the great right wing conspiracy plotted
to make her husband Bill's morals look spotted.
And later explained as she got around to it,
that Bill's Mama and Grandma made him do it.

Then she packed her carpetbag for New York State
where sadly they had none of their own to relate.
Then she and Bill freed the terrorists and blessed the vices,
kissed up to big labor and other liberal devices.

She would crush that great right wing conspiracy and beat old Rudy.
Because almost everyone knew the mayor was too goody.
But all of Rudy's problems began to surface, too.
So he resigned the race, and Rick came to the rescue.

With such a late start and little name recognition,
Rick needs great issues to overcome that condition.
I recommend two themes he trumpet from post to pillory.
First, he's from New York, and second, he ain't Hillary.

Happy 21st Birthday, Patrick

Enjoy yourself. You are in a wonderful
time of your life.
But having been over the road let me
warn you of the strife.
Headaches and set backs are inevitable –
they come to every man.
So learn from the bad. Stay on track,
Be true to your plan.

Set goals in life. Make plans to achieve them.
Dream the big dream.
Then live each day with enthusiasm
with head held high and a healthy self esteem -

Always remember in you heart that
God loves you.
You are special to Him, to your family
and me, too.
And love yourself too. Take pride in
who you are.
Then loving and serving other's will
be the par.
Don't ever stop learning. Seek more
knowledge forever.
Knowledge will serve you well
and brighten each endeavor.
Form the habit of doing what failures
don't like to do.
Good habits and discipline will
spell success for you.

And as success comes your way
with just reward,
you don't have to buy everything
you can afford,
Enjoy life but form a habit of saving
all you can.
Then feel the satisfaction of a sound
financial plan.

I love you. Have a great birthday
and a great year.
And I guess old Popa will
even concede you a beer.

All my love, Popa

My grandson Patrick Downing is now 29, married,
a father and successful salesman.

Kacey and Luke Downing

THE PROPOSAL

Early in our dating, Jo Ann and I assured each other that we were not looking for a serious relationship. Jo Ann had been single for fifteen years and was wrapped up in caring for her family. I had already had the love of my life. Neither of us planned to ever marry again. Even so, we hit it off from the start. I was becoming increasingly fond of her.

At Christmas time 1999, I knew I couldn't host all my family as Evelyn had always done. I rented condos at a Cucharo, Colorado ski resort. I hosted the family there. My kids and grandkids all wanted to know why that lady sent chili biscuits and cookies with us. Our family had a wonderful time in the snow, but I still didn't acknowledge any serious relationship.

I had decided to place my home on the market. I was tired of maintaining a yard, swimming pool and big house. I asked Jo Ann if she knew a reasonable painter to paint wood work in my bathrooms. She said she loved to paint. When she insisted on doing my painting, I began to ask myself, "Is this getting beyond casual?"

I started looking at retirement community apartments and high rise condos. A couple of those retirement communities had promotional parties for prospective residents. They had a free dinner and entertainment. I took Jo Ann to a couple of those events. I took a lot of kidding about taking advantage of "cheap dates." Jo Ann said she just couldn't picture me living in one of those small apartments. She was prophetic; I planned to go from my 3,000 square feet house to a 900 square foot apartment. Instead, I wound up in this 6,850 square foot place on Lake Whitney.

In February, 1999, I had some minor surgery. Jo Ann insisted on taking me to the hospital for the five a.m. check-in. She looked after me for the couple of days there, and then she and my daughter Sheryl brought me home. I knew then that I was getting into a serious relationship.

One afternoon, our group of Questers planned to go to a movie together. I told Jo Ann I would pick her up at 2:30 p.m. When the day of the date came, Jo Ann had remembered the date time as 1:30 p.m. Before picking up Jo Ann, I had gone into Dallas for some business. When I didn't show up at 1:30, Jo Ann panicked. I had always been 100% punctual. She decided that something terrible had happened to me, since I didn't answer my phone. I never answered my cell phone while driving.

Jo Ann decided to go break into my house to see if I had fallen or had a heart attack. She left Glenda at home and took Laura with her to find me. As I was driving to pick up Jo Ann, we passed each other going in opposite directions. We both stopped. Jo Ann ran to my car. She asked what had happened to me and had a tear in her eye. I told her that I was right on time, Laura said, "Mom, you are in love."

We finally confessed to each other that we were in love. When we first discussed the possibility of marriage, I told Jo Ann that there was too much age difference. The excitement of dating a woman twenty-one years younger was one thing, but asking a life commitment was another. It would be totally unfair to her.

Jo Ann insisted that our age difference made no difference to her. We discussed all the reasons why we should or should not marry. Just living together was not an option for either of us. Through this discussion, Jo Ann said she wasn't saying she would marry me until I proposed. I had to get a lot of things straight in my head before I could propose. But finally, I hand wrote my proposal in a card that had a picture of a lighthouse on it.

ELMER'S PROPOSAL

Although our love shines like a beacon in the night
with boundaries as vast as the sea and sight,
you told me I would have to ask.
So with romance at stake, I'll warm to the task.

While the ultimate goal hasn't been in doubt,
It's all those details, I've worried about.

Kids, cats, house to sell, merging our stuff,
finances, trips and announcements – they all make it tough.
When, where and how? There is so much to ponder.
But all the while, darling, my heart grows even fonder.

A journey of a thousand miles, they say,
starts with that first step and that first day.
And all the lights between here and there
can't all be green at the same time my dear.

So I'll just put first things first and make my plea.
Jo Ann, my love, will you please marry me?

Jo Ann said, "Yes."

TELLING THE FAMILY

On Mother's Day, 2000, I joined Jo Ann and her three children for a Mother's Day dinner. Jo Ann and I had just agreed to marry. We think they already knew, but we used the occasion to announce that we planned to be married. Avery Hammond, Laura Hammond and Charles Hammond seemed pleased. Avery is now married to Michael Rowles, and lives in Dallas, Laura is attending the University of Texas in El Paso, and Charles lives in Hillsboro.

A MOTHER'S DAY TOAST

Today, we honor someone very special, indeed.
Your Mother, who loves you unconditionally,
and is there for every need.
All those qualities that make her so special for you
have also attracted my affection. I love her too.

So today, let's make her feel like a queen
with actions that express our love, more than she has ever seen.
We raise our glasses to offer this toast with great emotion,
Mother, Jo Ann, we love you and promise our devotion.

I had said I would never marry again, but I have proposed and the proposal has been accepted. I guess I had better work out the details. One frightening thought was Jo Ann and Charlie had no health insurance since she left employment with EDS. A serious accident or illness could spell financial disaster.

Now that we were absolutely sure we wanted to make a life together, I didn't want a long engagement. First, I could include them in my group health insurance when we marry, and secondly at seventy-two years old I didn't have a lot of time to waste. We set the date for July 1st, 2000.

My calendar was already loaded. I had already made arrangements to go to the Arkansas Derby for three days and to the Kentucky Derby for three days. I had asked John and David to go to Alaska with me. John couldn't get away, but I had already made all the reservations for David and I to go May 29th through June 8th.

I was concerned about my kid's reactions, so I wanted to get them together for the announcement. David was flying to Dallas from Florida on May 25th. I invited all the family to come in for an early Memorial Day dinner on May 26th.

To deal with my own feelings, I had written a poem to Evelyn. I wanted to honor her one more time. I read that poem to my family both as Memorial Day recognition and as an announcement that Jo Ann and I planned to marry. It was no surprise to Teresa and Sheryl who lived close by. I don't know about John, but David was shocked. They were all shocked when I told them the wedding was just five weeks away.

EVELYN

Oh what beautiful memories you left for me.
A life of love and companionship, what more could be?
Oh yes, four children and nine grandchildren to be exact,
God's precious gifts for you and me, a legacy intact.

I can still remember us as mere children in love.
Thinking we were mature enough, heavens above
to marry. Though you were too young, you became my wife
only with God's mercy, we survived the problems of life.

They gave us six months, which we beat fifty years,
filled with good times and hard times, laughter and tears.
Remember saving three weeks to buy a deck of cards?
We entertained ourselves. There was no money for other rewards.

We were poor but so in love we didn't know it.
When blessed with a little success we didn't blow it.
Then we were blessed with children, and we heard some say
that children were raising children. Well, they came out okay.

You always supported me in whatever career I sought,
living in dirty little apartments, then in houses we bought.
Your handwork and loving touch made a home of each place
with warmth, food, love and laughter, a haven from the pace.

We enjoyed family, friends and each other with games and debates.
We traveled nine other countries and all fifty states.
From Alaska to Florida and to Vegas recreations,
we bought pigs, spoons and Christmas tree decorations.

And then suddenly I lost you and my whole world crashed.
Grief overwhelmed me and my spirit was smashed.
Loneliness filled every crevice of my being.
What a void you left Darling, what darkness I was seeing.

But God in his eternal mercy still had plans for my life.
The sun continued to rise, family strengths quieted the strife.

A dear friend referred me to a grief seminar to learn
how to resolve my grief and overcome the burn
in my heart and in time gradually say goodbye.
Life is for the living. There is still a sun in the sky.

At the church I found a class of wonderful senior friends.
I learned to worship again and receive the blessing He sends.
I learned to enjoy other singles, laughing and caring.
They are alone like me with life's burdens and joys sharing.

It's been over a year and a half now my love
of grief, resolution, renewal. And now with help from above,
I've grown strong enough to say goodbye, my dear
to the shackles of grief and move on to the life that's here.

I have found another that I love dearly and true,
And I sincerely believe that she loves me too.
Life has treated her with severe ups and downs
and she deserves happiness too, where love abounds.

I need her so much and I believe she needs me.
We will make a life together - - whatever time that will be.
I'm confident that God has blessed our love so true.
I pray for the blessing from our children and friends, too.

Family is so important to both Jo Ann and I
and we cherish many happy gatherings as time goes by.
Our marriage and my love for Jo Ann will never detract
from my love memories of you or the children. In fact,
your memory will always be honored by both of us
as this life goes on with love, family and trust.

Wedding Plans

After the wedding announcement, David and I left for Alaska and had a wonderful trip. We saw all the sights, caught some fish and made up for a lot of time we have spent away from each other.

When we returned I had a lot of work to do. Jo Ann had taken a job with Account Temps. She was on an audit that opened up a big can of worms. The problems in that company were requiring extensive overtime. Jo Ann said, "If we get married on July 1st, you are going to have to make the arrangements".

We had another problem. My house was on the market, but not selling. The Real Estate Listing contract did not expire until a couple of weeks after the wedding date. The lease on Jo Ann's apartment was running out in June. The landlord wouldn't take a month to month extension. I decided to take my house off the market if it didn't sell under the current listing.

Jo Ann did find a nice large duplex near where she lived. The duplex owner was nice enough to let us lease it with a provision that we could break the lease if my house didn't sell and I took it off the market. So, we moved Jo Ann and Charlie into the duplex.

I made arrangements with our minister, a hotel for our guests, a musician and the Los Rios Country Club for the wedding and reception. I even took Charlie shopping for a new suit.

There were so many people we would have loved to invite to our wedding, but we decided to keep it small and uncomplicated. We invited our immediate families. Since Jo Ann didn't have much immediate family, she invited three long time friends that were like sisters.

Mary Kathryn Anderson and Jo Ann had been best friends since they were ten years old. She lived across the street from Miss Albright in Fort Worth when Miss Albright first brought Jo Ann home with her. Marjorie Perry was Jo Ann's running buddy when they were both starting their careers in Houston. They are still soul sisters. After other successful pursuits, Marjorie completed law school and began a law practice after she was fifty years old.

When Jo Ann lived in El Paso, her best friend was Kathy Duermyer Tate. Their children were about the same age. They enjoyed many good times together then both suffered through painful divorces. Kathy now lives in Corpus Christi. She is very happy and successful in real estate investment.

I enjoyed meeting all these "sisters" that I had heard so much about. We invited all the guests to my home the night before the wedding. We didn't have a rehearsal, but we did enjoy grilling steak and some salmon David and I caught in Alaska.

Things were moving too fast to get nervous about the big day tomorrow.

Soul Sisters
Marjorie Perry, Jo Ann and Kathy Duermyer Tate

OUR WEDDING

Our small family wedding still had forty-two guests. We had the wedding, reception, music, dancing and a nice sit down dinner all at the country club so our out-of-town guests didn't have to travel from one place to another. It was a beautiful wedding, if I do say so myself.

Jo Ann and I had discussed writing our own vows, but opted for our minister's version. I did write some vows but saved them for the reception.

When I asked Jo Ann where she wanted to go for our honeymoon, she said anywhere we didn't have to catch a plane. She didn't want any tight schedules. I told her to be packed. We would leave from the country club on a motor trip.

On our wedding day evening, we made it to the Vernon, Texas Days Inn. Our wedding night dinner was at K-Bobs. How's that for class? Our destination was Lake Tahoe, with no hurry to get there. We wondered off course our second day to visit Jo Ann's mother's grave in Texoma, Texas. Jo Ann had spent many summer childhood days visiting her mother's family there. On our third day we wondered off at Gunnison, Colorado looking for the ranch where I worked when I was sixteen years old. We didn't find it.

We crossed Nevada on Highway 50 dubbed the loneliest highway in the United States. We weren't lonely. But the only place we could get reservations was at a speck on the map called Eureka. We were apprehensive, but it turned out to be one of the nicest stops on our trip. Eureka is a historic mining town and proud of its heritage.

Our hotel turned out to be just a year or so old and very nice. The town was celebrating the fourth of July. Just as we settled into our room, we heard some kind of explosion outside. We looked out the window, and a fireworks display was starting. We moved the dressing stool bench, just wide enough for two, over to the window. The window was wide enough for both of us. We looked out over Main Street toward a ridge where the fireworks were being detonated. It was like a front row seat at the theatre and this beautiful firework display was being staged just for us.

We had a good time at Reno and Lake Tahoe. We then went to Lee Vining, California our base for touring Yosemite National Park. Our return trip across Nevada was on the Interterrestrial Highway which is even more remote than Highway 50. By late afternoon, we hadn't found any place for lunch. We came upon a settlement consisting of a few mobile homes. But it looked like there was a restaurant on the highway.

As we pulled into the parking lot, we were delighted to see that it was the "Little Ailie-inn" which we had seen on various television shows. We were at the mysterious area fifty-one, the subject of many U.F.O. controversies several years ago.

Luckily, the place was open although we were the only customers. After we were seated, a little alien robot with flashing antenna lights came over to greet us. It turned out to be the owner's mother who delighted in greeting tourists in her alien costume. We had a visit with her, and enjoyed all the artifacts and posters on the walls.

We went on to Zion and Bryce National Parks in Utah and Mesa Verde National Park in Colorado. We enjoyed the wide open scenic west before returning home not knowing where we would live.

Jo Ann's Family – *Laura Hammond, Avery Hammond Rowles, Jo Ann, Elmer, Charles Hammond and Jo Ann's sister, Glenda Dodd*

Elmer's Family – *Kneeling: Danielle Downing, Emily Federspiel, Shaun Federspiel, Mary Mulhausen, Sarah Mulhausen. Standing: Jeffrey Federspiel, Betty Ruth Millus, Troy and Teresa Federspiel, Dominique Downing Barnhouse, Sheryl Mulhausen, Patrick Downing, Jo Ann, Elmer, John, Jeanne and Harold Mulhausen*

*"**Happy Couple**"- Jo Ann and Elmer*

Entertained on our honeymoon by Little Ali Ann

ELMER'S WEDDING VOWS TO JO ANN

I wed thee my darling Jo Ann because I love you.
And I feel assured that you truly love me too.
I promise to love you every day, striving to make life pleasurable.
And I'll love you in the evening with hugs and kisses immeasurable,

And throughout the night I promise to love you more,
even if you toss and turn, even if you snore.
And as the sun rises in the morn and we wake-up,
I promise to love you before brushing, combing and make-up.

I'll love you in the springtime as the blossoms bloom.
Even with the Derby calling, I'm your ever-loving groom.
And through the long hot summer; let's keep that loving thrill.
In the fall, between the Cowboys and
Breeders' Cup, I'll love you still.

When you need the warmth of love in winter, I'll be your nurse.
Because you are my love for all seasons, for better or worse,
richer or poorer, in sickness or health, I'll love you with all my heart.
And we will keep loving each other till death do us part.

CHOOSING A HOME

When we returned from our honeymoon, my home still had not sold. I took my travel clothes and personal articles and moved into the duplex temporarily. Charlie had one more year of high school. It was important for him to stay in JJ Pearce High School with his friends for his senior year. We did determine that he would be allowed to commute to school. Our landlord was true to his word, and would release us from the lease.

We took my home off the market and moved Jo Ann and Charlie to Plano. The school year of commuting the four miles to school was sometimes inconvenient, but no big deal. Charlie did graduate in the spring of 2001. We celebrated with his friends and all the family. His dad was able to come in from New Mexico to make the celebration complete.

Avery and Michael Rowles, Charlie Hammond at graduation 2001

Charlie is a big, good looking, cheerful and lovable young man. He makes friends wherever he goes. He also has retained many, long time, loyal friends. His mother, Aunt Glenda and two older sisters have spoiled him his entire life. With all his charm and wonderful qualities, study discipline was not one of them. He started in Community College but dropped out the first year.

He has had a series of juvenile type jobs. He's had the good sense to discard some bad habits and bad companions. Charlie has lived with us off and on. He considered the military but never went in. He worked in a health club and did become disciplined to body building. However, he never made a living wage on that job or had any benefits.

But now, as we get ready to celebrate his twenty-fifth birthday with a host of friends, I believe he is growing up. He has an adult job with benefits and paying enough for him to live. The job also provides opportunities for advancement. We believe he has the talent to become an effective sales person. Charlie lives in Hillsboro, Texas and has become active in his church. We love him and pray for a good life for him.

Jo Ann's sister Glenda has lived with us off and on. She is rarely content to live anywhere for very long. She is a dependable, hard worker and is very helpful to us when she is with us. She lives in an apartment in Clifton which is within walking distance of her job at Lutheran Sunset Nursing Home.

Jo Ann's daughters were both adults and living away from home when we met. Laura has had an extended visit, but they have never lived with us. Both girls have a strong appetite for education, and have worked and attended classes just about the entire time I have known them. Avery has completed a bachelor's and master's degree. She is now working on her doctorate, and is working with troubled children. Her husband Michael Rowles has a successful software business. They own a nice home in Dallas. We are happy for their success, but Jo Ann is still praying for some grand babies.

246

Laura has an indomitable spirit. As a child she had severe dyslexia. She suffered in school until the condition was identified and treated. She went to Brush Ranch, a wonderful private school to learn to overcome this handicap. Up until the 2007-08 school years, Laura had worked full time while taking part-time classes. She spent the summer with us and worked in the bed and breakfast. This school year she is going to school full time at the University of Texas at El Paso. She is making top grades and determined to complete her degree.

We are proud of Laura.

Happy 29th Birthday Laura

Dear Laura, we love you dearly and
admire your grit.
Your positive attitude is a delight
and your enthusiasm is a hit.

So keep that cheery smile, and to
your goals be true.
We wish you success and happiness.
Nothing's too good for you.

Have a wonderful and happy 29th
birthday Laura our dear.
And may your special day and year
be full of cheer.

Love,
Dad and Mom

Laura Hammond

My Thoughts on Mother's Day

I take pen in hand to honor Mothers
on this special day,
realizing that God's blessings flow
through Mothers more than any other way.

I can best express this thought by remembering
the mothers who have blessed my life,
from my Grandmother all the way
to my darling wife.

Precious memories go back to Grandma Haswell
a true Oklahoma Pioneer,
who was fun, feisty and self-reliant
till dying in her 98th year.

While teaching me humor as well as responsibility,
she was a loving Grandmother.
And when times were tough, she provided a
home when there was no other.

One of the brightest lights shining in Heaven
must be my Mother, Ruth.
By word and deed, she taught me positive
thinking, love and truth.

She raised and supported four children without
their father's assistance,
with gigantic faith, sacrifice, hard work
and persistence.

I can't recall ever missing a meal
due to Mother's efforts and prayer,
Even though we were very poor and the
cupboard usually bare.

Our clothes were hand-me-downs and there
was no money to spend.
Mother's attitude never let us feel poor and we
were stronger in the end.

Whatever good or whatever success I
may have achieved,
I owe to my Mother for all the
lessons and examples I received.

I also have loving memories of Evelyn my
loving wife of fifty years.
She was the wonderful Mother of my children
before her death left me in tears.

In addition to being a near perfect Mother,
she was at her best
in total determination that no want go unfilled
for the Grandkids in her nest.

Her ability to anticipate all her broods'
problems was uncanny,
and some how, some way, she solved
them because she was Super Nanny.

She is also in Heaven, loving and being
loved on Mother's Day.
All our family will honor and remember
her in a prayerful way.

Daughters, Sheryl and Teresa and
daughter-in-law, Jeanne as well,
have blessed my life with Grandchildren.
This fact I must tell.

They are wonderful, loving Mothers
in their own way.
I sincerely appreciate, honor and love
them on this Mother's Day.

As life goes on, God's blessings continue
flowing to me,
bringing me Jo Ann, a wonderful, loving
mother of three,

I am so thankful that Jo Ann has
become a Mother in my life.
She is brightening every day as my
loving wife.

While not replacing their Mother, she is there
for my children for whatever part
they wish her to play. I'm so thankful for
her gigantic heart.

And for my Grandchildren, she has become
Grandma Jo
with heart enough to include all mine
with her own. We all love her so.

Yes, Mother is the most beautiful word
in God's creation,
deserving our love, respect, honor
and admiration.

Sitting left to right: Grandma Clara Haswell on her 90th birthday
Standing left to right: Harold Mulhausen, Ruth Mulhausen, Betty Ruth
Millus and Elmer Mulhausen

MEMORIES

It must have been about 1971 in Shawnee, Oklahoma. Our youngest son, David, was about six years old. A magical thing was happening. Tens of thousands of monarch butterflies filled the skies, trees, branches and lawns.

David and I went for a walk to enjoy their beauty and marvel at this incredible event. I don't know if it's true, but somewhere I heard that we were experiencing a fifty year phenomenon. When I related that information to David, he stopped and looked me in the face. Then he said very seriously, "Dad, you won't ever get to see this again, will you?"

This last spring, twenty-nine or thirty years later, David and I went to Alaska. We enjoyed seeing all the sights and fishing together. "Lord, I don't know if these special moments will ever be repeated, but I thank you for the memories."

(Written in 2001)

David lands a king salmon in Kasilof River, Alaska June 2000

DEAREST JO ANN

Happy Valentines Day my dear,
I love you very much.
Your love brightens my every day
and I feel excitement in every touch.
I can't describe our love in words,
song, dance or even a whistle,
except to paraphrase Apostle Paul
in his Corinthians Epistle.

Our love has no envy, is long suffering,
kind and is not easily provoked.
Our love is not puffed up, has no rudeness,
boasts not and we are equally yoked.
Our love is unselfish, generous,
celebrates truth rather than evil or lies.
Considering the happiness of the other first,
is what our love implies.

Love is the greatest of all human experiences
of which the whole world sings.
And our love will never fail while believing,
hoping and enduring all things.

1st Corinthians Chapter 13

254

HAPPY BIRTHDAY CHARLIE

May your day be full of happiness and
joy, a day of perfection.
May you feel much love, security,
confidence and direction.

You know we love you very much and
God loves you too.
As you journey from boyhood to
manhood deciding what to do.

While you learn that freedom
isn't always free.
And learn that getting things you
want depends on what you plan to be.

Just remember, we love you and wish
you birthday cheer,
With hopes and prayers for your
success and happiness all year.

Love, Mom and Elmer

My daughter, Teresa Federspiel lives in Plano, Texas; a friend's reserve unit was called to active duty. The friend, a nurse was serving at a hospital in Germany where wounded from Iraq and Afghanistan were being treated. The nurse sent out a call for care packages from her friends in Texas. Teresa commissioned me to write a poem to include in the care packages — this poem was included in each package.

FREEDOM ISN'T FREE

I rise and sing the words "Oh say
can you see".
But do I really fathom the price that's
paid by others that I may be free?

As I stand, place my hand over my
heart and recite
"I pledge allegiance to the flag", do I
comprehend the cost of the fight?

Can I feel the misery of Valley Forge?
The grief for those left in Flanders Field?
How much precious blood has been shed
So our freedoms are sealed?

Normandy, Korea, Viet Nam and all
over the globe front and back,
our young, our best purchased our freedom
and now in Afghanistan and Iraq.

The price of freedom is misery, pain, blood
and loved ones' tears.
So let's honor all those who serve
past, present and in future years.

256

May we express our deepest gratitude to
those who defend us on land, air and sea.
May we always cherish our freedom,
because freedom isn't free.

To the men and women serving our country,
we express our deepest gratitude to you
for the price you have paid for us and
the red, white and blue.

Our prayers thanking God for you and
asking for your healing will not cease.
May we see a speedy and just conclusion
to this conflict and a lasting peace.

USING OUR TIME

When effective people have something
to do, they do it.
While some of us, seem to
never get around to it.

Always bogged down with some
urgent, overdue thing,
rather than concentrating on
things important and satisfying.

Or perhaps we just prefer a
recliner, comfy and soft,
maybe become a procrastinator
but just keep putting it off.

God gave each of us the same number
of hours yesterday.
But how effectively we used them
varies widely, it's safe to say.

I don't think I would rank very
high, if you would compare,
so becoming a better steward of
time should be a matter of prayer.

Lord help me manage. Give me
discipline, I ask of thee.
If I had a better handle on my
time, the happier I would be.

I know people don't plan to fail, they
just fail to plan.
With your help, I'll be a better
planner, I know I can.

Help me form the habit of putting
important things first in my day.
Help me overcome interruptions, time wasters
and plan busters that come my way.

Help me plan my work, work
my plan and grow in personal power.
I promise to make my time with
You my most important hour.

Woolaroc Museum in Oklahoma, Spring 2001
Sitting- Emily Federspiel, Elmer, Shaun Federspiel, Mary Mulhausen
Standing— John, Jeanne and Jo Ann Mulhausen

AVERY'S BIRTHDAY GREETING

Sweet Avery's birthday has
come and gone.
And alas, no birthday celebration yet,
not even one.

But Avery, your family wants you to know
you are loved so dear.
So we've gathered together
To wish you birthday cheer.

Although we are late for this
Birthday celebration tonight,
our love and greeting are still
sincere and bright.

And what about a gift for someone
so dear?
The non-shoppers came up with an idea
both practical and clear.

Mom's waiving the toll tag charges from May to October
that are such a bummer.
While wishing you a year of health and happiness, a
real hummer.

All our love,
Mom and Elmer

MOVING TO LAKE WHITNEY

After Charlie graduated from high school, we started thinking about where we wanted to live. We thought it would be better to live in our house rather than my house. We decided that we would like to live on a lake so there would be some activity for our families when they visit.

Jo Ann ruled out any of the privately developed lakes. She wanted to be on a large uncrowded lake for boating and skiing. When we looked at property on Lake Texoma, a realtor took Jo Ann by a Bed and Breakfast that was for sale in Sherman, Texas. We didn't want to move to Sherman, but that realtor planted a seed in Jo Ann's head.

When Jo Ann was a teenager, her mother owned a weekend place on Lake Whitney about an hour and half south of Fort Worth. Lake Whitney is a 23,000 acre impoundment on the Brazos River. It is surrounded by limestone bluffs and relatively clean. Jo Ann remembered all the good times at Lake Whitney when she was growing up.

We contacted the Coldwell Banker Real Estate Agency in Whitney. We talked to Linda Alesia Miller, who turned out to be a real pro. She had pretty well picked Jo Ann's mind before our scheduled day to tour Lake Whitney and look at properties. Linda knew we had seven children and nine grandchildren. She and Jo Ann also considered the Bed and Breakfast possibility so we could afford the needed space. My protests regarding price range were going unnoticed.

Linda had a place in mind but saved it until last. The place was a second home for a couple living in Dallas. It had four bedrooms with private baths, plus two suites with private bath and two bedrooms each. The couple had enjoyed the place as their children grew up, but all the children were now living out of state. As their interest waned, maintenance and yard up keep was also neglected. It was a lot of house for the money.

I would have told Linda to drive on, but Jo Ann wanted a better look. Jo Ann could see the possibilities and wanted the house. We made an offer contingent upon selling our place in Plano. Everything finally came together, and we moved to our lake home in April, 2002.

The Corps of Engineers owns the shore line of Lake Whitney so there are no private homes right on the shoreline. There are many beautiful homes on the bluffs overlooking the lake. Our back fence forms the property line between us and Walling Bend Park. The Corps operates the park. We are on the Bosque County or west side of the lake and have a beautiful view of the lake with the afternoon sun to our backs.

At first, we were just going to clear the brush and vines and clean up the place. But by September we embarked on major remodeling of the house, driveway and yard. It turned into a nightmare. Our contractor was incompetent and uncaring. It turned into a money pit.

We finally fired the contractor. It sure would have helped if I knew anything about building. We did find a skillful carpenter to finish and re-do a lot of things. Craig Blanchard also advised us on subcontractors to redo and finish other work. Stephanie Westbrook did a creative job of decorating.

We are proud of the finished job, and it only cost twice the original estimate. We have 6850 square feet of living space plus three decks and two porches. We have seven bathrooms and two more commodes and wash rooms. Four septic systems serve the commercial kitchen and the bathrooms. We have four air conditioning and heating systems.

We don't have anything luxurious or fancy. We just want all guests to feel down home country comfortable. We do enjoy having enough room for family gatherings. We also enjoy the clean air, bright stars, lake view, lack of traffic and wonderful neighbors.

When we moved to Bosque County, there was only one traffic light in the whole county. I'm sad to say that progress has arrived and now we have three. None of them are closer than eighteen miles to us though. Our mail address is Clifton, Texas, but we are about eighteen miles outside of Clifton. We are about equal distance from three home towns,

Clifton, Whitney and Meridian, our county seat. Whitney is across the lake in Hill County. It's only about six or eight miles as the crow flies but eighteen miles by highway. Waco is about forty miles away where we can obtain about anything we need.

On Kate's 100th Birthday Celebration

Warmest Greetings Aunt Kate on
this most special birthday.
With love and respect, we wish
you happiness in every way.

We are so thankful that Heaven
has waited this long,
so we can express our love serenading
you with birthday song.

You have lived life to its fullest
for a hundred years
experiencing thousands of joys
and thousands of tears.

Always serving God playing the
organ so beautifully,
and serving your family and others
so dutifully.

While your family and friends thank
God for your presence,
we pray his blessings you will
continue to experience.

MERRY CHRISTMAS

As we address each greeting, memories set out hearts aglow
and we are thankful for family and all the friends we know.

We wish you a season of great Christmas cheer
for you, and for all those you hold dear.

May our homes be filled with laughter and joyful sounds,
and may they be havens where His love abounds.

May we all claim the promises revealed by His birth
and may each of our hearts know peace on earth.

May the New Year bring health and happiness for you
and may God add his rich blessing to all you do.

Jo Ann and Elmer Mulhausen
From Lakehaven

OUR WEDDING BLESSING FOR YOU

Dear Trey and Danielle may your love
continue to grow.
May your joy and enthusiasm for each other
continue to glow.

Life will also bring you some inevitable
heartaches, too
So these are some traits and tools that
will carry you through.

Arm yourselves with love, honesty, trust
and sincere communication.
Link these together with faith for a happy life
of mutual dedication.

Be thankful for all the good times. Bear your
burdens, together.
Share the years, the tears, and the cheers
in all kinds of weather.

Young love is exciting and a beautiful
thing to behold.
We pray it will grow even sweeter,
and more serene as you grow old.

All Our Love, Popa and Jo Ann

Elmer, Danielle Downing Brooks, Trey Brooks and Jo Ann

HAPPY VALENTINES DEAR JO ANN

Some people bet on dice.
Some bet on cards.
Some even bet on
old "would be" bards.

Some people bet on horses
as you know I do.
But your best bet
is knowing I love you.

John and Jeanne have a lovely home in Tulsa, Oklahoma. On a recent visit, I discovered a strategically located crack in the commode seat in his guest bathroom. Since family members had their own bath rooms, I'm sure he was unaware of it. John is a very sensitive person. Of course I couldn't resist some kidding.

For his birthday right after our visit, I enclosed gift cards to a restaurant and Home Depot in his birthday card.

JOHN'S JOHN

I must warn you about John's john.
Your posteriors may be in danger if put upon
the commode seat in his guest bathroom.
An invisible crack could spell your doom.

If you aren't careful, it's a cinch,
your bottom will get a painful pinch.

Happy birthday greetings to a wonderful son,
although your facilities pinched my bun.
May this humble gift let you go out to eat,
then on the way home, buy a new commode seat.

All kidding aside, we love you very much,
May your birthday be full of cheer with a loving touch.

All our love,
Dad and Jo Ann

Zion United Church

When Jo Ann and I moved to Lake Whitney, we started looking for a new church home right away. We visited one Methodist Church, but decided to visit one or two more before joining.

We noticed a nice looking church out in the country about half way between us and Clifton. We discovered that it was an historic church founded by German immigrant farmers in 1891. At that time, it was associated with the German Evangelical denomination. Over time that denomination merged with the German Reformed church, the Congregational Church and elements of the Christian church to form the United Churches of Christ. The main theme of the U.C.C. is unity; for Christians of diverse traditions seeking one church on earth.

We joined the little country church. Many members are descendents of the original founding families, so there is great heritage. Our church in Plano had over six thousand members. It served our needs then because it had activities for specific groups. But moving to this church where an attendance of one hundred is a good Sunday has been a great experience. Our pastor was Dr. Charles Rice, a former Methodist. Dr. Rice retired at the end of 2007. We already miss Charles and Tanya who moved to be close to their grand children.

While sermons are important, we emphasize responsive worship more than other churches I have belonged to. I like that. Do I agree with all the church's theology? Do I agree with the way we do everything? The answer is no on both counts. I have never agreed one-hundred percent with anybody, not even my saintly mother or either of my beloved wives. We do enjoy the worship, the fellowship and channel of service. That's enough to make us love our church.

Our Sunday school opens with an assembly of all our classes. We have two or three hymns and a devotional thought. Some of we adults volunteer from time to time to bring a devotional thought. I don't volunteer often, but several poems in this book were written to help me convey a particular message.

This past year, I was concerned about both organizational and personal goals. I prepared a devotional thought and poem on goals. I think it adds to the quality of life for even retired people to have goals. Although I have always been goal oriented, it struck me that I didn't have a current goal. If I was going to lecture others, I should have a goal of my own. That's when I decided to write this book and get it out by my eightieth birthday. It's proving to be a bigger chore than I anticipated.

When our church paid the note on a building addition, our congregation president, John Thiele asked me to write something for the note burning celebration. The work on the addition had been done before we moved to the area, but I had heard stories about Joe Conrad heading up the effort. Joe was killed in a farming accident after the completion of the work. His widow, Nadine Conrad, is a treasured member of our congregation. Ludwig Conrad was a founding member and we still have several Conrad families who serve essential roles in the work of the church.

That poem at the note burning is one of several I have written to commemorate events in the life of our church or church members.

At various times in my life, I have enjoyed Bible study, but never read the Bible straight through; several times, I started to read cover to cover but I got detoured. I was talking to my sister, Betty on the telephone in January, 2007. She said that her resolution was to read the Bible through in one hundred days. That appealed to me as a nice, specific goal, so I decided to do it too.

My study Bible has 2,768 pages, so I decided to read about 30 pages a day. I included commentary and explanations as well as the scripture. It was a great experience. Studying by subject or specific passages is good, but reading straight through provides a great sense of context.

I believe the Bible. I believe all of it is the inspired word of God, but some passages may not be literal. Some scriptures are parables, illustrations and lessons. I have no problem reconciling creation, science and evolution. I believe in proven science, but not in every scientific theory. Infinity, time and space give me a headache, so my faith has to substitute for complete understanding. We either believe or we don't. Everything goes back to "In the beginning, God."

One Sunday every year our church has "Lay Sunday". Every part of the service is lead by a lay person. One year, I was assigned the benediction and wrote a poem for that. The next year when I was asked to deliver the sermon, it scared me to death. I am no preacher. I can hear a lot of my old buddies laughing at the thought. My first impulse was to resist. But, in reality, a sermon thought had been rattling around in my head. I agreed to do it.

I used the text about Jesus asking Peter three times if Peter loved Him. As an outline, I used our "bulletin" or order of worship. I believe that God asks us that same question, "Do you Love Me?" I talked about how we should answer that question with each step of the order of worship from the opening music, silent prayer, hymns, and prayer of confession, offering and sermon. I wrote the poem, "Do You Love Me" to summarize the point.

CELEBRATION IN WOMACK

We gather this morning, February ninth
two thousand three,
to celebrate: Zion United Church
is once again debt free.

About two and a half years ago our
congregation answered God's call
to build a new educational facility
and fellowship hall.

The work is complete. The bills have been paid.
what a wonderful story!
and now we meet for this joyful occasion
to give God the glory.

While we rejoice here, there is joy
in Heaven, too,
as Joe Conrad looks down at completion of
a cause to which he was true.

With zeal, dedication and by example,
Joe was the leader and inspiration
in financing and completing this building
so loved by our congregation.

The hundred fifty-four thousand dollar cost
was much more than raised.
and our history was to pay as we go,
so some were amazed.

That such a fiscally conservative membership
would go into debt - indeed,
assuming that debt was an act of faith
and response to a special need.

The note was for a hundred, seven
thousand dollar obligation.
though we planned to pay sooner,
it had a fifteen year amortization.

The work began and was completed. Dedication
was February eleventh, two thousand one.
that's exactly two years ago. Miraculously,
that note is paid and done.

Thanks be to God! Our congregation
has been richly blessed.
And we have responded by giving
of our very best.

But now after two years, that
note has returned.
So, with joy and thanksgiving, we gather
around to watch it burned.

SALUTE TO KYLE

We gather here on this
twenty-ninth day of May
To honor you – Kyle Schulze.
Congratulations and best wishes we convey.
We salute you Boy State Citizen,
Honor Society President, Pals Mentor,
Graduate and Clifton High School Valedictorian
for Two Thousand Four.

Your athletic achievements have also
brought you considerable fame.
As a Clifton Cub and clear back to the
little dribbler and the broom game.
As a hurdler, hoopster and quarterback,
you have demonstrated true grit
Overcoming serious injuries and working
hard to keep your body fit.

A partial list of awards you have
earned as you compete
Include All District, All State Academic
and outstanding Clifton athlete.
We are so proud of all you've done and
confident of what you'll do.
But we are most thankful for who
you are – for being you.

You maintain your Christian values
without fear of intimidation,
As you serve your church, school
community and nation.
And you remain humble, giving thanks
to your Savior and Lord,
For your heritage of church,
school and family accord.

You know your talents are gifts and
cultivated by Father and Mother.
And know you are loved as a son,
grandson, friend and brother.
Kyle, you are an inspiration for all
of us younger that you.
For your peers, you are a joy and
a friend that is true.

And for your elders, you are a source
of pride and admiration.
Best wishes on your studies as you
join that great Aggie nation.
Kyle, we honor you for who you are,
and for all you have done.
We offer our prayers and encouragement
for the future you've only begun.

Birthday Blessing

Emma Louise Conrad, best wishes on this your unique birthday.
Family and friends have gathered here to honor you in a special way.

On Easter Sunday, March twenty-seventh, nineteen thirty-two,
you were born to Henry and Emma Thiele Meinkowsky, a blessing true.
On that day when your family celebrated their Savior's resurrection,
you became a blessed part of the Meinkowsky family affection.

You joined siblings Verlia, Hester, Pauline, Nadine and H.L.
in that dark depression year, you were a bright Easter gift, a story to tell.
You grew up to be a lovely lady, but you were not too reckless,
because you were a member of Zion Church in Womack, Texas.

At Zion you were baptized, taught,
confirmed and served,
and still a vital member with love
and respect richly deserved.

You fell in love with Erwin Conrad,
and he made you his wife.
Along came Patricia, Alan, Don, Beth
and grandchildren to light your life.

You were a loving wife, a doting mother, singing, sewing and giving,
through good times and bad, happy and sad, always faithfully living.
When you lost Erwin, the grief was almost more than you could endure.
but with support and family love you survived with faith secure.

You have worshipped every Easter as 71 birthdays have come and gone.
How many times have you wondered if the two would ever again be one?
But Emma Louise, as you worship this Easter with your beautiful voice,
you and all of yours have an additional reason to rejoice.

Finally, after all these years, the moon and the calendar have aligned
so that we celebrate your seventy-third birthday and Easter combined.
The tomb is empty – the stone has rolled away.
We worship a risen Savior, on this glorious Easter Day.

Thanks be to God, today, March twenty-seventh, two thousand five,
He hears our prayers, our hymns and praise, He is alive!
And He joins us in extending our love on this special birthday.
Congratulations, Emma Louise, may God continue to light your way.

BENEDICTION

Precious Lord,
Thank you for your love, forgiveness
and presence felt in worship today.
And Lord, we have tried to express
our gratitude and love to you in every way.

As we leave the warmth and
fellowship of this Holy Place,
may the Holy Spirit go with us,
providing the strength and the grace

For us to honor and serve you,
deliver us from sin;
Keep us from harm and in your
loving arms till we meet again.

In Jesus Name, Amen.

DO YOU LOVE ME?

Peter had denied his Lord three times, that
dark and bitter night.
Jesus caught his eye, the cock crowed, and
Peter's heart became contrite.

Convicted of his sin; Peter wept bitterly
and repented with tears.
Jesus; arrested, tortured, crucified, became a
sacrifice for Peter's sin and ours in future years.

Peter was with the other disciples on
that glorious resurrection morn.
He was amazed, fearful and rejoiced that
morning when hope was reborn.

A few days later after breakfast with His disciples,
before ascending into Heaven,
Jesus called Peter by name, singling him out
from the eleven.

He asked, "Peter do you love me?" "Yes Lord
You know I love you."
Jesus asked three times, and Peter answered
with a heart anguished but true.

Jesus responded to Peter's answer three times,
"Peter, feed my sheep."
Peter learned that words and obedience must
combine when love runs deep.

I can see myself in Peter's shoes. I've stumbled,
erred and am often contrary.
Jesus knows my name. He knows yours, too.
And extends to us this same query.

"Elmer, do you love me?" and He asks you
the same question, too.
As we worship, may we leave no doubt,
"Yes Lord, we do love you."

John 21:15-17

WONDERFUL NEIGHBORS

One of the rewards for living in a rural area is great neighbors. Jo Ann and I visited Ralph and Reba Johnson, our next door neighbors to the south, before we bought. They gave us a run-down on the neighborhood and we liked them immediately. They proved to be great neighbors and kept us in fresh garden grown tomatoes that first year. Sadly, Ralph has passed away and Reba's health has given us a couple of scares. She is still a great neighbor and we love her.

The Lohmers live at the end of our street. They have lived in the area for a number of years. Pete works for the Post Office in Waco and Joyce teaches in Meridian. They are great folks. Jake and Eileen Crawford own the home across from us. They were excellent neighbors before moving to Fort Worth because of failing health. Their children maintain the place and visit occasionally. About half the homes in the neighborhood are owned by people living somewhere else and using this as a get-away. Our next door neighbors to the north live in Tulsa. We enjoy seeing Bob and Delores Mayfield when they get down here.

Chris and Robbyn Hensley live across the street from us. A couple of years ago, they brightened our neighborhood by bringing Zoey into the world. She is a darling little girl and makes Chris and Robbyn even more appealing as neighbors. A single man, Mark Shouletovich moved in next door to Chris and Robbyn a couple of years ago. Mark immediately established himself as a good neighbor. He is a P. R. representative of a large nursery company and brought us some nice surplus plants.

In 2006, Jo Ann cooked Thanksgiving Dinner for our fine dining club. When we learned that Mark was not going home to Illinois for Thanksgiving we invited him to be our guest. Our friend Tiffany Swanson is a beautiful girl who sometimes stars in our community theatre. She managed the pest control company we use and is a fellow Rotary member with Jo Ann. She enjoys coming out here and helping Jo Ann on occasions. She worked for the Lakehaven Thanksgiving dinner. There was an immediate attraction between Mark and Tiffany.

They started dating. They married Thanksgiving week, 2007. Jo Ann and I had the honor of standing in for Mark's family. They make a delightful couple. Now we not only have Tiffany as a friend, she is our neighbor.

Bill and Mary Gossett lived next door to Mark. We and the Gossets belong to the same church. During the same Thanksgiving week that Mark and Tiffany married, Bill Gosset passed away. Bill had a series of serious illnesses. Bill was a retired educator. He lived a good, full life, and we really miss him. Mary is a dear friend, good neighbor and fellow church member.

Jeff and Ann Hollinger live on the street dead ending onto our street. We belong to the same church, and they are great neighbors. Jeff has become my horse-racing companion. We both really enjoy the sport.

Lenny and Janet McCain live on the same street just north of us. Lenny is a retired Southwestern Bell Manager. When I served on the board at our Community Association, I noted that we were an aging board. Another board member and I stepped aside from running again and talked Lenny and his friend, Bobby Creech into joining the board. They added a lot of energy and accomplished a lot. Lenny became president of the association in 2008. We really enjoy having Lenny and Janet as neighbors.

Walt and Debby Lane live next door to Lenny and Janet. They are a lot of fun and great neighbors, always ready to lend a helping hand.

We have such a great neighborhood, I hate omitting anybody. George and Eileen Foley who own the water system, Don Benda, Mel Roberts, Charles Hall, all the Winnetts, Walt Schwarzer, Dana Eoff and Lori Lewis are all great neighbors.

We have great neighbors in nearby subdivisions also. We especially appreciate those we have worked with in the Civic Association like Fred and Esther Hodge, Terry and Sandy Lyons, Melvin and Liesa Musgrove, Fred and Gwen Owens, Cecil and Bonnie Sedberry, Bill and Nell Sims,

Paul and Mary Wagner, Julian and Wanda Wilson, Bobby and Sherry Creech, Joe and Linda Bates, Ginny Duda, Bud and Jo Ann Fricke, Bill and Betty Black, Fred and Kelly Spanibel and many others.

Dolores Miller, Bob and Judy Ashew are neighbors in other subdivisions close by, that introduced us to the Conservatory in Clifton. Dolores has since married Marvin Marek. We enjoy their families as well as them.

Fellow church members James and Lyn Boyd live in the nearby King Creek area. Lyn wrote a children's book "Muffin's Potato Soup" last year. She was an inspiration for me to write this book. Carl and Theresa Surley live in that same neighborhood. Theresa has a therapeutic massage practice. She is currently giving Yoga lessons to Jo Ann. In September, we spent a week exploring Big Bend Park with Carl, Theresa and their friend Jo Barnett. We shared a guest home in Terlingua Ghost Town and had a great time.

Sandy Bogovich seems to have unlimited energy. She and Robert operate a small weekend restaurant, look after their rental property and she also works as a reporter for the Bosque County News and is a fellow Rotarian with Jo Ann. She still makes time to do odd chores for Jo Ann. She has agreed to proof read this manuscript if I ever finish it.

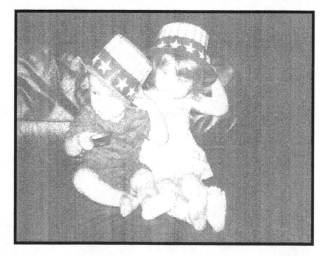

Great grandchildren Luke Downing and Amelie Federspiel

THE RHYTHM OF LIFE

The sun sets. The sun rises. The seasons come and go.
The tide comes in. The tide goes out. Things die. Things grow.
The rhythm of God's creation continues. It will never end.
On Thanksgiving Day this year, we lost a neighbor and dear friend.

At the same time, great-grandchildren
visited with life still to race.
And then a wedding, our hearts were
warmed by the newlyweds embrace.

We experienced God's rhythm
of life all in one week,
From despair to hope, from tears to joy,
from boisterous to meek.

Family together, babies, a wedding,
a death: all call for prayer.
Lord thank you for the life of Bill Gossett,
giver, teacher a man of care.

We pray for Your loving arms to
comfort Mary in her grief.
Thank you that Bill has found rest.
He's with You because of his belief.

We pray your blessings on the marriage of Tiffany and Mark.
May their love endure good times and bad times, daylight and dark.
Please bless Alex, Amelie and Luke with love and protection.
May they come to know You. Bless their parents' direction.

Thank You for all Your blessings, for Your love, Your care.
Thank You, dear Lord, for hearing this prayer.

Elmer Mulhausen
12-01-07

Ecclesiastes 3:1-4

Ordinary People

God has work to be done. He
sends out the call.
But how often does He hear
this old stall?

I don't know how. I am
not equal to the task.
I'm just an ordinary person,
so don't even ask.

What ever He asks us to do,
He will also provide a way.
And even ordinary people can experience
joy of service when we obey.

Ordinary people, doing extraordinary things –
that's the way God gets things done.
Each talent, each gift, each effort
combined as one.

As we go about God's work,
may whoever sees us
know that we are ordinary people
who have been with Jesus.

Acts 4:13

THAT INNER SELF

Our self-image is a magical and fragile thing.
When it's healthy, we work, create, dance and sing.
But when it's low, we can't seem to do anything at all.
We are ineffective and down - we try to run and only crawl.

How can we raise our spirits when we are down?
It helps to have a friend with a smile rather than a frown.
Friends remind us of our worth and let us know we are not alone.
Remember God made us in His own image and loves us as His own.

At times medical help may be needed, but don't forget to pray
for a healthier spirit, for love, for purpose, for a brighter day.
Become a giver as well as a taker. Love a cause more than self.
Be enthusiastic, only if acting. Get involved. Get off the shelf.

And remember, we also affect the spirits of others.
So don't tear down, but lift the spirits of our brothers.
The responsibility is even greater for parents, bosses, teachers,
business owners, officials, mentors, managers and preachers.

Management may require that we see people as they are,
But leaders see them as they can be when pointed to a star.
Help people see their worth. Help them stay in the race.
Remember, even Moses was once a basket case.

That delicious yogurt was made with help of a germ,
and that beautiful butterfly was once a worm.
When we give someone a healthy self-image to live up to,
God will reward us with a brighter spirit, too.

Proverbs 12:25

On one of my turns to deliver opening thoughts in our Sunday school, I prepared by reading Hebrews 11 and 12. The text in Chapter 12, verse 1 compares life to running a race. I envisioned the ancient Greek athletes running in late evening with blazing torches carried overhead. They passed the torches on like relay runners today pass the baton.

RACE OF LIFE

Runners' line up for the race, their flaming
torches light up the sky.
While a great heavenly host of saints
look down from on high.

The saints have already finished the
race and passed on the fire.
They kept the faith, fought the good fight
and have a crown to inspire.

Now the race has started and the runners
strive to do their very best.
As each succeeding runner takes the
torch in turn, victory is the quest.

The shouts continue from above, "Let he who
has the light, pass it on!"
And I watch my favorite as he runs with
love and grace till his part is done.

It took all his remaining strength
to pass on the flame.
Then he prayed, "Lord, may my race of
Life, glorify your name."

OUR COMMUNITIES

It is amazing how quickly one can get involved in a rural community. Our first affiliation was with Zion United Church. It is about halfway between us and Clifton in the Womack community. That's just an area of farms on highway 219.

Shortly thereafter, we joined the West Shore Civic Improvement Association which serves the unincorporated town of Laguna Park and areas on the southwest shore of Lake Whitney. This organization provides community center building for voting, meals on wheels, flu shots, health screenings and all kinds of community meetings.

Our association raises funds for the volunteer fire department, the First Responders, and the Laguna Park Library. This last year, we started a drive to get a deputy assigned solely to this area. The County Sheriff's budget couldn't afford it. We raised funds to supplement the sheriff's budget in order to equip a deputy to live in and patrol our area. We also sponsor a huge clean-up campaign each year with the cooperation of our county commissioners and the corps of engineers. I enjoyed my time on the board of our association.

Jo Ann joined the Rotary Club and is now serving as president of the Bosque County Club that meets in Clifton. We support the Annual Angel Tree that provides Christmas for needy children, Bark that cares for pets and pet adoptions and the Family Abuse Council which cares for abused spouses and is raising funds for a shelter.

A couple of years ago, we learned that the corps of engineers was closing our adjacent park. We rallied citizens to protest. We called ourselves the Friends of Walling Bend Park. When Congressman Chet Edwards came to the park to make a public announcement that the park would remain open, it was suggested that there should be a citizen's organization that kept communication open with the corps. That group became "Friends of Lake Whitney." Our friend, Tom Schenk is president and Jo Ann is Vice President.

The Friends of Lake Whitney had a great variety of goals but had no idea how many property owners around the lake had grievances against the corps of engineers. The organization has primarily become a communications tool between property owners and the corps. Lake management meets regularly with the "Friends" and the needs and problems of both sides are discussed. We don't always agree, but we are talking.

We are also members of the Bosque Conservatory which sponsors the arts in our county and area. It is amazing how much culture there is in this small, rural county. We have great local artists and art galleries. The conservatory sponsors great art shows and all kinds of classes. It also sponsors our community theatre which puts on tremendous shows. I'm amazed at the Conservatory's ability to raise money and enhance the quality of life in our county.

Jo Ann's most passionate volunteer calling is C.A.S.A. or Court Appointed Special Advocates. It is amazing how many children's lives and futures are in the hands of the courts. C.A.S.A. volunteers undergo extensive training. Judges appoint them to investigate and advise the judge on what's in the best interest of the child. Jo Ann's work fills a tremendous need. She has had some very troubling cases and some very happy endings. In some cases she keeps a mentoring relationship with children after cases are closed. As I write, we have an adolescent girl visiting for the weekend.

Last year a widow and good friend suggested that our church establish a single adult Sunday school class. Doris Jennings and her deceased husband had met many years ago in such a class. The Questers Class had meant so much to Jo Ann and I that we supported Doris' suggestion. The other single adults in our little church didn't have much interest. As the three of us tried to recruit new potential members in our rural area, we discovered that the single adults who were interested were already established in their own churches.

The idea for a class in our church didn't materialize, but we decided to invite single, Christian adults to dinner once a month. No formal organization has formed as yet. We just provide a dinner and a place to fellowship; if they organize recreational events or Bible Classes that's up to them. Last month we had fourteen participants. They pitched in to contribute to the costs of the dinner and we all enjoyed getting together.

It was never our intent that we become a dating service, but Dave Ponewash met Louise Bartek here for dinner. They have since married and are very happy. Lakehaven is in danger of getting a reputation as a place where good people meet their future spouses.

From a business standpoint, we belong to the Clifton Chamber of Commerce and the Lake Whitney Chamber of Commerce. We also belong to the Heart of Texas Bed and Breakfast Owners' Association. Just recently we were appointed to the Lake Whitney Board of Tourism, a new organization that will promote and advertise the lake.

Our contributions to the large, established charities have really suffered. It is so much more satisfying to contribute to causes that don't have the huge administrative costs and where you see directly how funds are used. In a rural community, you can get involved quickly.

The past three summers, I have served on the Bosque County Appraisal Review board. It takes about eight or nine weeks, two days a week, for us to hear citizens' appeals to the appraisal of their property for tax purposes. It has been an honor to serve with some outstanding citizens as we try to conscientiously weigh all the facts and reach a decision.

Raymond Whitney and A. G. "Buzz" Jordon retired from the board after my first year. We were all saddened when Paul Murphey passed away after my second year on the board. Bill Beck, Joe Birdwell and Charles Goodwin joined Jeanne Cosper and I on the board. In 2008, we are just being joined by Robert Evinger.

As with every job, sometimes we are snowed under and other times people don't show up. During those times, we swapped stories. In my first year, Buzz was the principal story teller prompting the "Good old Boys." Last year Charles regaled us with stories about his law enforcement days. That inspired "Evening News."

Every October, Charles and his wife, Kathy, entertain family, friends and neighbors at the Goodwin family fish fry and barbeque. Two or three hundred people gather on their beautiful spread in Bosque County. It is truly a great event

EVENING NEWS ANALYSIS

The Hollywood Madame did so good doing bad,
that getting busted really made her mad.
While lawyers argued pros and con,
she threatened to release *her* book of john.

That news caused such alarm among the high and mighty,
that all charges were dropped by noon on Friday.

TEXAS GOOD OLD BOYS

Buzz and Humpy were the pride of Kopperl, Texas.
They ran up and down the Brazos, wild and reckless.
Truly a couple of good ole boys in days gone by,
they could beat any pair under the Texas sky.

They hunted every creature in their Brazos River empire,
then toasted their toes around an old camp fire.
They terrorized coons all night long,
and listened to the hound's woeful song.

Using their hands, nets, telephone or a fishing pole,
they gave the catfish no chance in the old fishing hole.
The land, the fish and the game were true joys
for Buzz and Humpy, true Texas good ole boys.

Buzz was fearless and never backed down from a fight,
but one day, he made a mess, a pitiful sight.
He told his Dad he knew how to castrate a calf,
but he had to sew up a gash before enjoying a laugh.

The good ole boys grew up. Each one developed a spread,
while working full time so they could get ahead.
They raised families and herds. They tended the land
while always lending their neighbor a helping hand.

Buzz always has a story about things he has not forgotten,
about hunting, fishing, fighting, picking cotton,
putting whiskey in a calf's milk, cutting hay,
or buying and selling cattle, his stories make the day.

There was a day when fists might settle a score,
but with gray hair and by-passes, they don't do that anymore.
Now, the boys will beat you in a game of forty-two,
and bet they can negotiate a better gas lease than you.

The Serenity Prayer – *by Reinhold Niebuhr*

God grant me the serenity to accept the things I cannot change; courage to change the things I can; and the wisdom to know the difference. Living one day at a time; enjoying one moment at a time; accepting hardships as the pathway to peace; taking, as He did, this sinful world as it is, not as I would have it. Trusting that He will make all things right if I surrender to His will; that I may be reasonably happy in this life and supremely happy with Him forever in the next. Amen

MAKING IT PERSONAL

The *Serenity Prayer* is wise and beautiful to read,
but, for it to change my life, to really fill my need,
I must personally and sincerely make it my prayer.
When I do, He lifts my anxiety and burdens of care.

My prayer may not change the world, the land and the sea,
But thanks be to God, my prayer can surely change me.
When there are no answers, when ruin litters the road we trod
there is only one solution. We must - "let go and let God."

When I pray the *Serenity Prayer* and truly seek His way,
then joy replaces gloom and blue skies replace the gray.
In prayer – thankful, repentant, forgiven and clean;
forgetting failures of yesterday, confident of tomorrow – and serene.

Living for the beauty of the moment and feeling His peace,
questions, indecision, things I can't change, I release.

Phil. 4:6 and 7:

SENSES OF CHRISTMAS

We love the wonderful sights of Christmas:
Nativity scenes, angels, stars, all the decorations,
the tree, smiles, children' eyes and beautiful illuminations.

We love the wonderful sounds of Christmas:
"Silent Night", "Little Town of Bethlehem", "Hark the Herald Angel
Sing",
"Holy Night", "Come Let Us Adore Him", "Glory to the Newborn
King."
Hearty greetings, children laughing, all the mirth,
sounds of joy as we celebrate our Savior's birth.

We love the wonderful tastes of Christmas:
Ham, turkey, dressing and gravy making the juices flow,
candy, cakes, cookies, pies and a kiss under the mistletoe.

We love the wonderful memories of Christmas:
Family and friends, warm thoughts with every card received and
addressed,
Of childhood, life, times of want, times of plenty, thankful that we
are blessed,
Of those gone on before, of sadness and of joy,
a moment to reflect and revere the birth of that Baby Boy.

We love the wonderful feelings of Christmas:
Gratitude for all we have; health and zest for living,
compassion for those without and a spirit of giving.
Love of family and having them near
makes Christmas special, full of joy and good cheer:

Our love goes out to you and all you hold dear.
We wish you a Merry Christmas and Happy New Year

Love to all,
Jo Ann and Elmer Mulhausen

HAPPY BIRTHDAY SHAUN

Are you ready for some football?
Our grandson Shaun is.
He plays center on two winning teams
He's a real whiz.

So, Shaun here's wishing that the
balls bounce your way.
May you have plenty to cheer about,
and a very happy birthday.

May the candles be as bright as
the love around you glows.
May you have a wonderful, healthy year,
as your happiness grows.

All our love,
Popa and Jo Ann

I'm appalled at the popularity of the prosperity preachers. Yes, God wants us to prosper, but that shouldn't be the focus of prayer and the Christian life. God doesn't always answer with a yes. Sometimes the answer is no or later.

YES - - NO OR LATER

Dear Lord, please give me a new Lexus to drive
and a mansion with servants to pamper me when I arrive.
Give me more talent so I can have riches and fame.
And I need a little more time to enjoy life's game.

I impatiently waited for a response from the heavenly skies.
My Lord's answer was both loving and wise.
My son, prosperity can be a blessing or it can be a curse.
Granting your prayer might help or make life worse.

I love you too much to give you more than you can bear.
Your time, talent and treasure must bring good, not be a snare.
How have you used the gifts I have already bestowed?
How much have you given to share the load?

Stewardship of what you already have is one way I measure.
What are you doing now with your time, talent and treasure?

Luke 12:13-15

Lakehaven Bed and Breakfast

Before we completed our remodeling and decorating, Linda our real estate agent and friend asked us to house a couple of her clients. We protested that the property wasn't finished, and we had no insurance. Well, Linda is a friend and she is persuasive.

Two long time friends, Judy Dooley from Dallas and Susan Roler from Austin were meeting to look at property on Lake Whitney. They stayed with us. As a result those two old friends and later their husbands also became our friends. Richard and Judy Dooley built a beautiful home nearby. Richard is moving his real estate law practice down here and will practice from his home on the lake. Susan and John will continue to live in Austin because of her psychology practice.

After completing all the work, we opened our Lakehaven Bed and Breakfast in the spring of 2004. (www.lakehaven.biz). From those first, pre-opening guests, we have learned this is a business of meeting and enjoying people.

Our training has been on the job training. We did get some helpful ideas from Helen Hubler who owns Riverbend Bed and Breakfast near Clifton. We thanked Helen for being so gracious to potential competitors. She told us that Bed and Breakfasts don't really compete. Each one is unique. We have learned that is true and share experiences with our owner's association.

Lakehaven is different. We are not a historical marker. We aren't luxurious. We are down home, country comfortable. Our food is exceptional. Our spacious public areas allow people to stretch out and feel at home.

Since Jo Ann is a gourmet cook, we operated a fine dining club for a while. We had dinner parties for members and guests. The parties started at 6:30 with a social hour and an array of appetizers. Then we had a nice sit down gourmet dinner. The finale was a selection of at least three desserts and more social time until around 10:30. It was great fun and responsible for at least ten of the thirty-five pounds I have gained since marrying Jo Ann.

Our members also loved it, but we discontinued the club for several reasons. The only reason that counts is Jo Ann's re-occurring back problems. This market wouldn't support hiring another chef. We can hire people for other chores around here, but the cooking for fine dining is special. Our members became good friends and we miss having them.

We have had all kinds of Bed and Breakfast guests. All of them are special. We have had guests from Norway, India and Pakistan. We have had three very interesting authors on book promotion tours. Dr. Charles Russell wrote *"Undaunted"*, the story of a Norwegian single woman's adventures in frontier Texas (Clifton is the Norwegian capital of Texas).

Eric Latham wrote about his adventures as he literally walked coast to coast raising money for cancer research (www.takestepswithapurpose), Eric is an extra-ordinary young man and continues to raise money for cancer research.

Susan Atchison wrote *"Spirit Walk,"* a Mother's glimpse of Christ in everyday experiences (Tate Publishing). We have really enjoyed meeting and visiting with these authors, and all of the interesting guests we have had visit us at Lakehaven.

Dear Guest,

Welcome to Lakehaven. We hope to make your visit with us a memorable and pleasurable time. Should you need anything, please do not hesitate to let us know.

So that we can better serve you please complete the following Breakfast Selection form and place the completed form outside your door before retiring for the night.

Your hosts,
Jo Ann and Elmer Mulhausen

Breakfast Selection For:

_____

Breakfast will be served with seasonal fresh fruit, Southwest potatoes, and your choice of *ANY* of the following:

(Please check your choices. On egg servings, please indicate number of eggs.)

_____ Bacon _____ Sausage _____ Canadian Bacon

_____ Pancakes _____ Pancakes with blueberries

_____ French toast _____ Fluffy, flaky old fashioned oatmeal

_____ Eggs Benedict _____ Eggs Florentine (Eggs Benedict with spinach and sautéed mushrooms)

_____ Scrambled eggs _____ Fried eggs _____ Poached eggs

_____ Omelet with: ____Bell Peppers _____Onions _____ Ham

_____ Spinach _____ Mushrooms _____Tomatoes

_____ Cheddar cheese _____ Swiss cheese

_____Toast _____ Biscuits ____ English Muffin

Approximate time you would like breakfast served: _____

Would you like a wakeup call, and if so, at what time? _____

Lakehaven's Breakfast Selection Form

CHHS – Year 2000 Reunion

Not long after Jo Ann and I were married, Capital Hill High School had a "Fabulous Forties" reunion in Oklahoma City. Jo Ann was sport enough to join me in attendance. She actually seemed to enjoy all these older people who had been a part of my life.

On Sunday morning, this reunion closed with a memorial service honoring all the deceased. They actually printed a listing of all who had died from those 40's classes. The numbers were overwhelming. My first wife, Evelyn, was included. Most all the buddies I ran around with were also included.

On the way home, Jo Ann and I agreed that we would never take life and health for granted. We vowed to be thankful for each day.

When we got home, I wrote "Morning Prayer." Somehow, we lost that first version. I have just finished re-constructing it the best I can remember.

As I finished, my grandson, Patrick Downing, and his wife, Kacey, arrived for a visit. They brought my first great grandson, Luke, for a visit. This is our first meeting. He is nearly three weeks old, and precious. They have just moved from Austin to Denton, Texas.

MORNING PRAYER

Lord, this morning I didn't see my
picture on the obituary page.
I thank you because the majority of those
I saw were younger than my age.

I can't question your infinite wisdom
and your plan.
You take some to be there with you and
leave me in this land.

Don't get me wrong, Lord. I'm in no hurry
to leave this life.
I'm happy here with my family, friends,
home and wonderful wife.

Sometimes I just wonder what you might
have in mind;
when my first love and all my high school buddies
have passed on, leaving me behind.

I just figure you must have me here
for some reason.
Please let me know what to do as I
prepare for another season.

May I always reflect Your love and keep
respectful of You and Yours.
Help me have a sense of humor and encourage
others, be one that re-assures.

Of course I know that one day on that fateful
page, my name will appear.
I just ask that You make me a blessing
as long as You keep me here.

Psalms 118:24

With all the news coverage, when Jessica Lynch came home, I wrote this piece for my own emotions. I never sent it to her. Even though I served only a short time and saw no action, I remember coming home. This is for the thousands who have served their country and came home. My only regret is that I never found anyone to put this piece to music.

HOME COMING

Oh Jessica, Jessica! Where have you been?
It's so wonderful having you home again.

While a little girl with pretty golden locks,
and wearing bright cotton frocks.
You answered the call of the red, white and blue,
to become a soldier, too.

Oh Jessica, Jessica! We are so proud of you
and the other men and women serving, too.

In a distant land in the darkest of night,
suddenly, you joined the fight.
Your body broken, enduring bitter pain,
fears and tears, you restrain.

Oh Jessica, Jessica! Do not despair.
Your fellow Americans joined you in prayer.

Then taken prisoner in that distant land,
how much abuse can you stand?
When you were saved in that daring rescue,
we rejoiced along with you.

Oh Jessica, Jessica! Begin to heal.
The wondrous dream of homecoming is now real.

Then came stories making a hero of you,
you said, "I'm just a soldier, too."
May God and time heal your body and heart,
Be happy, you've done your part.

Oh Jessica, Jessica! Where have you been?
It's so wonderful having you home again.

FAITH

Do I believe the Bible? Yes, I certainly do.
I believe it is the inspired Word of God. Don't you?
Yes, it is a collection of inspired writers over the ages.
Some stories are literal; others illustrate a message on their pages.

I have no trouble reconciling evolution and creation.
Species continue to evolve with God's coordination.
Some believe the world came to be by happen stance.
But I'm confident that God's plan ruled and not by chance.

Yes, I get a headache contemplating eternity and space.
But faith allows me to accept it. It's a settled case.
Faith and acceptance allows God's love to enter our hearts.
Then with confidence and peace we enjoy creation's parts.

A black cow eats green grass under a blue sky
and orange sun. I don't understand how or why,
but she provides me with white milk, red meat,
yellow butter and orange cheese, that's good to eat.

Do I understand all that I believe?
Of course not, only bit by bit God lets me receive.
Faith believes the unproven and unseen.
We either believe or we don't, there is no in between.

Faith is acceptance and grows as we view the beauty of God's earth.
Faith grows with each expression of love, each loss and each birth.
Faith grows after each storm, as stars re-appear in the sky,
and plants emerge with new life. My faith will live on even after I die.

Hebrews 11: 1-3

THE AFRICAN CHILDREN'S CHOIR

On two occasions we have been blessed by housing the African Children's Choir while they performed in our area. All are orphans and support their home and schools in Africa by taking year long trips to perform.

They came to visit from a far away place,
dancing and singing with beauty and grace.
They spread God's love and message world-wide,
and came into our home a short while to abide.

They came with loving hearts and loving smiles
on a mission journey of thousands of miles.
They work together, all doing their parts,
but most of all they came into our hearts.

God speaks with love and grace then sometimes with fire,
and inspires us through the African Children's Choir.

DECISIONS

We come to many forks along the road of life.
Where do I go to school? Who do I take for a wife?
Choose a doctor, dentist, and lawyer. Choose a congregation.
Where shall I live? What should I make my occupation?

Should I buy that home? What kind of car should I drive?
What kind of friends do I select? For what goals do I strive?
Some people are always takers. Others choose to give.
Some choose habits that destroy health. Others choose to live.

The course of life is shaped by each decision made.
Thought and prayer is needed to avoid being dismayed.
And sometimes the road of life is too narrow to turn around.
If we can't go back, we better make each decision sound.

The biggest choice - what do we do about God in our life?
Do we choose to believe? Do we choose peace or strife?
And God gives each of us that free right to choose.
Do we choose Him? Or do we choose to lose?

Joshua 24:15

A Few Things I have Learned over the Past Eighty Years

I didn't create these sayings. I learned all of them from someone else. I wish I could credit each one, but I have a bad memory. The important thing is, I tried to incorporate them into my own philosophy and practice.

Don't be obsessed or worried about whether people love you or not. Be obsessed with loving others.

Diagnose before you prescribe.

I can't remember learning much with my mouth open.

Aimlessness is not a good human condition.

Everyone needs goals, even retirees

First you set a goal, and then you plan how to get there.

If you can't plan your whole year, then plan the month.
If you can't plan your whole month, plan your week.
If you can't plan your whole week, plan Monday.
If you can't plan Monday, plan the first hour— the first hour is the rudder of the day.
The first hour sets the pace – it sets the tone.

Every career has pleasant activities and also necessary, sometimes unpleasant chores. The successful person makes it a <u>habit</u> to do what failures don't like to do.

If a person or a company risks an investment to provide me a job, the least I can do is strive to make a profit for my employer. The best way to always be employed is to make a profit for the employer.

There must be employers before there are employees.

There is a fine line between ambition and greed. Quality of life demands that we find that line.

On Selling

Nothing happens until somebody sells something.

If the phone isn't ringing in your business, start dialing, or as Winston Churchill said, "If the wind isn't blowing, start rowing."

In selling or in leadership, your ears are more important than your mouth.

In selling or in leadership, questions are more powerful than statements.

Product knowledge, friendliness, personality, and resourcefulness are all important traits, but time control is even more important. We must learn to push the start button.

It is fulfilling to sell your product but even more fulfilling to find a need and solve the need with your product.

On Leadership and Management

Forgive me for dwelling on insurance management but that's what I did for thirty-two years. I was made a manager before I could even spell it, but I had a lot of help along the way.

You manage things, but you lead people.

Don't let managing interfere with your leadership.

Managers see people as they are. Leaders see people as they can become. Both views are necessary at different times.

You motivate people by making them believe in themselves.

The best managerial advice comes straight out of the Bible. He who would be first must be servant to all.

> The power of synergy is attained when you meld the goals/interests of the organization (owners), the customer and employees. That was a natural at State Farm because policy owners own the company. Our three-way partnership consisted of:
>
> (1) The policy owners (2) the agency force and (3) the company and employees.
>
> You aren't a leader until people follow you.
>
> It is very difficult to follow someone that is unpredictable or wishy-washy. It is hard to believe in someone that isn't sure what they believe. How can you trust someone that says one thing, but body language indicates they feel another way. We want leaders that walk the talk. We want leaders with integrity. A person with integrity feels, believes, talks and acts in a straight line. That's a person in whom you can confide, trust and follow.
>
> A leader knows where he/she is going, knows why and makes a plan to get there.
>
> A leader surrounds himself/herself with quality people.
>
> A leader doesn't have to know everything. They just need to know where to get the answers.
>
> A leader doesn't have to be skillful at everything. He/she finds people who do have the needed skills.

Cash Value Life Insurance

Although many financial writers criticize cash value life insurance, my life insurance is the highest quality property I have ever owned. When I was young, I didn't have an investment problem. My problem was protecting my family in the event of my early demise or disability. I also had a savings problem.

By buying as much permanent cash value life insurance as I could afford it and paying premiums by payroll deductions, I solved both problems. I don't have anything against term life insurance. I had to buy that in order to afford the protection I needed. But I have lived. All those term policies and premiums are gone. My cash value in permanent policies is multiple of the premiums paid.

I haven't paid premiums on these policies for decades. The dividends pay the premiums. And there are enough dividends left over to the purchase paid up additions that keep increasing my protection and my cash value. Of course your policies must be from a high quality company. I recommend State Farm but there are many high quality, dividend paying companies.

Your cash value can form the foundation for other investment opportunities. If you have $100,000 of life insurance cash value, you can borrow that $100,000 and pay it back in complete privacy. There is not even a bleep on any credit report company records.

You can borrow that $100,000 with:

1. no credit application or decision by anyone;
2. at a pre-determined prime interest rate;
3. with repayment on your own terms, or interest only or wait until your death;
4. as long as you keep the policy in force, you can get the money and pay it back without creating any taxable event.

I'm not aware of any other type of property where these four points are true.

INVESTING

My first efforts to invest were to invest in myself. Even before I could legally borrow and sign contracts I had a fling in the home improvement business with my cousin, Bill Tubbs.

While working for Western Electric Company, Evelyn and I bought a small neighborhood grocery store in Oklahoma City. She planned to operate it while I helped part-time. That venture failed, but we repaid the credit union every dime. That was important because my father-in-law, J.C. Crow, had co-signed the note.

When I went into the insurance business, I invested everything I had into my agency, both as local agent and as a manager. I established a financial base with a solid life insurance program. It wasn't until later in my career that I took advantage of deferred compensation and 401K programs.

Later in Shawnee, Oklahoma, and in Columbia, Missouri, Evelyn bought a dress shop and called it Carrie's Fashions. The social aspect and going to market was great fun, but that business turned into a tax write-off too.

It wasn't until I retired that I got involved with purchasing individual stocks. A good friend and colleague, Cliff Galaway, told me about the Bowser Report in 1994. This report researches stocks that are selling for under $3.00 per share (www.thebowserreport.com).

I started buying one company at a time when I had spare funds. I invested about $600.00 on each issue. In a very few years, sales proceeds left in the portfolio funded all new purchases. The last time I added money to the portfolio was following the September 11, 2001 attack. The market took a dip at that time.

Since then, I have been withdrawing profits to invest in our construction and operating our B & B. Those profits have ranged from 13% to 28% each year.

This portfolio is quite modest by most standards, but has been handy.

THE BOWSER REPORT

Every month I await the Bowser Report in the mail.
Then I buy Max's company of the month without fail.
But big shot experts say, "don't buy a low price stock."
Max Bowser is a rebel, and has developed quite a flock.

Max recommends gems less than three dollars a share.
The experts say, "buy and hold, forget they are there".
Max says, "Buy to sell at a profit, they won't be up forever."
So, I sell when the time is right, even those I hate to sever.

Max calls we subscribers his buckaroos,
because we don't follow those experts, we do as we choose.
Max does the research. We might add a personal touch,
but by following his game plan, we have never profited so much.

CHEERFUL GIVING

God loves a cheerful giver,
the scriptures say.
So can you imagine giving any
other way?

Obeying God in giving provides
peace of mind.
Sharing in the cost of God's work
brings joy and cheer combined.

Giving from our hearts is an expression
of our love for Him.
Worship, just like prayer, and joyfully
singing a favorite hymn.

How much should I give? The question
comes to me.
How much did He give me? How much
can I give cheerfully?

How much will test my faith
and make me rely on His will?
To grow faith, I must exercise
Faith, His will fulfill.

Whether we give from plenty or have
only a widow's mite,
It gives joy to know that either gift is
precious in His sight.

So, Zion membership, united in
faith and cheer
will underwrite our church's budget
for the coming year.

2nd Corinthians 9:7

Back Surgery for Christmas

Our appointment at the Zale Lipsky hospital was for 5:30 a.m., December 17, 2007. On Sunday night, the 16th, we just couldn't get to bed. We had a business function at Lakehaven and then family company following that dinner. When all the company left, Jo Ann didn't feel like packing for the hospital, so we set the alarm for 2:00 a.m. to allow time for preparation and the two hour drive to Dallas.

I just happened to wake up at 3:30 a.m. Either we did not set the alarm properly or it malfunctioned. We rushed around and got on the road in record time and were only twenty minutes late getting to the hospital.

In Jo Ann's three previous back surgeries, Dr. Kevin Gill fused her vertebrae along with the needed mechanical support. This time, the damaged disc is too close to a fused joint. He didn't want to fuse any more vertebrae. He inserted an artificial titanium disc.

The surgery started at 7:00 a.m. I sat prayerfully in the waiting room until Dr. Gill came in at almost 8:30 a.m. He assured me that everything went well. They would call me when Jo Ann was ready to go to her room. My faith was beginning to wane by 10:45 a.m., when I received a call that I could go up to room 507.

Jo Ann was sitting up in bed. She had combed her hair and applied make-up. Only the IV's and drainage tube in her neck hinted that she had been in surgery. I started to telephone the list of people who asked to be informed, but Jo Ann insisted on making those calls herself. She was very happy and thankful that all her neck, back and shoulder pain was gone. She had regained feeling in her hands. Within an hour she dragged her IV as she walked to the bathroom.

Her recovery was miraculous, but there was one small problem. The surgeon worked on her spine from the front, so arteries, esophagus and breathing channels had to be held out of the way. She had a very sore throat where the breathing tube was inserted. That problem was deemed to be normal and temporary.

319

On Tuesday morning, I woke up at 4:00 a.m. to find Jo Ann packing to go home. Dr. Gill came in about 6:15 a.m., removed the drainage tube and released her. We were out of the hospital by 9:00 a.m. and home well before noon. What a remarkable recovery!

Jo Ann's throat continued to bother her however, and we noticed swelling by Wednesday afternoon. When her breathing became difficult, we finally talked to the doctor. He faxed a prescription for a cortisone dose pack, but our small town pharmacies were already closed. Somehow, we got word to the Brookshire's pharmacist in Clifton. He came back after hours to fill the prescription.

Jo Ann's breathing was much better on Thursday morning, but she was still speaking in a whisper. She had a C.A.S.A. court case in Meridian, and I couldn't believe she planned to go. This was the final hearing on one of her cases that had a happy ending. She went. Then she drove to Clifton for a Rotary meeting and grocery shopping for all our holiday guests.

Jo Ann is like a worm on a hot rock. Finally, on Friday and Saturday she rested in bed and let our dear neighbor, Tiffany Shoukletovick, clean house. We really appreciate Tiffany's help because we had a full house of B&B guests on the weekend, then a full house of family and friends for Christmas.

Jo Ann's Christmas surgery was very successful, thanks to a lot of prayers and a very skillful surgeon.

Alex Becceri, Kathleen, Amelie and Jeff Federspiel,
Christmas morning 2007

HAPPY NEW YEAR

Our traditional holiday activities got off track this season.
Jo Ann's back surgery on December seventeenth was the main reason.
So Christmas 2007 has come and gone.
We received many beautiful cards and loved every one.

Jo Ann did make a remarkable recovery thanks to God's will.
We are also very thankful for the surgical talent of Dr. Gill.
We thank you for your intercessory prayer,
and Zale Lipsky Hospital for their excellent care.

Reflecting upon God's wonderful Christmas gift lifted hearts
but we gave up on sending Christmas cards after false starts.
Now, we do want to wish you a Happy New Year.
May two thousand eight bring you health, success and cheer.

Jo Ann and Elmer Mulhausen

I have always been goal oriented. Aimlessness is not a good human condition. But, as I prepared a devotional thought on goals for our Sunday school opening, I realized I didn't have a current goal. That's when I decided to write this book. When I announced that goal to our Sunday school, I was on the hook.

THE GOAL

The men were laboring in the hot sun.
I approached and asked a question of one.
"What are you doing sir?" if I may ask.
"I'm laying brick," he said, returning to his dreary task.

I asked the same of a second man, blonde and tall.
As he brushed sweat from his brow, he said, "I'm building a wall."
My curiosity was not satisfied, so I asked a third.
This brick layer looked enthusiastic and assured.

He was actually enjoying his work and I asked why.
"I'm building a beautiful cathedral that will reach toward the sky.
It will be God's House, and I'm gladly doing my part."
I marveled at how having goals affects our heart.

Some know what, others know how. Blessed are those who know why.
May God bless me with a goal until the day I die.

DECEMBER MAN

I can recall that in the last days of Popa Crow's life, we dreaded ending a visit. As we prepared to leave, he would always start to cry. Then of course Nana Crow would join him. It was like he thought each visit would be the last time he would see us and his grand kids.

As I navigate the December of my life, I better understand Popa Crow's emotions. My faith in the here after has spared my children and my grandchildren from my tears, but reality tells me that I must savor life's special times because each one could be the last.

I thank God for every great memory, for excellent health, for long life and each additional pleasure allowed. In September, I learned that my knees can no longer handle a mountain hike. Energy, hearing, eyesight and stamina wane. I'm a December man.

I used to joke that my goal was to live to age 114 then get shot by a jealous husband. Jo Ann made me change that goal. She said that I gave Evelyn fifty years so my goal should be to give her fifty years also.

SOMETHING FUNNY

Something funny happened on
the way to my 80th birthday.
I decided to write a book
and announced it one Sunday.

That's funny all right, remembering
life's hard and funny times.
And I struggled trying to
refine all those crude rhymes.

It may seem funny to some
that God forgave my sinful deeds.
But, I am thankful that He did
and fills my daily needs.

I am aware that I'm living
the December of my life,
and that each laugh and each joy
experienced with my loving wife
may be my last. But I am in
good cheer and not crying.
Because I don't plan to spend
the rest of my life dying.

May be a funny thing,
but I plan to live until I die.
When this book is done,
May God give me another goal to try.

There will come a goal I do not
complete, that I know.
But I have had a wonderful life,
and I'm ready to go.

God's grace, two loving wives, family,
friends and a great career,
Thanks Lord, but give me one more
funny thing before I'm out of here.

THE CAPPER

I better put a cap on this tome if I have any hopes of finishing by my birthday. I do hope that if you are still reading, you have found something of interest. I may be accused of going to all this trouble just to see my name in print.

I have tried to include the names of a lot of people important to me. However, the years have been long and the numbers great. I know I have omitted some very important names.

But, there is only one book that is really important to have your name in. That is God's Eternal Book of Life.

It is my prayer that your name is written there.

EPILOGUE

Well, here it is December 2008. I thought this book would be out by my birthday in May, but I didn't understand all of the delays and technicalities of the publishing business. Well, a couple of more funny things have happened in my second eighty years that I need to record.

First my family threw a big 80th birthday bash for me in May. I was surprised, thankful, honored and humbled. My grandchildren did the heavy lifting under the buck sergeant leadership of Danielle. Friends and family attended the party in Lewisville, Texas, from as far away as Tulsa and Houston. Some friends dated back to the sixties and some I had not seen since Evelyn's funeral. The kids even made reservations for the travelers.

The kids had pictures all over the place and even made a video. Now I know where photos were that I couldn't find for the book.

The second important thing is that Jo Ann and I have added another family member. As part of her volunteer work with CASA, two years ago Jo Ann began mentoring a young girl named Ashley. Jo Ann was first drawn to Ashley after learning about Ashley's history of being abandoned by her birth parents at age three and of the many problems she was experiencing as a result of being shuffled around in over seventeen different CPS foster home placements during her short, at that time, eleven years of life. Jo Ann and Ashley have developed a real bond of love and trust. In November 2008, when Ashley was faced with moving into another placement by CPS, we decided enough was enough. We wanted Ashley to become ours in the hope that we can give her the experience of knowing the love and stability that comes from having a "forever home".

Jo Ann has raised three children and worked many years as a CASA volunteer. I have raised four children and have had four grandchildren and C.W. Vowell live with me at one time or another. Ironically, the state may require us to take parenting classes. Oh well, maybe I'm old enough now to learn how.

Made in the USA
Lexington, KY
15 March 2011